The

Vice Admiral Richard Bell D...
of the most important charac...
Despite a traditional naval education – he was among the last
cadets to be trained under sail – he was quick to grasp the potential
of aircraft. After World War I he continued to promote the flying
interests of the Navy and, as the first man to regularly land and take
off from carriers, he did much to prove the value of shipboard
aviation. He retired from the Navy in 1941 and died in 1966.

SAILOR
IN THE AIR

**Vice-Admiral
Richard Bell Davies**
VC, CB, DSO, AFC

Introduction by David Hobbs

Seaforth
PUBLISHING

This edition first published in Great Britain in 2008 by
Seaforth Publishing,
Pen & Sword Books Ltd,
47 Church Street,
Barnsley S70 2AS

www.seaforthpublishing.com

British Library Cataloguing in Publication Data
A catalogue record for this book is available from the British Library

ISBN 978 1 84832 011 6

First published by Peter Davies, London, 1967

Printed and bound in Great Britain by Creative Print & Design, Blaina.

CONTENTS

Introduction

Richard Bell Davies was the outstanding personality in the development of aviation within the Royal Navy. He made the very first deck landing on HMS *Argus*, the world's first flush-decked aircraft carrier, and refused, unlike the majority of his contemporaries, to transfer to the newly formed Royal Air Force in 1918. In a career that spanned over forty years he was taught seamanship in a sailing vessel as a Dartmouth cadet, learnt to fly at his own expense in 1911 and achieved high command in the newly re-formed Air Branch in 1939. In between flying appointments he served in a number of conventional warships throughout the world and these memoirs are full of fascinating stories that recall an era that has now passed into history. The journey by train from Charing Cross to Manchuria, changing at Moscow and Mukden, in order to take up an appointment in the cruiser *Minotaur* on the China Station at the end of which he arrived only twenty minutes late to be met by three sailors, who had engaged a rickshaw for his luggage, stands out as an epic from an era which cannot be repeated today.

These memoirs were first published in 1967 shortly after the author's death at a time when the Royal Navy was in shock after the cancellation of the CVA01 aircraft carrier project, to have been named *Queen Elizabeth*. They are a rich source of historical information about the Royal Navy in general but more particularly about the development and progress of aviation within the Service. They are written in a modest and light-hearted style and contain a wealth of factual material that brings events to life in a clear and logical fashion.

He had been taught to fly at his own expense, while on leave from the battleship *Dominion*, at the Graham-White Flying School at Hendon. The course cost him £50 plus a £25 deposit against damage, repayable if he had no 'smash-ups' while flying. His first flight in a naval aircraft in 1912 was in Admiralty Aeroplane Number 1.

The design and development of aircraft and their operation from shore bases was rapid and Bell Davies was part of it. He served in the Royal Navy's first aircraft squadron at Eastchurch in 1912 as Executive Officer, or Second-in-Command, under the colourful Commander Samson and deployed with the squadron to France in 1914. He served in the Gallipoli Campaign and in France again before appointments to sea as senior aviation officer in the seaplane carriers *Campania* and *Furious* from 1917, in their days the largest and most capable aircraft-carrying ships in the Grand Fleet. It had at first been assumed that seaplanes operated from the water would suffice for fleet operations but they proved difficult to hoist in and out and Bell Davies became a leading exponent in the development and installation of flight decks from which wheeled aircraft could take off and land. In addition to his skill as a pilot, he had a flair for administration and the tact and diplomacy with which he organised the use of his small number of flimsy aircraft in support of disparate military and naval operations was noted by a number of senior officers, especially in the Dardanelles.

In the early days of aviation, actual experience in the air was considered more important than military rank gained by seniority or 'time-served'. Career officers serving as pilots were, therefore, given two ranks: their 'normal' naval rank and a 'flying rank' used within the Naval Air Service when appointed to flying duties. Thus a substantive Lieutenant RN could be appointed to flying duties as a 'Flight Lieutenant', 'Flight Commander', 'Squadron Commander' or 'Wing Commander'. Bell Davies himself rose rapidly through the flying ranks himself and was a Wing Commander RNAS by 1916.

After the embryonic Naval Wing of the Royal Flying Corps was re-formed as the Royal Naval Air Service in 1914, all pilots wore the RNAS eagle badge over the curl of their left sleeve lace; flight and squadron commanders were denoted by stars over the lace and wing commanders by three 'stripes' in their sleeve lacing. On reverting to general service, officers reverted to their naval rank. Bell Davies was involved in early discussions with Winston Churchill, the First Lord, about what sort of uniform short-service pilots should wear and was keen to see their position within the Naval Service emphasised; and an indication of what early flying was like is demonstrated by his forced landing in Number 33, following a broken inlet valve on the engine, in the Sheppey Marshes during a trip to Whitstable to obtain a barrel of oysters for Churchill's lunch at Eastchurch.

Bell Davies will always be associated with the development of aircraft as strike weapons, capable of seeking out and attacking the enemy at ranges far beyond those that a warship's own guns or torpedoes could achieve. He was awarded the DSO for an attack on U-boats alongside the mole at Zeebrugge on 23 January 1915, during which he was severely wounded by a bullet in the thigh 'handling his machine for an hour with great skill in spite of pain and loss of blood'. Later in the year he was awarded the VC for an attack on Ferrijik Junction, a point on the strategically significant railway line that ferried German supplies to Turkey. On 19 November one of his squadron pilots was shot down near the junction and Bell Davies landed next to the burning wreckage of his aircraft to pick him up and fly him to safety 'crouched on all fours between the rudder bar and the engine bearers with his head bumping on the oil tank'. The Admiralty described the feat as one 'that can seldom have been equalled for skill and gallantry'.

From 1917 onwards he played a considerable part in the development of aircraft carriers that could operate their aircraft in the open sea in all but the worst weather. He was appointed Wing Commander in *Campania*, a converted Cunard liner that could launch aircraft from a platform 245 feet long built over the forecastle, but she had no means of landing them back on and they had to land on their floats on the water. Recovering them meant stopping the ship so that they could be attached to a crane and hoisted inboard, an evolution that meant the carrier losing station in the fleet and being desperately vulnerable to enemy action while stopped. In August 1917 Squadron Commander Dunning landed a Sopwith Pup on a similar deck on the new *Furious*, a converted battlecruiser. This proved that wheeled aircraft could land on a ship at sea under ideal circumstances but Dunning's death at the third attempt showed just how ideal those circumstances had to be. Bell Davies transferred to *Furious* after her modification with a landing deck aft of the bridge and funnel, but attempts to use it mostly failed because of the turbulence over the deck caused by the ship's superstructure and funnel gases. Both ships were involved in anti-Zeppelin patrols in the North Sea and Bell Davies spoke out against the futility of waiting for the enemy to take the initiative, urging instead that aircraft from the carriers should strike at the Zeppelins' bases. He got his way in July 1918 when Sopwith 2F1 Camels attacked Zeppelin sheds at Tondern destroying *L 54* and *L 60*, the first effective strike by carrier-borne aircraft in history. By then the RNAS had been subsumed into the Royal Air Force and Bell Davies had the flying rank of Lieutenant Colonel. He advised Rear Admiral Phillimore, the Admiral Commanding the 'Flying Squadron' of the Grand Fleet, on a variety of aviation topics and, with his unique experience, was chosen to carry out the first flying trials in *Argus*.

Although Dunning had landed on a ship over a year earlier and trials had been carried out on a 'flight-deck' marked out on the Isle of Grain Naval Air Station, Bell Davies had to work out the best technique for himself and then practice it to perfection in a Sopwith 1½ Strutter before carrying out the first true carrier landing in the Firth of Forth on 24 September 1918. At first the trials involved landing on the bare steel deck. Later, fore-and-aft 'retaining' wires were installed which were intended to engage hooks on the aircraft undercarriage and hold it on deck after landing. The trials also involved the construction of a wood and canvas 'island' on the starboard side of the deck, amidships to see if such a structure was acceptable to pilots. Bell Davies thought that it gave an accurate indication of height above the deck in the final stages of landing and actually improved matters. Since 1918 virtually every aircraft carrier in the world's navies has adopted this arrangement.

After the Armistice, Bell Davies refused the offer of a commission in the RAF and remained in the Service he loved. His experience was to be invaluable and followed a career that alternated between service at sea and in the Admiralty where he strove to get the best out of the flawed system of 'divided control' that plagued naval aviation between 1918 and 1939. There is evidence that many officers, including Oliver Swann, subsequently regretted their transfer to the new Service but felt that they had 'burned their bridges' behind them and so could never go back. Their loss was to damage the Royal Navy's ability to fight the Second World War effectively. Sea appointments included a spell as Executive Officer of the battleship *Royal Sovereign* and command of the cruisers *Frobisher* and *Cornwall*, the latter on the China Station. He stood by the new carrier *Eagle* while she was building on the Tyne but, surprisingly, did not command a carrier between the wars. The memoirs give a fascinating insight into this difficult period which has received insufficient coverage from historians.

Full, undivided control of the aircraft embarked in the fleet was returned to the Admiralty after the Award by Sir Thomas Inskip, the Minister for defence Co-ordination in July 1937. By then Bell Davies had improved his knowledge of manpower management serving as Commodore of Devonport Barracks and was ideally placed to play a key role in the transfer after his promotion to Rear Admiral in 1937. After a spell in charge of the Selection Board that interviewed candidates for aircrew training in the new Air Branch he was appointed as the first Rear Admiral Naval Air Stations, RANAS, late in 1938 charged with establishing the new shore-based infrastructure that was to take over from the RAF in May 1939. He was responsible for much more than the day-to-day administration of the growing number of air stations and it must have given him keen pleasure to watch the Skuas of 800 and 803 Naval Air Squadrons take off from RNAS Hatston in Orkney at 0430 on 10 April 1940 to attack and sink the German cruiser *Königsberg* in Bergen, the first major warship in history to be sunk by aircraft.

These are the memoirs of a man who not only served through a period of unprecedented change but was instrumental in making them work; not only was he there when so much happened but he was a driving force in making sure that the new ideas worked in practice. 'One of the first naval pilots'; 'one of only four naval pilots to be awarded the VC'; 'the first man to land on an aircraft carrier'; 'the man who organised the transfer of air administration from the RAF back to the Royal Navy'; 'a driving force in the development of strike warfare'. These are just some of the epithets that apply to a remarkable man. In an age when the origins of naval aviation and the tribulations it suffered under divided control between 1918 and 1939 are largely forgotten, the re-publication of these memoirs a century after the first events described in them is most appropriate. The factually accurate but amusing and interesting style in which they are written will attract a wide variety of readers.

Commander David Hobbs MBE RN (Retired)
Former Curator, the Fleet Air Arm Museum, Yeovilton

1
Schoolboy to Snottie

My fourth term at Bradfield was the Easter term of 1901 and I was now ready to sit for the Navy Examination. Bradfield and Clifton were the only two public schools whose Navy classes were officially recognized, and although I had been old enough to sit in the previous term my form master had decided, rightly, that I did not at that time stand a chance of success. I had not worked nearly hard enough.

To take the examination at all it was necessary to secure one of the nominations, the majority of which were in the gift of the First Lord of the Admiralty; he allotted most of them to specifically naval schools and of these Foster's and Littlejohn's were the chief. When my headmaster applied for me to the Admiralty he was told that all nominations had been allotted; fortunately, however, there was an ancient custom in the Navy whereby each captain on being appointed to his first command was allowed to nominate one boy to sit for the examination. He heard from the Admiralty that a Captain Baker was just being appointed to the cruiser *Blake* and it was suggested that an approach should be made.

I had no parents to write to Captain Baker for me, both having died before I was six, but my uncle who had brought me up, Dr Edwin Clifford Beale, a throat and chest specialist to the Victoria Park and Great Northern Hospitals, sent him a letter and I received the nomination. I never met Captain Baker, but about thirty years later I met his son, who told me that his father had always felt responsible for getting me into the Navy and had therefore taken an interest in my progress.

The examination took place about mid-term. It lasted four days and was held in the Examination Hall on Savoy Hill in London. About 300 boys competed for 65 vacancies. At the end of term when I went off for the Easter holidays my form master gloomily remarked that he fully expected to see me back again when school began. But towards the end of the holidays I heard to my great surprise that I had passed and was thirty-seventh on the list.

So next term found me at Dartmouth in the *Britannia* where the curriculum, spread over four terms, had remained unchanged for very many years and consisted almost entirely of mathematics and seamanship. The Admiralty had just decided to modernize the course – although this had not been put into practice when I joined – so that cadets were no longer to be taught sail drill or running rigging; we had our full measure of the myriad names of standing rigging, little of which specialized knowledge was to be of any use in my later career.

First-term cadets were known as 'news' and lived in the two-decker *Hindustan* which was moored ahead of *Britannia* and was connected to her by a bridge. Second-, third-, and fourth-term cadets were described respectively as 'threes', 'sixes', and 'niners' – these representing the number of months that they had been on board at the start of each term.

In those days the playing fields which now belong to the Royal Naval College were already in use. Also available were skiffs and four-oared gigs for the cadets to take out on the river for the afternoon, and some clinker-built sailing cutters and two schooner-rigged yachts, in which I spent as much time as possible, were there to use on half holidays. I was desperately keen to be handy aloft, but I found to my disgust that I had a bad head for heights. I did everything I could to cure this by spending a lot of time clambering about *Britannia*'s single mast, and to a certain extent I succeeded.

The College itself was under construction. While I was there only the sick quarters were completed, but the foundations of the main building came into being, the stone being laid by King Edward VII. I remember how he arrived in the royal train at Kingswear and crossed the river in the regular ferry steamer which had been painted all colours of the rainbow for the occasion.

Into the hollow foundation stone before it was lowered into

place was put a casket; this contained a specimen of every coin of the day from £5 to a farthing. Tapping it with a mason's mallet, the King in his rather gruff voice and with his peculiar way of rolling his *r*'s in his throat declared it 'well and trrruly laid'.

During my last term, in the summer of 1902, we went for a week's cruise in the barque-rigged sloop *Racer*. Although we had not officially been taught running rigging or sail drill we had picked up a good deal, and there were some excellent petty officer instructors to push us around. Cadets worked the mainmast and the ship's company the foremast and mizzen. I was told off for the main t'gallant yard.

There are three ways of going aloft: run, walk or crawl. The right way is to run. You must in turn work right hand and foot together, then left hand and foot, never raise your hand higher than your shoulder and you must stand up straight. But you have to learn to walk before you can run, and the same technique applies to walking. Crawling was anathema and there were no rules whatever. I could run a few steps but after that I generally missed a ratline. I could walk sedately but rather slowly. But I was a master crawler. I had discovered that once into the futtock shrouds nobody could get past you provided you stuck your knees and elbows well out. So my technique was to run a few steps, walk a few and then crawl like mad for the futtocks. It worked very well.

The *Racer* took us first to Plymouth. We shortened sail and went in under steam. It was my first view of Plymouth Sound and we saw it at its best. The old *Impregnable* lay at a swinging berth off Mount Wise. There were two brigs in the Sound, one of which was getting under way. It all looked much as it must have done in Nelson's day. I was standing on the poop admiring the view when the commander called me. He said, 'See that brig, boy? What's she doing?'

'Getting under way, sir.'

'I know she's getting under way, but what's she doing just now?'

'She's braced to box, sir, for casting to starboard. Her anchor must be nearly away.'

'Oh! So yer know that much, do you?'

I felt that approbation from Commander Beatty was praise

indeed! From Plymouth we sailed to Mevagissey and lay at anchor off the little harbour. The next morning we got under way under sail. Beatty told us it would probably be the only time in our lives that we should see it done.

Soon after that I was shifted from the t'gallant to the topsail yard and one day we were introduced to the operation of reefing topsails. For this the yard-arm man becomes 'Jack outside the lift', lying out with no footrope to stand on and no jackstay to hold. In this position one has to lean out and reeve the earring through the reef cringle. It was a post of honour which I coveted.

When we were sent up I used my crawling ability to the full and managed to get first on the yard and slide out to the mark, a white line painted on the quarter of the yard, beyond which none may go until the order to lay out is given. Arrived there, I was safe to be yard-arm man.

Once when I reached the yard-arm, I managed to wriggle past the lift and get one leg over the yard. Then I suddenly realized that I had bitten off a lot more than I could chew. I had only partly overcome my fear of height and it came back with a rush. The place seemed so beastly unfriendly and bare. No jackstay, no footrope, no lift, no anything. I was supposed to sit on the yard-arm but instead I lay prone and scared stiff, gripping it with my thighs and embracing it with both arms in a hug which would have been a credit to a grizzly bear.

It was while I was in this position, sweating with fright, that a cheerful voice behind me remarked, 'You're all right, sonny.' I could not have agreed less. It was the captain of the main top, who had strolled out along the yard poking cadets into their proper places with his bare toes, and who was now standing close behind me with one hand on the lift. After a few more encouraging remarks he said even more cheerfully, 'Now then, son, one 'and for yourself and one for the Queen.' (It was over eighteen months since Queen Victoria had died, but the old slogans still persisted.) Somehow I managed to release one arm and push the hemp tail of the earring through the reef cringle and over the fairlead. I thrust it feebly behind me; somebody took hold of it, and the deed was done. I do not remember how I got back on to the footrope, but I do remember the intense relief at being there. I came down to the deck triumphant but subdued, and firmly

4

determined that next time somebody else should be 'Jack outside the lift'.

Racer returned to Dartmouth. It was the last time that cadets made a cruise in a masted ship. The following Term spent their last term in a training cruiser, and masts and yards were on the way out.

I had been keen on the seamanship part of the course and must have worked reasonably at mathematics, as in the final examinations I just kept my place, passing out thirty-seventh as I had passed in.

I spent the summer holidays at Arisaig on the west coast of Scotland, sailing, fishing, and picnicking amongst the islands. While there, I received my appointment to the 2nd-class cruiser *Diana* (see illustration) on the Mediterranean Station, with orders to take passage out in the SS *Menes* of the Moss Line, embarking at Liverpool early in September. I had gained a little sea-time as a result of the exams and so became a midshipman before the *Menes* arrived in Malta. I was not let off the traditional ceremony however as my cabin mate, Percy Ridler, managed to get hold of a ship's biscuit which he smashed on my head while I was still asleep.

Lord Chatfield marked that year 1902 as one which saw the start of a great many changes and reforms in naval thought and practice. Sir John Fisher (Jacky) had only just gone to the Admiralty as First Sea Lord when I joined *Diana* in September, and the changes at that time were still limited to thought. The general routine in ship and fleet had remained the same for very many years.

The sailors' meal hours were probably based on the habit of working-class England in the early nineteenth century. There were three official meals. Breakfast at 5.15 a.m., dinner at noon and supper at 4.15 p.m. after evening 'Quarters'. But from 8 a.m. till 8.20 there was a break known as 'Stand Easy' during which the men had to shift from 'night clothing' into the 'rig of the day'. But habits had changed. The sailor of 1902 used his official breakfast-time to drink a mug of cocoa and tried to eat a reasonable breakfast in his twenty minutes stand easy. Of course there was no time for a smoke after it. I suppose the early nineteenth-century sailor did not smoke: he chewed. So the perpetuation of this routine encouraged the continuance of chewing and spitting.

The routine was also objectionable in increasing petty offences. 'Quarters, Clean Guns' lasted till just before 'Colours' at 8 a.m. so that the men went below with hands covered in oil and brass polish. The temptation to slip away early in order to clean up was great. Equally so was the temptation to slide off later for a quiet smoke. This piled up the defaulters list.

The leave system was also archaic. There were three classes: first or special, second or general and third or limited. Special leave men were the petty officers and such older men who had not blotted their leave record over a stated period. General leave men were the great bulk of the ship's company. Limited leave men were, and still are, a nuisance. Even general leave was only given once a month and consequently was looked on as an opportunity for a spree. The younger unmarried men had no other chance to spend their money so they spent it on drink. The amount of drunkenness on general leave nights was shocking, and many of the younger men felt that if they were not 'up before the bloke' for drunkenness next day, they had wasted their opportunities.

The subsequent reform of the meal routine and of the leave arrangements made an immense difference to the daily life of the sailor, and the latter had a remarkable effect in reduction of drunkenness. The reforms coincided with an increase in football fields and other recreational facilities, and the opening of beer canteens at many places where the men could get decent beer instead of the firewater of the local pubs. The reduction in drunkenness between 1902 when I joined the *Diana* and 1906 when I again went to the Mediterranean Fleet as a sub-lieutenant was astonishing.

Another thing which made life hard for the sailor was lack of washing facilities and the issue of fresh water for the purpose. The water issue was in the hands of a party called the special pumping party, whose activities were supervised by the midshipman acting as assistant navigator – hence his nickname of 'Tankie'. There was nowhere to wash clothes or scrub hammocks except the upper deck, and nowhere to dry them except clothes lines on the fo'c'sle. Monday night was scrub-hammocks night and Tuesday and Thursday wash-clothes nights. If for any reason a sailor missed the routine night it was extremely difficult for him to catch up. Even if he could obtain permission to do his washing out of routine and to dry it out of sight under the boat deck, he still had to wangle the washing water; and washing presented nearly as many problems to officers as it did to the men. The introduction of drying-rooms in ships made life much easier for everyone.

The fleet was still painted in the old colours: red boot-topping, black sides, white upper works and yellow masts and funnels, the latter known as mast colour. But experiments were going on with colours to reduce the visibility of ships. During the winter of 1902–3, orders came to paint all ships grey, except destroyers, which remained black in home waters and white in the Mediterranean.

On arrival at Malta the *Menes*, in which I had been taking passage, secured at the Fishmarket in Grand Harbour and in due course the *Diana*'s sailing pinnace came alongside to collect our sea chests and ourselves. There were two besides myself, Percy Ridler and A. M. Y. Dane, naturally known as Amy. We had already arranged ourselves in round-jackets and buckled on our dirks and, on reaching the ship, reported ourselves to Commander Colomb who then introduced us to Captain Slade. Ceremonies completed we were told we could 'sling our hammocks' for the rest of the day, an old expression meaning we should have no duty and could settle in.

Next day we were told off for duty. I was allotted to the quarter-deck division, 4.7 inch battery, second A.D.C. (or 'doggie') to the commander, and the 1st cutter. We were lucky in the senior members of the gun-room, and there was none of the bullying and excessive caning which was such a bad feature in many gun-rooms then. The sub was Culme-Seymour, a very nice fellow and the senior midshipman was Tommy Greenshields who was one of the greatest characters of his time. The first duty I had to perform was to stand between Greenshields and the commander so as to hide the hole in the seat of the former's only pair of trousers.

I was rather overawed by my boat. The *Diana*'s 1st cutter was a survivor from an obsolete class of boats known as barges. She was 34 feet long and pulled 14 oars. She had the usual two-masted

7

cutter rig, with dipping-lug forward and standing-lug aft, but the sail area was very much bigger than that of the instructional cutters in *Britannia*. She turned out to be one of the best sailing boats in the fleet. The *Diana*'s only power boat, called a steam cutter, was a completely open boat except for a canvas canopy over the bow sheets and another over the stern sheets. She had to be hoisted at davits, and was seldom used except for towing liberty boats on the monthly general leave days: a nasty and rather dangerous class of boat, though there was one worse – the steam gig.

Soon after we joined, we sailed for Suda Bay in Crete. There, in company with other ships, we had to land small-arm battalions to attend a ceremony and march past Prince George of Greece at Canea, the capital. It was a longish march along a rough and stony road and after the ceremony was over and we had left the ground, our battalion was halted for a stand-easy and permission was given to take off boots. In my company at least half the men chose to complete the march back with their boots slung round their necks by the laces.

Much has been written about the inefficiency of naval gunnery prior to the reforms of Fisher and Percy Scott. But it was not true, at any rate in *Diana*, that no interest was taken in fighting efficiency. The trouble was that the Navy had inherited a tactical idea which had come down from the days of short-range guns of doubtful accuracy. The idea was to smother your opponent by a heavy volume of fire at close range. Practice at long-range moving targets was therefore neglected.

There were some other ancient ideas which were due for scrapping. The Marines and the four seamen divisions were quartered at the great guns, but there remained the fifth division composed of the daymen or idlers as they were then called. This division, by tradition, fell in as boarders armed with boarding pikes, tomahawks and cutlasses. Naturally the artisans in the division were needed for repair parties, so the idlers remaining available as boarders were mostly cooks, stewards, bandsmen, etc. In the Mediterranean these were Maltese and were selected for their skill as cooks, waiters and musicians rather than for their physique.

In one ship the captain's steward was English, being an ex-corporal from the Brigade of Guards, invalided for flat feet. So of course he was told off to take charge of the boarders. When admiral's inspection took place, the ship was cleared for action, ship's company at General Quarters and the 5th division of boarders drawn up in the waist. The admiral, walking round, came suddenly face to face with a line of small Maltese armed to the teeth with their ancient weapons. He exclaimed, 'Good Heavens! What is this?' With a crash the ex-Guardsman came to attention and barked out, 'England's last hope, sir.' It may have been that incident which finally eliminated boarders. But though boarders vanished, tomahawks and boarding pikes lingered on for many years. The former, nicely polished, made decorative trophies, and the latter excellent corner posts for football.

Diana came back to Malta for the winter and remained there, except for an expedition to deal with brigandage in the Riff provinces of Morocco. At Malta the ship's berth was close to the Corradino Steps, at the bottom of which there was an establishment which was a sort of offshoot of the dockyard. The Maltese dockyard mateys employed there were summoned to work by a steam whistle attached to the archway above the gate. The whistle started to blow at 6 a.m. each day and continued till 6.30 when work started. It was particularly resented by the navigator who said, with justice, that as he always had disturbed nights at sea he was entitled to sleep in peace in harbour. Tommy Greenshields, who from his general beefiness was known as the Ox, decided to put an end to this nuisance. Landing at Corradino Steps late one night, he climbed up the archway and detached the whistle from its steampipe. Next morning there was a cloud of steam over the gate but no noise. There were no dockyard mateys either as their motto appeared to be 'No whistle, no work'.

The part played by goat's milk in engendering Malta or undulant fever was not understood at that time. It was thought to be due to the body becoming chilled. There were rows of coat pegs in the customs house, and everyone intending to return to his ship after sunset had to take a great-coat ashore which he could hang in the customs house, but had to put on before getting into a boat after dark. Bighi Naval Hospital actually kept its own flock of goats to supply patients with milk, and it was not at all

9

uncommon for a man to go into hospital with a broken arm and come out with Malta fever.

It was about the end of February 1903 that the fever bug attacked me. First a sore throat followed by a temperature and then I was packed off to hospital. I was lucky in that Bighi was then in charge of the Deputy Inspector General of Hospitals and Fleets, Porter, commonly called the Deputy. Porter was afterwards Medical Director General, and was responsible for the reform of the Naval Nursing Service. He was determined that the fever patients in Bighi should have proper nursing in spite of a very inadequate staff. There were so few nurses and sisters that most of the nursing had to be done by sick berth attendants, and Porter drove them hard.

By late March I was on the mend and was discharged to the Navy's only hospital ship, *Maine*. She was filled with Malta fever patients and sailed for home, calling at Gibraltar for a few hours and reaching Portsmouth on 1 April. There we were packed off into Haslar Hospital. It was a gloomy place. The officers' wards were in the front of the old building and the rooms were small and dark, usually four beds to a room. The staff seemed to be even more inadequate than at Bighi, there being one nursing sister for all officers' wards. About the only person we saw with any frequency was the messenger. These messengers, who were mostly naval pensioners, appeared when you rang your bell and would fetch a sick berth attendant if you said you were feeling really ill: otherwise they brought in and cleared away meals and would buy anything you wanted.

I took a long time to recover strength after the fever and it was August before a survey board passed me as fit for duty. I was appointed to the battleship *Magnificent*, second flagship to the Channel Squadron lying off Bangor in Belfast Lough.

The Channel Squadron had for a long time been used as a training squadron and consequently always had a very high proportion of boys and ordinary seamen in the ships' companies. As the men in the ships were for ever being changed by drafts from the barracks there was no need for ships to be paid off and recommissioned. The start of the *Magnificent*'s commission was therefore lost in the mists of antiquity.

The vice-admiral in command in the Channel was Lord Charles

Beresford (Charlie B.) and his second-in-command was Rear-Admiral Sir Hedworth Lambton, who afterwards changed his name to Meux. The captain was Sackville Carden, very tall and dignified, who was later to command the Mediterranean Fleet during the Dardanelles campaign; but the officers who made the greatest impression were the commander, 'Blinker' Hall, and the first lieutenant, 'Quex' Sinclair. Reginald Hall, a most remarkable man, was at that time regarded as about the smartest commander in the Service and a very taut but just hand. His nickname of Blinker came from a nervous habit of snapping his eyelids. Sinclair was about as big a contrast to Hall as it is possible to imagine. Nobody could call his normal appearance smart. Being a torpedo specialist, he naturally affected the greatest contempt for anything that smacked of the parade-ground, which was of course the concern of the gunnery officer. His nickname, Quex, came from the curious nasal drawl in which he talked and which was suggestive of the slow quacking of an elderly duck. But in his own peculiar way he could be just as taut a hand as Blinker.

While Blinker never swore, Quex did so continually, but always contrived to give his bad language a humorous twist. He was a master of apt expressions and also of blistering, though amusing, sarcasm.

When the ship was at Invergordon that winter, small-arms companies were landed for a route march. The terrain was very muddy. On return the men were fallen in on the quarter-deck and the gunnery officer reported to Blinker before they were dismissed to go below; but Quex intervened and asked if he might say a few words. Blinker agreed and Quex proceeded to harangue the assembled company: 'Well, you've all had a nice walk ashore with your guns, and I expect you've enjoyed it; but if you think I'm going to have the standing part of Invergordon taken down to my mess decks, you're mistaken. You'll all take your boots off and scrub them well before you go below.'

He then gave Blinker a torpedoman's salute with two fingers and slouched off.

The association of these two lasted on and off throughout their careers. Blinker, as captain, got Quex as his commander; when Blinker made a brilliant success of Naval Intelligence in the first German War, Quex was first his assistant and later his successor,

The senior watchkeeper was Bobby Monsell, the only naval officer since Lord St Vincent to become First Lord of the Admiralty. Another character amongst the officers was the junior lieutenant, Sillen, nicknamed Bosun. He had just got his second stripe having been senior sub in the gun-room for a long time. He ran the large boys' division and was determined to keep a high standard of cleanliness and smart appearance. But he had found difficulty in making all the lads keep their hair cropped close. The accepted price of a haircut by a lower-deck barber was then twopence. Sillen found that he was always meeting the excuse 'No tuppence, sir.' So he entered into a financial arrangement with the barbers by which he underwrote the twopence himself, and the boys could get a haircut on tick. I saw the dénouement of this arrangement. He stopped in front of a boy and said, 'I told you to get your hair cut. Why haven't you?'

'No tuppence, sir.'

'That won't wash. Out knife, instructor, and cut this boy's hair.'

The petty officer, with a broad grin, pulled out his clasp knife and grabbing a handful of hair, proceeded to saw it off. After that Sillen's boys had the closest-cropped heads in the fleet.

Not long after I joined, the squadron lay for a few days in the Downs where it was caught by a sudden strong westerly gale. The battleship *Mars* had a sailing cutter in at Deal waiting to bring off officers. When it tried to make the ship, close-reefed, it was driven to leeward and *Mars* had to get under way in a hurry and pick the boat up.

Some time before, Quex had given me the job of assistant navigator (Tankie) and had told me off to command the steam pinnace; jobs normally given to senior midshipmen. On this same day I had been sent in the pinnace to the storeship *Tyne* to draw stores which included two heavy spars and the gale came on just as we reached the *Tyne*. It was impossible to stay alongside because of the sea which had got up very suddenly, so I was given a grass line from the stern, and, as we rode to that, the stores were lowered over her counter. Somehow or other in the course of this the spars let go and drifted astern. As soon as I had embarked the rest of the stores therefore I went after the spars, but it was a job to get hold of them in the heavy sea, and during my efforts the boat got beam on to it for a moment or two. Although she was quite a good seaboat, she had a long thin funnel like a young factory chimney which promptly went over the side. We got hold of the spars however, and using them as a sea anchor, rode to them, while we rigged up a contrivance of broom handles, boathooks and canvas round the funnel base, to stop the water getting into the uptake.

When I returned to the ship, all ladders had been triced up, but a wire jumping-ladder had been put over from the gangway platform and a senior midshipman was suspended on the end of it. He dropped into the boat and said, 'Hop it, youngster, I'm taking charge.' I felt very indignant but there was nothing for it but to climb up the ladder. When I reached the quarter-deck I found Blinker waiting for me and he snapped out, 'I've no fault to find with your handling of that boat, but under these conditions I must put someone with more experience in charge.' Of course my indignation evaporated. That was typical of Blinker. Everyone was afraid of him, but he would take any amount of trouble to remove any possible cause of legitimate grievance or avoidable discomfort.

I had another instance of that, arising from the perennial nuisance 'wash-clothes'. It was only later that I realized the set-up. The ship had been carrying out a series of gunnery practices both in daylight and after dark, and this had caused us to miss several routine wash-clothes nights. Blinker realized that there must be a lot of dirty clothing in the men's bags and that many would have no clean clothing for Sunday, which would make for trouble. Normally, wash-clothes and the subsequent rigging of clothes lines was carried out in all ships simultaneously. So he asked permission by signal for the ship to be out of routine for the purpose. That day I had the first dog watch and presently Blinker came on deck with his telescope. He trained it on the flagship *Majestic* and stood watching her.

Then he said to me, 'See that ship, boy? There's a battle going on between common sense and old-fashioned prejudice over there. See that flag?' (The affirmative was hanging at the dip.) 'If that flag goes up, common sense wins. If it comes down and the negative goes up, then old-fashioned prejudice wins.'

Presently the affirmative flag gave a jerk and shot upwards.

13

Blinker clapped his telescope shut, snapped his eyelids, and barked out, 'Got it'. Then, all in one breath, 'First part of port watch reeve clothes lines, special pumping party serve out washing water, hands to scrub and wash clothes.'

There was a big tactical exercise in 1904 in which the Mediterranean, Channel, Home and Reserve Fleets all took part. At its conclusion the combined fleet moored in Lagos Bay in the south of Portugal. There were eight lines of heavy ships and, when leaving Lagos for further exercises, the *Magnificent* nearly caused serious trouble. We were leading one of the eight columns of ships in close order. I think it was the fourth or fifth column, and thus nearly in the middle. Owing to a wrongly delivered message, the bridge wheel and telegraphs were disconnected at a time when the fleet was just completing a turn. Out of control, we charged diagonally through at least three lines of battleships. How our neighbours avoided us I don't know, but there must have been some pretty prompt and drastic action.

Another catastrophe, which might have been a major tragedy, took place soon afterwards. Charlie B. (Lord Charles Beresford) determined to give his squadron thorough practice in manœuvres at night without lights. We were in the southern half of the Bay of Biscay, and something went wrong, with the result that the battleship *Hannibal* rammed her next ahead, the *Prince George*. She struck broad on the port quarter, her ram cutting deep into the *Prince George*'s after torpedo flat, the largest compartment in the after part of the ship; the upper part of her stem tore a great rent in the plating almost to the level of the upper deck. The fleet was stopped, and both admirals Beresford and Lambton boarded the *Prince George* for a conference. It was about 10 p.m. and, luckily, fine weather with a smooth sea. *Prince George*'s bulkheads held but through the ventilating system water was flooding the after compartments, one of which contained the steam steering engine. At the last minute before the collision both ships had put on full helm, and the shock had severed all connections in *Prince George* between wheel and steering engine. The situation was saved by the chief engineer of the *Prince George* who went down into the rapidly flooding compartment and, working the steering valves by hand, got the rudder amidships. The admirals then decided to send the *Hannibal* back to England as she was only

14

slightly damaged, and to try to get the *Prince George* into Ferrol on the north coast of Spain. Charlie B. hoisted his flag in *Prince George*.

The channel into Ferrol was well buoyed for ships of normal draft, but the *Prince George*'s stern, deep in the water and going deeper, drew at least 40 feet by the time she reached harbour. So a cruiser was sent ahead to sound out a 40-foot channel and mark it by anchoring boats. *Prince George* went ahead soon after midnight, steering with her screws, the rest of the squadron escorting her. Reaching Ferrol with the canopy over the stern-walk almost flush with the water, she was moored near the Spanish Royal Dockyard.

The technical details of that salvage became something of a classic, as most of the work was done by the fleet's divers, working within the ship in water which became like pea soup. A wooden cofferdam was built inside the ship to cover the damage, supported by a forest of shores. Then the armoured cruiser *Sutlej* went alongside to provide extra pumping power, and her stern came up. The *Prince George* finally returned to England under her own power.

When the ship that I was in, the *Magnificent*, became due for a refit, her ship's company was transferred to her sister ship *Victorious*. Having reached the age of eighteen and ceased to be a 'wart' (the name by which a midshipman fresh from Dartmouth was known), I was in fact senior 'snottie' in *Victorious* and was promoted to being in charge of a picket boat. These 56-foot boats were the finest steam boats that the Navy ever produced. Capable of 17 knots and perfect to handle, they could stand up to almost any sea. They could be armed with a 3-pounder gun forward and a .45 Maxim aft, and could carry two 14-inch torpedoes in dropping gear.

The trips that I enjoyed most were those for mail distribution round the fleet when my boat was duty steam boat. At Gibraltar these trips came in the evening. The Marine postmen would collect their ships' mail at the post office and assemble at the Ragged Staff Steps, where the duty steam boat collected them. Then it was a race round the fleet, into which the postmen entered with enthusiasm. The art was to choose the route so as to have to turn round as seldom as possible, and, on approaching each gangway, to reverse engines from full ahead only just enough to check the boat's way while the postman jumped for the gangway platform. After several gangways had been smashed, authority stepped in to stop the mail race, which was a pity.

At this period Captain Percy Scott's revolutionary ideas for improvement of naval gunnery were gaining ground at the Admiralty. One of them was for provision of centralized control for the main armament. Soon after I joined the *Victorious*, a Fire Control Committee under Captain Doveton Sturdee,[1] was formed to experiment along these lines. The ship's company of the *Victorious* happened to be suffering from an outbreak of measles at the time and all leave had been stopped; so she was put at the committee's disposal for experimental purposes. As my action station had been on the fore bridge, working the small navigational range-finder, I was added to the committee as range-taker. The primitive arrangement we devised was in fact the forerunner of the intricate, electrically-operated fire-control system that was later developed.

The three machine-guns in the fore lower top were dismounted and struck below, and the range-finder hoisted up there. As telephones were found unreliable, a large number of leather suction hoses were drawn from the dockyard and used as voice-pipes between the top and various gun positions. The idea of an intermediate transmitting station had not then occurred to anyone and we tried to run the whole control from the top. One of the *Magnificent*'s officers, Dumaresq, had invented the instrument for calculating deflection to which his name was given, and there were also several rate-of-change-of-range clocks of different types to be tried out. Gunnery experts from the fleet and from the Admiralty came on board in numbers, and were by no means unanimous in their views. Sturdee kept arguments within bounds by a mixture of tact and sarcastic humour. Many years later, after the Falkland Islands Battle, when Sturdee had command of one of the Grand Fleet battle squadrons, he asked me to dinner, and reminisced about that committee. He said the Admiralty had been very wise to appoint an ex-torpedoman as chairman, for if he had been an ex-gunnery man himself, it would have been much harder to keep control of the experts.

[1] Later the victor of the Falkland Islands Battle.

Towards the end of the year 1904 the Admiralty caused the Channel Squadron to become the Atlantic Fleet. The *King Edward VII* class of ships were completing and *King Edward VII* herself replaced *Majestic* as fleet flagship. The *Magnificent*, having completed her refit, was commissioned as a private ship by Captain A. M. Farquhar and I was once again appointed there.

During the last few months of my time in *Victorious* there had been a change round of snotties' duties and I had been given a cutter. High authority had decreed that the fleet must become silent. No verbal orders were to be given in boats and they must be controlled only by hand signals. I had a particularly good crew in that cutter, but *Victorious* was a west country ship and no west country man yet has been able to carry on for long in silence. We were particularly smart in such dog-watch evolutions as 'out kedge anchor', etc., and were usually first boat to complete; but the volume of conversation which accompanied our efforts met with disapproval, and my leave was constantly being stopped for not preventing it. The coxswain and crew were very sympathetic about the leave, but I told them that so long as we were always first boat, I did not worry.

Soon after I rejoined *Magnificent*, a parcel arrived from the *Victorious*. It contained a meerschaum pipe wrapped in a signal form on which was written: 'From the 1st cutter's crew. When you are tired of the Maggy come back to the Vic.'

I valued that pipe and kept it a long time. It eventually fell out of my pocket into the Pearl River off Canton and was lost.

2

Officer's Training: Greenwich and the Mediterranean

Early in 1905 I began to hear stories in Gibraltar about my *Diana* shipmate, Tommy Greenshields, the Ox. He had passed his acting sub's courses and been appointed junior sub in a battleship. The senior sub, lord of the gun-room, was one of those who delighted in making the lives of warts a burden to them. Soon after the Ox joined, the sub was amusing himself one evening by making them 'grope for offal' which consisted in their carrying out various manœuvres on all fours under the gun-room table while the sub took swipes with his cane at their exposed parts. The Ox had not been in the mess when this started but hearing what was going on, he came in and remarked to his senior, 'Unless you stop that I'll make you eat your bloody dinner under that table for the rest of the commission.'

As he was so obviously capable of carrying out the threat, that form of amusement stopped.

While we were at Gibraltar there took place the Dogger Bank Incident in which the Russian Baltic Fleet, on its way to the Far East and destruction at the Battle of Tsushima, opened fire on the fishing fleet, thinking they were Japanese torpedo boats. The fleet became very warlike for a time; but what affected us locally at Gibraltar a good deal more was the stranding of the repair ship *Assistance*.

Gunnery practices there were usually carried out inside the Straits off Tetuan Bay, ships anchoring for the night under the lee of Cape Negro. One night there were five battleships in

18

the anchorage besides the *Assistance* when the wind suddenly shifted to the north-east and blew hard. The repair ship dragged her anchor, then drove ashore on the sand and soon bedded herself well into it. Efforts to tow her off failed and it was found necessary to lighten ship.

Owing to the position she was in and to the seas, it was not easy to send working parties on board by boat; but as the ship formed a breakwater they could be more easily embarked from the beach. Ships took it in turns to lie in Tetuan Bay and land working parties at Cape Negro where they marched along the beach. As it was Moroccan territory they could not be armed, but the Sultan provided soldiers to act as escort. The chief Riff brigand at the time, named Valiente, being a man of considerable enterprise, fixed up a most creditable ambush for our working party. As soon as trouble started the Moroccan soldiers took to their heels whereupon Valiente selected the two officers of the party as prisoners and sent the ratings on their way.

One of the two was our Marine officer, Hatton, who with his colleague apparently had quite a good time as Valiente's guest while pressure was brought to bear on the Sultan to pay the ransom demanded. It took about three weeks before the financial arrangements were completed that enabled Hatton to rejoin us.

There had been several unsuccessful efforts to tow the *Assistance* off, and after further lightening, *Magnificent* was ordered to take on the job. We dropped both anchors as near the *Assistance* as was safe and got two tow lines of 6½-inch wire across to her. Then we hove in on our cables until the wires were taut, went ahead and worked up to full speed. There was a tremendous strain on the wires but no sign of the *Assistance* moving.

Captain Farquhar stopped engines and came aft to the after shelter deck. He arranged a chain of messengers to pass orders to the bridge and fo'c'sle, sent the commander on to the quarter-deck to watch the wires, and a leadsman to take soundings. Then he ordered both cables to be veered and the engines put slow astern. As we moved astern the wires slackened up and the soundings shortened, but he continued until there cannot have been more than a foot of water under our screws, and the wires were resting on the bottom. Then having had the quarter-deck cleared, he ordered full speed ahead, at the same time heaving in on both cables.

It seemed a miracle that wires or bollards could stand the jerk which followed when the tow came taut. The *Assistance* listed over and her bow moved seaward. That must have broken the suction of the sand, for the movement continued and she slid slowly into deep water. She had steam up, so we cast off the tow and escorted her to Gibraltar. I looked at her bottom in the dry dock. There was no hole, but the plating had been corrugated throughout the whole length. No less than five captains incurred 'Their Lordships' displeasure' over the *Assistance* affair. Captain Farquhar was not one of them.

We had a very nasty gun accident while carrying out the newly introduced gun-layer's test firing. I was away at the time in the picket boat with a cutter in tow containing the target party and spare canvasses. The ship was carrying out a series of practices, firing 6-inch guns singly. Half-way through the run I saw what appeared to be the flash of a gun, but no splash of projectile followed.

What had happened was that there had been a 'hang-fire'. When the gun-layer called out 'misfire', the breech worker had immediately flung open the breech, whereupon the cartridge had exploded. Intensive drill at the loading machine had produced almost automatic action amongst the guns' crews who were desperately anxious to achieve a high rate of fire.

The breech worker was killed instantly by the brass cartridge case. Most of the gun's crew, as well as some men on the mess deck outside the casemate, were badly burned, several of them dying later. It led to a change in the 'misfire' drill, whereby a compulsory pause was imposed before opening the breech of a misfired gun.

By the time the *Magnificent* got back to Plymouth to give Christmas leave, I was due for my seamanship examination, followed, if successful, by promotion to acting sub-lieutenant and the course at the R.N. College, Greenwich. After some delay, a board of two captains and a commander was convened. As I was the only candidate, they gave me a gruelling lasting the whole forenoon and I awaited their verdict with much anxiety. They awarded me a first-class certificate however and I celebrated it by giving a dinner party at the old Globe Restaurant in George Street to such of my friends as had not already gone off on leave, and I took the midnight train to London.

The Greenwich course at that time consisted of two parts. At the end of Part 1, there was an examination in which you could star, pass, or fail. If you starred, you went on to Part 2 and a second examination at which you could earn a first-, second- or third-class certificate. If you passed without starring you were awarded a third-class certificate and went on to other courses. This was about to be changed. Future batches of midshipmen would have to learn the substance of Part 1 at sea and would plunge straight into the Part 2 course at Greenwich. The result of this was that in ships where the majority of the midshipmen would come under the new scheme, school hours on board had been increased and the mathematical standard raised by the naval instructor.

But this had not happened in the *Magnificent*, so that I found that in my class at Greenwich at the beginning of 1906 the great majority were a long way ahead of me in mathematics, and that the Greenwich instructors were suiting their lectures to the majority. In other words it was mostly far above my head. My old term mate, Archie Southby, found himself in the same fix. We agreed to work together and to go in for a course of cramming. We would have no chance of a star but must aim for a pass.

There was a retired chaplain and naval instructor named Robinson who lived in Lewisham who undertook cramming. His name was well known then, as he was the author of a number of school books on mathematics. We arranged to go to him on several evenings a week between 6.30 and 9. This, of course, meant missing dinner in mess, so we used to eat a sandwich supper in a bar which was attached to a minute music hall in Greenwich called Barnard's Palace. We generally found the manager of the music hall, Mr Kent, also having his supper there and having made friends with him, he often asked us in to watch the show.

Barnard's Palace boasted two boxes at stage level and Mr Kent usually occupied one of them. He was always magnificently arrayed in frock coat with an enormous buttonhole, and a very shiny top hat. Parties of medical students from the London hospitals used to come to Greenwich for a fish dinner at the Ship Inn and they usually finished up at Barnard's Palace, taking the other box. The party was apt to be a bit hilarious by the time they came to Barnard's, and Mr Kent used to watch with anxiety. When the noise in the opposite box was too much for him, he would thrust the top hat well back on his head, button up the frock coat, and with a 'scuse me gents', would go out.

Next minute the curtains of the box opposite would be pulled to with a jerk, the noise of battle would break out and queer-shaped bulges appear in the curtains. Then all would become quiet and the curtains would open on an empty box. Mr Kent would return polishing the top hat, to remark apologetically, 'I don't like spoiling a bit of fun, but they was going too far. Quite spoiling the show they was.' As a chucker-out, he was second to none.

The acting subs at Greenwich were all my contemporaries and mostly my old term mates. There were also the newly entered Marine officers. The subs claimed the exclusive use of the large ante-room but their claim was disputed by the Marines, who periodically invaded it. The result was battle. The Marine who always most distinguished himself in these frays was a short thick-set lad, so fair as to be almost albino. His name was Wildman-Lushington, called 'Lush' or 'Spot-White' for short. He afterwards became one of my best friends. I. T. Courtney was another, and both later were among the early aviators at Eastchurch. A third Marine there whom I was to know well later was Thoroton.

Subs and Marines were allowed two late nights a week. On all other nights they had to be in college by 10 p.m. To ensure this the main gates were shut at 10 p.m. and anyone coming in later had to pass through the porter's lodge and sign his name in a book. There were four captains studying at Greenwich at the time, and when they came in late they merely said 'Captain' to the porter and passed in without signing. Thoroton discovered this and made a practice of always saying 'Captain' to the porter, and as he looked a great deal older than his years, he soon came to be known as such.

The ruse worked very well for a time as the real captains seldom came in late. But the inevitable happened. All four captains came in late one night and so did Thoroton. Of course the Porter arrested the fifth man who said 'Captain'. It was not Thoroton.

Thanks to the cramming with Robinson, Southby and I passed, though without starring, and gained our third-class certificates. All the rest starred. The result was that for the future courses we were separated from our term mates and were classed with the tail end of the Term which had preceded us.

In the early summer of 1906 the Admiralty decided to exercise a partial mobilization of the Reserve Fleet in conjunction with large-scale manœuvres. My appointment for mobilization was to the old destroyer *Zebra* in reserve at Chatham. I was on leave, fishing in Scotland, when the telegram came. I set off for Chatham, arriving at the barracks in the middle of the night and joining *Zebra* in the basin at daybreak. *Zebra* was one of the early 27-knot destroyers and an abominably wet ship at sea. In reserve her only permanent officer was a warrant engineer. I found that the captain, Lieutenant T. N. James, had come on board the night before and the gunner arrived soon after me. The engineer was busy raising steam and drafts of men from the barracks arrived at intervals. As soon as we had steam, we got under way and moved into the lock, and the rest of the ship's company joined there. On the way down the Medway I divided the sailors into their watches and the two leading seamen tossed up for the middle watch as we passed Sheerness.

After a few hours anchored at the Nore, James was ordered to take two other destroyers under his command and proceed to Guernsey. With the gunner's help I had got a station bill made out, and we went to quarters to see if the guns and tubes would work. They proved to be in good order. James decided that, as I was latest from school, I had better be navigator. We passed through the Downs and along the south coast and then took a departure from St Catherine's Light.

It was night, and as soon as we lost sight of the light we ran into thick fog. We were a bit doubtful about going on, but decided to try to fix our position by picking up the Hurd Deep with the sounding machine. We were lucky to pick it up at the point where it narrows to about a quarter of a mile, which gave us an exact fix. At daylight the fog cleared and we sighted Guernsey.

There we received orders to go to Alderney, and James decided to take his command through the Race. It was a lovely morning and the spring tide was running at full strength so the Race was a fine sight. According to the chart, a beacon in a field ashore was one of the leading marks for the entrance to Alderney. I thought I had spotted it, got it on the correct bearing and the *Zebra* proudly led the party in and anchored. When I looked for the beacon to use it for an anchor bearing, it had vanished from its field and I saw it being driven down a lane by a small boy. We had brought our fleet in on the bearing of a cow.

We found the rest of our reserve flotilla there and another from Plymouth. One of these ships was commanded by G. P. Leith whom I met for the first time. His destroyer had been in dry dock at Plymouth when mobilization was ordered. He had joined her on a Saturday night, when no dockyard assistance was available, but by Sunday morning he had flooded the dock, floated out its caisson (gate), and taken the ship out, making a signal to the Admiral Superintendent as he left that he had 'observed the caisson of the dock to be adrift in the Hamoaze'.

The manoeuvres included a destroyer attack on Spithead in which several flotillas took part, followed by a visit to Milford Haven where we joined the Atlantic Fleet, in which most of the pre-dreadnought *King Edward VII* class were to be found at that time. It was sunset as we came in and the battleships looked impressively huge in the fading light, drawing from one of the sailors the remark, 'That bloody Kaiser ought to have a look at this little lot.'

Following a trade protection exercise off the south of Ireland we had a taste of Atlantic weather in which, even at slow speed, the *Zebra* seemed able to scoop the best part of each swell on to her fore deck and then, sitting on her tail, chuck the whole lot on to the bridge. The manoeuvres at an end, we paid the *Zebra* off into reserve again.

There followed for me the pilotage course, held at Portsmouth Naval College (later the Navigational School), next to Admiralty House, the gunnery course at Whale Island, and torpedo course on board the *Defiance* at Devonport, where we lived in the barracks. Courses ended with 1906 and I had collected second-class certificates for pilotage, gunnery and torpedo to add to my solitary 1 for seamanship and 3 for Greenwich.

Having thoroughly enjoyed my time in *Zebra*, I was keen to go on in destroyers, and visited the Admiralty to ask for appointment to one. There was no Naval Assistant to the Second Sea Lord responsible for officers' appointments in those days. Instead there were two Admiralty clerks and they had an undesirable amount of power. Very shortly after this a captain was appointed as Naval Assistant and the clerks no longer interviewed officers applying for appointment. It was alleged that the immediate cause of the reform was the fact that one of the clerks was seen to be suffering from a black eye. My own interview with the clerk resulted in my appointment to the destroyer *Ariel* in the Mediterranean Flotilla and I was ordered to take passage out in the old cruiser *Scylla*, commissioned to do a trooping trip to Malta and Hong Kong with relief crews. She sailed early in 1907.

I found the *Ariel* in dry dock, with officers and ship's company berthed in the 'Cruiser', a wooden corvette lying in Dockyard Creek. The captain was Lieutenant L. N. Turton and I found him one of the most difficult people to serve under whom I have ever met. I think that he was very highly strung and one never knew what to expect. One day he was full of praise for everything; the next nothing in the ship was right. I came to the conclusion that praise and blame depended entirely on the state of his nerves, and I wished that I was back under James.

The *Ariel* was a 30-knot Thorneycroft ship with beautiful lines. With white enamelled hull, grey funnels and mast and a shiny glass ball on her masthead, she was a real picture. The flotilla was commanded by Commander Fitzroy-Talbot in the destroyer *Mallard*, and the old ironclad *Orion* acted as destroyer depot ship and also drill ship for the Malta R.N.R. The flotilla berthed in Lazaretto Creek.

That spring after I joined *Ariel*, King Edward paid a visit to Spain and it was arranged that the Royal Yacht *Victoria and Albert* would meet him at Cartagena to take him and the Queen on a Mediterranean cruise. *Ariel* and *Desperate* were ordered to Cartagena to add to the general gaity of the scene.

We left Malta in company, Turton being senior officer, and almost at once ran into a real westerly gale. The only reasonable thing to do was to go dead slow and wait till it blew over, but Turton soon grew impatient and sent up orders for high speeds. That resulted in damage to the ship and the burning up of a lot of coal to no good purpose, and we had words and unpleasantness over it.

When it eventually became clear that we should run out of coal before reaching Cartagena, Turton decided to put into Bugie for fuel. All we could get there was a kind of patent fuel made into black bricks, which produced maximum smoke for minimum steam; but the stay gave us a chance to repair some of the damage, and it also allowed the gale to blow over. The bridge and chart table had been completely wrecked and we had to ditch the remains and navigate from the 12-pdr. gun platform.

After coaling (or rather bricking), we got to sea in lovely weather but with a considerable swell left by the gale. Soon after leaving I had a request from the ship's cook to come and look at the galley. The big steel T-bar, which was one of the main strength members of the hull, ran through the galley and it was making an ominous movement each time the ship pitched. I collected the chief engineer, and between us we chipped the layers of paint away to find that the flange of the bar was cracked right through. There was nothing we could do about it; but there could be no more driving the ship into big head seas.

We reached Cartagena much later than intended, and having secured head and stern between buoys, had hastily to paint over the side which would be visible to the royal yacht, while we took in coal from lighters on the other side – the only time that I have coaled ship and painted ship simultaneously. We had not finished coaling when the Royal train arrived, when we dressed ship over all, arrayed ourselves in No. 1 dress (cocked hats for officers, white sennet hats for ratings) and manned ship – still with black faces.

We got back to Malta without further mishap and reported the damage, but before any decision was come to, we were sent to Naples to collect a King's Messenger. When we returned from that expedition we found that an exercise was being worked out to test the defences of the Grand Harbour. It was to be a night attack to test guns and searchlights and most of the flotilla had already covered their white enamel sides with a coat of black

26

paint. The general idea was that a 'forlorn hope' of two white-painted destroyers, of which the *Ariel* was one, was to make an obvious dash at the harbour entrance, while black-painted destroyers sneaked in on either side. The other white-painted destroyer in the 'forlorn hope' was the *Bruiser*, Lieutenant Preston.

I did not like Turton and we had had words several times over pilotage and navigation, but I am sure that he was not to blame for what happened that night. Malta's breakwaters had just been built and were not yet complete. Turton told me to find out what lights were on the arms of the breakwaters. I found out and told him that there was a temporary red oil light marking the end of the port breakwater arm.

I was on the bridge with him as we made our approach, the *Bruiser* being astern, but acting independently. Turton picked up the dim red light at a considerable distance and I saw it too. Setting course to pass the end of the breakwater, he rang up full speed. Almost at once every searchlight of the defence was switched on, completely blinding us. Turton held on his course and speed, trying to resight the dim red light in the glare ahead. Eventually he saw it, but rather broad on the port bow, and I saw it too. He altered course slightly to port, to pass the end of the breakwater close on his port side. Then, suddenly, the middle of the breakwater appeared right ahead.

A second red light had been placed at the shore end of the breakwater as a warning to road traffic. The red light marking the end of the arm was completely swamped in the searchlight glare and this second light was unknown. The *Ariel* hit bows on, at about 22 knots. It is astonishing how mild steel can concertina. The bows just seemed to fold up for about fifteen feet which produced a buffer effect and the shock was not severe.

Turton had rung for full astern. The engines had no time to respond before she hit, but they pulled her off the rough blocks of concrete at the foot of the wall and we backed astern and stopped. There was a strong westerly wind blowing along the shore and a considerable sea. Ricasoli Point sticks out from the coast about half a mile from the breakwater. *Bruiser* came up from astern and promptly reported to the flagship *Bulwark* what had happened. Preston then tried to take *Ariel* in tow. I went out on what was left of the fore deck with a party of sailors and we

27

got a wire from the *Bruiser* secured. But *Ariel* was down by the bow and there was a lot of motion on both ships. The wire came taut but parted.

Turton then said he would try to get into harbour under his own power. Wheel and telegraph connections had gone, so I went aft to get the hand wheel manned and arrange a chain of messengers to pass verbal orders from bridge to engine-room. I had very little hope of success in this because our bows were going rapidly deeper and I was certain that both screws and rudder were nearly out of water. As I went aft, I told one of the leading seamen to collect a few sailors and clear away the derrick and hook on the spreading slings of the Berthon boats, and to have oars and crutches put into the boats.

Since the order revealed the seriousness of our situation I gave it very quietly; but in a few moments it had a remarkable result. Up till then there had been the usual amount of talking among the men; but now there came a sudden and complete silence. The men remained alert and obeyed every order, but they stopped talking.

The attempt to move the ship under her own power failed. The bow was going still deeper and the screws and rudder were useless. Preston in the *Bruiser* had realized that the only chance of getting *Ariel* into harbour was a dockyard tug with a heavy towing hawser. He made a series of signals urging this and I read the signal log afterwards. His final signal read: 'Bruiser to Flag. Send tug immediately.' Quite a nice signal from a lieutenant to a full admiral!

When it was clear that *Ariel*'s engines would not get her in, Preston decided to try and tow her stern first. I was aft on the 'bandstand', as the after 12-pdr. gun platform was called, having been passing orders to the hand wheel. I stayed there while we got the after warp wire across to the *Bruiser*, but it parted at once when the strain came on. By this time *Ariel* was very close to the rocks of Ricasoli Point, and Preston decided to come alongside. He brought *Bruiser* up between the rocks and *Ariel* – that is to say on *Ariel*'s lee side – and placed his bridge abreast *Ariel*'s where Turton had remained. What passed between them I don't know, but the order to abandon ship was passed aft along the chain of messengers. I repeated it from the bandstand.

Ariel's stern was then practically out of the water, and swaying rapidly from side to side. *Bruiser* also had a lot of motion, so the two sterns kept coming together with a bump and then swinging apart. As soon as the order to abandon was given, the men climbed over the berthing rails and took their chance to jump as the ships swung together.

In *Ariel* that queer complete silence persisted, but the moment the men landed on *Bruiser*'s deck they turned and started shouting advice to their shipmates. I saw Ward, the chief engineer, come from the engine-room hatch and he told me the engine- and boiler-rooms were clear. I saw him jump and as by that time *Ariel*'s upper deck seemed to be almost clear of men with the last few outside the rails and preparing to jump, I climbed over the rails right aft. There was no difficulty about jumping, but I was nearly deafened by the amount of advice and nearly pulled in two by the amount of assistance given.

I started forward to report to Preston but saw Turton with the coxswain beside him was still on board. They were right forward by the foot of the bridge ladder. I heard Preston urging Turton to jump but neither he nor the coxswain moved. It put Preston in a very difficult position, as both ships were drifting on to the rocks, and Preston had two ships' companies on board. At last he had to go astern and clear out, leaving Turton and the coxswain still on board.

I felt very badly about this as, if it was somebody's duty to stay with the captain, it was obviously the first lieutenant's rather than the coxswain's. But at the same time it seemed unreasonable for Turton to have stayed. It could do no good, and in fact resulted in risk to the *Bruiser* and in the death of the coxswain.

It was some days before I heard what had happened on board *Ariel* after the *Bruiser* left her. Turton was naturally reluctant to talk about it, but he gave me a general account. *Ariel*'s sunken bow had grounded on the rocks, leaving her stern high and swinging in and out. There was a unit of the Royal Artillery stationed in Fort Ricasoli and a number of gunners came down to the shore with ropes. They formed a chain and waded out into the surf as far as they could and succeeded in heaving a rope to the *Ariel*'s stern.

Turton and the coxswain secured the end on board, and Turton urged the coxswain to haul himself ashore on the rope. He started, but after a few yards was swept off the rope and disappeared. Turton was badly shaken by this and said he went down to the wardroom where he had a glass of sherry and a cigarette. Later he came up again and, finding the rope still secure and the gallant gunners still manning the other end, he hauled himself ashore without difficulty. After Turton left, *Ariel* gradually filled and sank, breaking in two just before the foremost funnel.

For some reason the Admiralty in their official announcement said she was damaged, but did not say she had sunk. Naturally the Press got hold of the real facts which resulted in considerable publicity and questions in Parliament. I think this was rather lucky for Turton, because 'Our Naval Correspondents' all stressed the point that if destroyer attacks were to be effective, destroyer captains had to be encouraged to take reasonable risks in peace-time exercises. Also as the Admiralty did not admit that the *Ariel* was lost, it enabled the affair to be dealt with by court of inquiry, instead of by court martial. The court duly sat, but I don't think the findings were published. Anyhow Turton was not seriously blamed, and in due course was promoted to commander.

It was decided to salve the *Ariel* and bring her into dock for scrapping. The method used was that of cutting her into three pieces using gun-cotton hose; big mooring lighters then lifted the sections and took them into a dry dock. The *Ariel*'s crew assisted the dockyard people and we found it an interesting and amusing job. The foreman of riggers was an eighteen-stone Englishman named Billy Fisk. His principal charge-hand was a minute Maltese named Manoel. They worked together as a perfect team using a mixture of English and Maltese and, between them, got the maximum of activity and noise out of the Maltese riggers. I picked up a certain amount of Maltese while on this job, and was surprised to find that a number of nautical words which I had always regarded as purely English, were in fact more truly Maltese: 'avast' and 'veer' for instance. I believe these words were originally Phoenician.

Once the three bits of *Ariel* were in the dock, it was pumped out and we proceeded to take out all stores and fittings and then pull her to pieces. As the main sewers from Ricasoli discharge into the sea just about where *Ariel* sank, it was a smelly business and large tanks of disinfectant were lowered into the dock; the stuff was always called by the sailors 'disconnectors'. Thus *Ariel*, having entered the dock through the gate, left it over the wall. The last thing to leave was one of the boilers and we hoisted a paying-off pendant on it.

The salvage operations had lasted throughout April and May 1907, during which time I had lived on board the *Orion*. Wanting to continue in destroyers, I pulled as many strings as I could to try and get appointed to another in the same flotilla, but I failed. Instead I was appointed to the armoured cruiser *Bacchante*, flagship of the Mediterranean Cruiser Squadron.

3

Turkish Troubles and Taut Superiors

The *Bacchante*'s captain was Ruck-Keene and the admiral, Sir Henry Barry. I found that I was the junior sub-lieutenant, the senior sub being Horatio Westmacott with whom I became good friends. I spent two years in the *Bacchante*, the first as sub-lieutenant in the gun-room, after which I gained my second stripe and moved up to the wardroom.

The most interesting experience of the commission was a visit to Constantinople organized for officers of the fleet during the summer cruise of 1907 in the Levant. The commander-in-chief, Admiral Sir Charles Drury, and his wife went up the Dardanelles in the ambassador's yacht *Imogene* – a naval despatch vessel, with a naval crew, command of which had recently been taken over by a Commander Taylor, who was squat and very broad with a short neck, red face and big hooked nose; naturally his nickname in the Service was Punch. The hospital ship *Maine* took the remainder of the party, collecting the members from the ships of the fleet which were scattered among the Greek islands. I went with our admiral's secretary and the parson of the *Bacchante*. We decided that we would take rooms in the Pera Palace Hotel and do the thing in comfort as the *Maine* was pretty crowded.

At that time Germany was trying to secure a dominating position in Turkey, and the Berlin–Bagdad railway project was being pushed hard. Our ambassador was Sir Michael O'Connor, a tall handsome Irishman, who was doing all he could to maintain British prestige with the Sultan, Abdul Hamid II, against the efforts of the Germans; but the Germans were making headway.

O'Connor was using every possible device to regain influence and he knew that anything mysterious always intrigued Abdul Hamid. So he sent word through the Imperial Dragoman that a very great Englishman had arrived in Constantinople and that the ambassador sought permission to present him to the Sultan. He also asked to be allowed to withhold the name of the great man until the presentation was made, as he was sure that the Sultan would recognize him at once. Taylor, *Imogene's* captain, who knew nothing of this, was bidden to come to the embassy in full dress in order to be presented to the Sultan. With the ambassador he was driven to Yildir Kiosk; there O'Connor entered the audience chamber, made his bow to the Sultan, and then led Taylor forward without speaking. To the astonishment of the court, and to Taylor's embarrassment, the Sultan jumped off his throne and hurried forward, holding out both hands, exclaiming, 'Ha Meestaire Ponch, Meestaire Ponch, How do you do.' Up went British prestige.

The visit to Constantinople was interesting. The parson, Dalzell, was well up in Byzantine history and we did the sights thoroughly. The Sultan gave a banquet to which we as well as the whole diplomatic corps were bidden. At Yildir Kiosk a broad staircase with very wide, shallow steps led from the entrance hall to the floor above, on which were the state rooms. The staircase was lined on either side by the Imperial Guards standing with rifles at the present. They were all six feet tall, in magnificent uniforms with the Sultan's monogram embroidered on their tunics. They had old-fashioned long rifles with toasting-fork bayonets and wore tall red fezzes; they stood like statues. It was a very impressive entrance.

We were then ushered into a large ante-room with big folding doors at one end, where we stood around for some time. Finally a magnificently arrayed major-domo appeared, accompanied by two almost equally gorgeous flunkeys who stationed themselves at the folding doors. Everyone stopped talking and when the major-domo decided the silence was complete, he announced in a booming voice: '*Sa Majistat li Sultan*' and the folding doors were flung wide open. Framed in the opening was a solitary little figure in a black clerical frock coat and black trousers with a very tall crimson fez on his head. He stood still for quite a while with a sly smile on a very yellow face; in fact he looked exactly

33

like the many cartoons of him in *Punch*. After the senior officers had been presented to him, he led the way into the banqueting-room with the C-in-C and Lady Drury and we all sat down to a tremendous dinner.

After dinner we returned to the ante-room where we lined up along the wall. The Sultan bowed and disappeared through the folding doors, whereupon the major-domo produced a tray of little gold medals, one of which was presented to each of us by one of the Turkish Ministers. That concluded the ceremony and we departed down the wide staircase, juniors first. I was among the first down and stood in the hall looking up the stairs. It was a fine sight. The Sultan's band was playing a march, the Imperial Guard were at the present on each step, and the staircase was a river of people in every sort of full dress uniform, Ministers, ambassadors, and Turkish and British naval officers.

The Turkish equivalent of writing your name in the book was to attend the Selamlik. This was the Sultan's weekly visit to his private mosque on Fridays. The mosque stood in the grounds of the palace, so it was only a short drive from the Yildir Kiosk down a wide private road lined with troops. Visitors stood on a stand beside the roadway. The Sultan drove in an open state landau, and as he passed each company of soldiers they called out in unison the equivalent of 'God save the King'.

By the beginning of 1909 I had completed two years in the Mediterranean, and though very happy in *Bacchante* was beginning to feel that I should like a spell at home. In the spring the battle-ship *Swiftsure* was transferred from the Home Fleet to the Mediter-ranean and arrived in Malta one lieutenant short of complement; *Bacchante* was one in excess, so an appointment to the *Swiftsure* arrived for me. I was indignant about this, the more so as the *Swiftsure*'s commander was E. C. Carver who had the reputation of being the hardest driver in the Service. I went to Captain Ruck-Keene who was sympathetic and consulted Rear-Admiral Henry Jackson who had relieved Barry. He was also sympathetic and I joined *Swiftsure* with an assurance that I should not be left there very long.

I found out all I could about Carver's reputation before I joined, and it was not encouraging. He was a magnificent seaman, a good all-round athlete, utterly fearless but an overbearing bully.

I gathered that to allow yourself to be rattled by him was fatal, and that if he thought that you were scared of him he would go on bullying at every opportunity; his nicknames were 'Spuddy', 'Nutty' and 'Nigger' owing to his swarthy face; in *Swiftsure* he was always Spuddy.

The *Swiftsure*'s captain was C. F. Thursby who had recently relieved Christopher Craddock.[1] The story was that Craddock had applied to be relieved because he felt that he could not go on serving with Carver as commander without bringing him to a court martial. On joining I reported to Carver and at once told him that I had already applied to leave the ship.

Swiftsure and her sister ship *Triumph* had been designed for the Chilean Navy but had been taken over by the Admiralty while on the stocks. They were armed with four 10-inch guns in two turrets and ten 7.5-inch hand-worked guns on the broadside. They also had two hydraulic cranes amidships for working boats. In the stowed position the two jibs of the cranes were swung inboard leaving about a ten-foot gap between them. It was said that Carver had once jumped the gap. I never saw him do it but can quite believe it of him. Carver had worked the ship to a very high pitch of smartness, particularly at all harbour drills. He had achieved this partly by his personal driving and also by his ingenuity. He had been especially clever in making use of the hydraulic cranes in most evolutions. His driving was however not always successful, sometimes resulting in putting the sailors into a sulky, half-mutinous frame of mind when everything went foul. They certainly hated and feared him, but most of them could not help respecting him.

Swiftsure had a very big quarter-deck, and consequently a much larger awning than most ships. Spuddy had worked out a very neat way of spreading the great stretch of canvas, which, when properly done, resulted in the awning being spread and hauled out taut in under two minutes. But sometimes I saw him take the whole forenoon spreading and furling that awning, so that the whole ship's company was in a thoroughly mutinous frame of mind.

The atmosphere in the wardroom was murky. There was a

[1] The gallant but ill-fated commander of the British squadron at the Battle of Coronel.

clique of the officers who had agreed never to sit next to Spuddy at meals. If he sat beside one of them, that individual got up and told the Marine waiter to bring him some sandwiches into the ante-room. Quite obviously, *Swiftsure* was not a happy ship.

Soon after I joined, a sing-song had been organized and a stage was being rigged at the after end of the quarter-deck. This necessitated raising the quarter-deck awning, and to do this a pair of sheers had to be rigged aft to lift the ridge rope. I was on watch, and as we were in half-whites, I had on clean drill trousers, frock coat, sword belt, and carried a telescope and a pair of white kid gloves.

As usual Spuddy had taken charge of the job and had all the quarter-deck men round the sheer legs. Presently I heard an outburst of profanity from Spuddy and then a roar of 'officer of the watch'. When I got to him he was glowering at the petty officer captain of the quarter-deck, who was quaking in front of him. Pointing at the petty officer, Spuddy shouted to me, 'Look at it! Look at it! Calls itself a petty officer and can't pass a sheer head lashing. Shin up those sheers and show this miserable lubber his duty.' This was to the senior petty officer of the division and in front of all his men.

Remembering that I must never appear rattled, I slowly divested myself of my kid gloves and sword belt, put down the telescope. I slung the coil of lashing over my shoulder, divided the skirts of my frock coat and then, straddling one of the spars which were projecting over the stern, worked my way out to the cross and passed the lashing, apparently to Spuddy's satisfaction. But the spars had lain for many months on the boat deck and were thoroughly sooty. The state of my drill trousers was nobody's business.

Early in 1909, the Turkish revolution broke out. The Young Turk Party seemed to carry the country and the Army with them. The newspapers hailed it as the 'bloodless revolution'. But besides being Sultan of Turkey, Abdul Hamid was Khalif of Islam. When it seemed that he was completely deserted he raised the cry that the khalifate was in danger and religion threatened. The revolution ceased to be bloodless. The first sufferers were the Armenians and massacres on a large scale started.

The *Swiftsure* was ordered to Mersina on the Armenian coast where we duly arrived and anchored off the town. The massacre there had been stopped, largely due to the efforts of Colonel Doughty-Wylie, the British consul. The Turkish police were doing their duty and the town was quiet. But during the disturbance, numbers of dead Armenians had been thrown into the river and the corpses had drifted out to sea. For many days after our arrival we had to keep a boat ready to tow floating corpses clear of the ship.

The principal town in the district was Adana, about forty miles inland, where the Turkish Vali (Governor of the province) had his residence. It was connected with Mersina by a railway – German owned – and the small town of Tarsus lay half-way between the two. Conditions were particularly bad in Adana where there were British and American Christian missions, and Doughty-Wylie had decided to go there as soon as Mersina had returned to normal. The consulate dragoman happened to own a large house in Adana. Doughty-Wylie appropriated it, hoisted a large Union Jack over it and announced that it was the British consulate.

He went off to interview the Vali, demanding a guard of Turkish soldiers to enable him to evacuate British and American women from the missions and to keep the mob from the consulate and other British properties. The Vali was sitting on the fence. Fanatical Moslems supported the Sultan, and the Vali was appointed by the Sultan. The young Turks on the other hand, were progressive and might be expected to frown on massacres. But which side was coming out on top?

The Vali was all for masterly inactivity, and he told the consul that everything was quite all right and that there was no disturbance to worry about. Somehow the consul persuaded the Vali to come out into the street and see for himself. Just then there was an outburst of shooting. The main post office happened to be close by, with a nice solid counter behind which the Vali promptly took cover, followed by the consul. Shortly afterwards two unfortunate Armenians who also tried to take cover there were murdered in the post office. As a result of this, the Vali provided the consul with a small guard of Turkish soldiers and a bugler.

With these Doughty-Wylie intimidated the immediate

37

neighbourhood of the consulate and then proceeded to patrol the town, with the bugler producing martial noises at frequent intervals. Meanwhile Mrs Doughty-Wylie had joined her husband and, helped by the women from the missions, had turned part of the dragoman's house and some other buildings into a hospital, which was rapidly filled with wounded Armenians. By the time *Swiftsure* arrived the consul had very nearly stopped the massacre single-handed. But trouble was liable to flare up again at any moment.

The immediate need was for doctors and orderlies for the hospital, to be followed as soon as possible by an armed party for the protection of lives and property. Spuddy arrived with the doctors and Marine orderlies to make arrangements for a camp for the armed party. Having installed the medical party in the consulate he left to look at a camp site. As he came out into the street a two-wheeled cart full of oranges, driven by a Turk, splashed muddy water over his trousers. At once he shouted for the Marines. 'Stop that cart. Pull out that man. Unharness that horse. Capsize the cart,' he yelled as oranges rolled all over the street.

The consul being anxious that as many British officers in uniform as possible should be seen about the town, I visited Adana for a day and went round the mission hospital. It was not a pleasant spectacle and showed up the Turk's most fanatical and brutal side; the sight of children who had been cruelly assaulted made me furiously angry.

The *Swiftsure*'s arrival at Mersina was followed by that of an international fleet. The first to arrive was the German light cruiser *Lübeck*, followed by an Austrian and a French cruiser, then a Russian gunboat and finally by a Turkish cruiser as a result of the final success of the Young Turk Party and the collapse of Abdul Hamid.

The presence of this international fleet in Turkish waters seemed a pretty good guarantee against any further massacres, but Turkey was in a pretty shaky state, and there was a reluctance to depart. I think most countries kept ships there in order to watch what the ships of other countries did, but whatever the suspicions of the various Foreign Offices might be, the naval officers soon made friends.

The *Swiftsure* was the only ship with a band. In the evenings we kept open house, and parties from all ships came over to listen to the band and to take part in kitchen lancers. It was most amusing to listen to a Frenchman and a German being icily polite to one another in English. As usual in pre-war days, it was the Germans with whom we got on best, and it was there that I first got to know von Schroeder, a lieutenant in the *Lübeck*.

When I had formed a party one afternoon, to go seine-net fishing and have a picnic, von Schroeder inquired if he could join. We had taken one of the cutters, the coxswain of which had asked to come. It was a beautifully kept boat, with the gratings and woodwork scrubbed spotless with sand and canvas. When we sailed alongside *Lübeck* to drop our guest, von Schroeder requested me to stay there for a few minutes, and going on board, he presently reappeared at the head of the gangway with most of *Lübeck*'s petty officers. He told our coxswain in English that he had brought all the petty officers to look at his boat, to see how a boat should be kept.

It was while we were at Mersina that something occurred between the captain and commander which resulted in Spuddy being ordered to his cabin under arrest. The result was an immediate slackening of the ship's discipline, but the arrest only lasted a few days, and Spuddy was restored to liberty one evening after Quarters with unmistakable effect. At that moment there was some job to be done for which the first lieutenant had both watches on the quarter-deck, and the men were lounging and talking. I was standing with my back to the after hatch on the starboard side when I heard it open behind me. Suddenly I saw the men stiffen and fall silent and then behind me there was a roar from Spuddy, 'Both watches on the fo'c'sle.' For about twenty minutes he kept them running from one end of the ship to the other, and there was no further slackness.

During the stay at Mersina, we had been exercising the guns' crews and carrying out sub-calibre practice with a view mainly to the next gun-layers' test. I had one of the 7.5-inch batteries. They were excellent guns but needed very large crews for the projectiles had to be raised by hand-worked grabs and then traversed on an overhead tramway to the loading tray. To keep up a high rate of fire needed thorough drill. We had a dummy loader system rigged on the upper deck and I had managed to work up keen competition amongst the gun crews, as to which could achieve the best rate of fire.

The gun-layers' test took place when we got back to Malta and we had almost a replica of the *Magnificent*'s gun accident. The crews were enthusiastic and the rate of fire of the first two guns had been well above average. The crew of the third gun to fire were all out to beat their predecessors, but after a couple of rounds, the gun missed fire. The gun-layer gave the correct order: 'Still!' But the breech worker's reaction was automatic and he flung the breech open. Standing just behind the gun, I could see the black crater in the base of the cartridge. There was no time to think. Instinctively I went at the breech worker in a soccer charge. He staggered away, and before I could get hold of the breech lever, one of the rammer numbers grabbed it and slammed it shut. We reported a misfire, and when the gunnery officer came to the gun, I told him what had happened. After one look at the chalk-white face of the breech worker, he said that no good purpose was going to be served by making that man a defaulter, so we agreed to say no more about it.

I had an example of Spuddy Carver's astonishing guts when I was on watch one afternoon in harbour. The physical training P.O. was taking a class of would-be 'springers' on the quarter-deck. They had the parallel bars rigged and, while the class was standing easy, one young sailor took a run at the bars and jumped them clean. Spuddy, who was standing near me, saw it and commented, 'Did you see that, could you jump those bars?' I replied that I certainly could not. He said, 'I ought to be able to; let's have a try.' He took a run at the bars, caught his foot and came down a real purler; he picked himself up, took another run and came down just as heavily. He came up to me and said, 'I'm funking it, that's what the trouble is, just funking it.' He told the P.T.I. to leave the bars just where they were while he went below and shifted into flannels. When he came up he had another try with the same result. Then he had the bars unshipped and made two of the class hold one bar at the correct height. He cleared that easily. Then he had both bars held at the proper height and again cleared them. Finally he had the bars replaced and jumped them clean.

In the summer of 1909 the Mediterranean Fleet came home to carry out manœuvres with the Atlantic Fleet, and at the end of them, the Mediterranean ships were sent to their home ports to give leave. Before the time came for *Swiftsure* to sail back to the Mediterranean I was relieved, and after spending the five weeks' foreign service leave due to me, I was appointed to the armoured cruiser *Cressy*, Captain Walter Cowan.[1] Walter Cowan had a great career in the Navy and was rightly admired and respected. He mellowed in later life, but as a young captain he had the reputation of being a taut hand, not much less so than Spuddy Carver, though in a different way. I began to wonder if I had not gone from the frying-pan into the fire.

I found that Walter Cowan was quite as difficult as I had expected. He demanded a very high standard (which nobody objected to), but seemed quite unable to express praise or appreciation of a good effort. This inability to praise, combined with a peevish voice and a nagging manner, made Cowan unpopular with junior officers and blinded us to his good qualities. Besides the very high standard he set himself and everyone else, he was a remarkable ship handler with wonderful judgement. Unlike many expert ship handlers he was always ready to leave his officers of the watch in charge, and he seldom interfered with them except to avert catastrophe.

As a lieutenant he had spent most of his time in command of small craft, which perhaps accounted for his good ship handling. He had commanded a gunboat on the Nile during Kitchener's advance into the Sudan and was there at the time of the Fashoda incident – when Kitchener had found a small French force under Major Marchant occupying that place, with a French armed steamboat patrolling the Nile. After due protest, Major Marchant had agreed to be carried down to Cairo in a British gunboat and Cowan had taken him down. Cowan told me that Marchant had carried the steamboat in sections right across Africa on the heads of porters. Besides the steamboat he had similarly transported a number of cases of champagne and, during the trip

[1] Later Admiral Sir Walter Cowan, Bt.

to Cairo, insisted on sharing a bottle with Cowan every night at dinner.

Cowan had also served with the Naval Brigade during the South African War, being attached to Lord Roberts's staff for a time. When *Cressy* was in Torbay that summer, Lord Roberts and his daughter were staying in one of the Torquay hotels and Cowan invited them to lunch. I happened to be on watch when they arrived and after presenting Garforth, the commander, Cowan beckoned to me and introduced me to Lord Roberts. The field marshal shook hands and inquired how long I had been in the Navy; I told him eight years. His rather severe features crinkled into a most kindly grin. He said, 'Eight years, eh? They caught you young enough, didn't they?'

The *Cressy* was lucky in her officers, particularly Plunkett (afterwards Drax), the torpedo-man, and her gunnery officer, Inman. She also had a very remarkable boatswain, Mr Job. A native of Totnes, he clung firmly to the speech of South Devon all his life. In those days the seamanship examination for the rating of petty officer was always conducted by the boatswain. A young leading seaman, one of the boatswain's mates, had applied to take the examination, and I happened to be on watch while Mr Job was examining him.

It soon became apparent that things were not going well and presently Mr Job made a gesture and the candidate started to walk away looking depressed. As he went, the boatswain called after him, 'There yew goes Tweedly Wee. Dooty hands fall in: that's all yew knows and it's – all – you're – bloody well – fit for.' It seems doubtful if an examination board, with the more elaborate system of today, can make more abundantly clear the reason for a candidate's failure.

The boatswain's naval creed was a simple one: the efficiency of the fleet depended on the ships' companies. Their efficiency depended on the standard set by the petty officers. It was the boatswain's duty to maintain that standard.

But, as he once explained to me, there were exceptions to the rule. 'One ship I was in, cap'n's coxswain was a leading seaman. Cap'n wanted him rated up, so he come afore me for examination. But he don't know nawthing, so course I fails him. Month or two later up he come again. Don't know no more than before so

42

I fails 'im again. Next thing I hears, cap'n's got him in his cabin teaching him some seamanship hisself. Well, I thinks, cap'n's losing peace o' mind over this. That be worse for ship nor what one bad petty officer would be. So next time he come up I sez to him, "Yurr! 'tis Sunday, see? Cap'n's been to church. Got his Sunday pants on. After church, reckons he'll go ashore. Sends for yew, takes off his Sunday pants, gives 'em to yew to fold. How d'yer set about it?" "Oo!" he sez. "Bring two top buttons together. Give 'em shake up like. See seams is in line. Put 'em over me arm, fold 'em this way, fold 'em over that way. Put 'em in drawer." "Right," sez I. "Petty officer yew."'

Although *Cressy* involved very hard work, there were times when life became boring, particularly when lying at Black Stakes – a most depressing spot in the Medway – for long spells in winter. I bought a second- or third-hand motor car, a Royal Enfield of about 1900 vintage. In it Thoroton, *Cressy*'s Captain of Marines, and I toured most of Kent on days off, and broke down everywhere. I also took up German. When in company with the German cruiser *Lübeck* at Mersina I had found that nearly all her officers spoke good English; since none of *Swiftsure*'s officers spoke German, I thought I would try and teach myself enough to pass the preliminary examination for interpreter.

Von Schroeder and I had corresponded, so I took to writing to him in German. He replied with considerable amusement, and also sent me German papers and books. The *Cressy* paid off suddenly and unexpectedly in the spring of 1910 and, as I had received no new appointment, I found myself on half pay. It was a good chance to tackle my German seriously. I went home to my uncle's house in London and arranged to take a course of lessons at the Berlitz School. After about ten days of cramming German, no appointment having arrived, I wrote to von Schroeder, still in the *Lübeck*, that I was coming to Kiel for a week.

At Kiel I installed myself in an hotel, then got a shore boat to take me out to the *Lübeck* which was lying in the fiord. On board, the officer of the watch told me that von Schroeder had been appointed a few days before to the naval gunnery school at Sonderborg, but that my letter would have been forwarded to him, gave me the address of the school, and advised me to telegraph. The next day I received a telegram from him inviting me to Sonderborg for the week-end and saying a room was engaged for me at the only hotel.

I travelled by train and spent Saturday and Sunday with von Schroeder, dining in the mess on Saturday. On Sunday, after a long walk through very lovely and heavily-wooded country, we joined a large party for a *Krebsfest* in the *Ratweinhalle*. *Krebs* is the local freshwater crayfish and is excellent; the quantity provided and consumed was impressive. They were brought in in large tureens with a forest of whiskers sticking out at the top. You grabbed the *Krebs* by his whiskers, dismembered him with a special implement and devoured him. As fast as one tureen was emptied, another appeared. The drink was Rhine wine, served in tall green glasses. I can strongly recommend a *Krebsfest*.

With von Schroeder's help I had obtained a berth in the coasting steamer for return to Kiel on Monday morning. When I said goodbye, I asked him what sort of an accent I had produced. He replied with a grin, '*Erschrecklich*,' which I understood to mean 'frightful'. Back in Kiel, I found that von Schroeder had written to many of his friends, and I was very well looked after. His father was at sea, being second in command to Prince Henry of Prussia in the High Seas Fleet: but his mother asked me to supper so I met the family and many of their friends.

Amongst the naval officers I met at that time were Valentine, who became a notorious U-boat captain, von Mohr, who was one of the school's staff officers, and Felix von Bendermann, the son of a retired *Grossadmiral* who had started life in the old Prussian Navy, before there was a German Empire. The Imperial Dockyard was very new then and believed to be the most up-to-date in the world. I was very keen to see it. So I wrote to the flag lieutenant of the Port Admiral, explaining who I was, and asking for a permit. I received a prompt and polite reply, saying that the admiral would have been delighted to arrange a visit but that he would need authority from Berlin, for which there was no time. He suggested that I should visit the Krupp Yard instead. I carefully prepared a speech in German, and then hired a fiacre to take me round the head of Kiel Fiord, as both yards were on the opposite side to the town. At the yard gate, I was stopped by a man in a cloth cap. I delivered my speech; he listened attentively and then said he would go and ask. He reappeared with a man in a bowler hat. Once more I delivered my speech; again he listened till the end and said he would go and ask. This time a man appeared in one of those hard felt hats – half bowler and half top hat. Off went my speech again. At the end he said '*Verboten,*' so that was that, and I went back in the fiacre.

I had been invited to dine with a number of naval officers at the Imperial Yacht Club that evening. I told them the story of my attempted visit and they insisted that I should repeat my speech yet a fourth time. It was received with great applause; but when the tumult had died down, von Bendermann insisted that it was all nonsense to say that I could not visit the Imperial Yard and that he would take me round the next day. He came for me in the afternoon and we drove round the fiord in a fiacre. If anyone spoke to us, he said, I was to say that I was his cousin from Hamburg. I had been rather doubtful about going, seeing that I had been refused by the Port Admiral, but von Bendermann said he knew that I was there as a friend and not as a spy and that I had no intention of making any official report of my visit. That was true enough, as I had always believed that the average naval officer could not learn anything of real value from a casual walk round a dockyard.

The yard was beautifully clean and well kept, particularly the machine and fitting shops. Presently von Bendermann asked if there was anything more I wanted to see. I said that we had not visited the building slips and that I should like to see them. He said that they were confidential and that even German officers in uniform were not allowed near without a pass; but he immediately added that we would certainly go and look at them. I protested, but he insisted and led the way to the head of one of the slips. One of the early German dreadnoughts was being built there, the frame of the ship being complete but no side plating. Within the frames and rising from the inner bottom to the armoured deck was a fore and aft armoured bulkhead, obviously anti-torpedo protection covering the main magazines and also the engine- and boiler-rooms. I knew that our contemporary ships had no similar protection. This discovery put me in a very awkward fix. I had more or less given my word that I was not going to report on what I saw. But did the Admiralty know of this detail in German design? I thought about it for a long time after getting back to England, and eventually concluded that it must be known, particularly as the ships were visible from ships in Kiel Fiord. I decided to make no report, but to talk about my visit a lot with senior British officers. This would salve my conscience.

Many years later, when Sir Charles Madden was First Sea Lord, I told him the story and asked if the Admiralty had that information in 1910. He said that they knew all about it and that serious consideration had been given to incorporating similar protection in our contemporary ships, but it would have involved a considerable increase in beam and would consequently have made all our existing dry docks obsolete.

The naval construction branch of the German Navy was given a very much better position than that which the Royal Corps of Naval Constructors then held with us. The constructor manager of the Imperial Yard was the executive head of the yard. Constructors always wore uniform and the senior ones all had official residences. All dockyard craft were under the orders of the constructor manager. This latter point added very greatly to the importance of constructors in the eyes of the German naval officers, because if they wanted to get from the yard to the town without the long drive round the fiord, they had to have permission to cross in a constructor's boat. This von Bendermann decided to do when we left the yard. We waited at the landing place for some time until the constructor manager himself appeared. Von Bendermann clicked heels and saluted, presenting me as his cousin from Hamburg, and requested a passage across to Kiel. The great man was himself about to cross and graciously allowed us a seat in his boat. Evidently feeling it necessary to entertain this civilian cousin, he held forth on the wonders of his yard all the way across. I sat and said '*Ach so!*' in an awed voice, at intervals.

I think that the German officers had been tickled at the idea of a junior British officer visiting them unofficially and on his own initiative. They had all been particularly friendly and hospitable and I had thoroughly enjoyed my time in Kiel. On getting back, I applied to sit for the preliminary interpreter's examination and succeeded in passing, but I never had a chance to follow it up.

4
Fleet Manœuvres and Flying

Soon after my return from Germany, I got an appointment as
watchkeeper to the battleship *Dominion*, Captain Morgan Singer,
in the Home Fleet. I had acknowledged the appointment and
received orders to join, when to my great astonishment I received
a letter from Walter Cowan. He said he was being given command
of the new cruiser *Gloucester* and offered to take me with him. I
had been under the impression that he had no use for me whatever. As one commission under Cowan ought to be enough for
anyone, I replied thanking him warmly but saying that I had
already had orders for joining *Dominion*.

The *Dominion* was a very happy ship with a particularly good
lot of officers. It was here that I first made friends with L. A.
Montgomery, whose sister was one day to be my wife, but by
the time I was married, he alas had died, going down in the *Good
Hope* at the Battle of Coronel. The commander was David Tom
Norris. Soon after I joined, we started summer manœuvres,
which were to finish up at Mount's Bay, where King George V
was to hoist his standard in the *Dreadnought* and take the fleet to
sea for some set-piece tactical movements.

Admiral Sir William May, who was the C-in-C, had continued
the strict orders for silence in the fleet, which had been initiated
by Lord Charles Beresford. The fleet duly anchored in Mount's
Bay and that evening I took over the first dog watch. Presently I
heard sounds of cheering coming from ships inshore of us, so I
hurried to the fo'c'sle to keep our men quiet. But the cheering
was spreading from ship to ship. When I reached the fo'c'sle I
found everyone gazing shoreward to try and see what it was all

47

about. The cheering continued to spread; then I saw two little lines in the sky low down over the shore. It was Claude Grahame-White in a Farman biplane, heading seawards over the fleet.

By that time the whole fleet was yelling, the men crowding the *Dreadnought*'s upper deck making as much noise as all the rest. Grahame-White continued to fly out to sea, heading for the *Dreadnought*, which, with the other battleships, was farthest away from the shore. At about 300 feet he circled round the flagship and then headed back for the shore. It was the first time an aeroplane had flown over the fleet and the first time an aeroplane had even been seen by the great majority. The enthusiasm was tremendous, the cheering continuing until the machine landed. Evidently the C-in-C felt it to be an occasion when the silence rules could be broken.

Bad weather set in and the fleet moved to Torbay where the King came off to the *Dreadnought* and took the fleet out, one of the very rare occasions when the fleet has been manœuvred by the Sovereign in person. Unfortunately a fog came down and the programme soon had to be abandoned. Parting company, the *Dreadnought* groped her way into Torbay so that the King could land: the rest of the fleet followed later.

During the autumn cruise, a notice appeared in the Press, that Mr Frank McLean had two aeroplanes which he was prepared to put at the disposal of naval officers who wished to learn to fly. He would provide instruction for them and only stipulated that they must become members of the Aero Club. I had been tremendously impressed by Grahame-White's flight over the fleet. The *Dominion* was an east country ship using Sheerness as her home port and Frank McLean's aeroplanes were at Eastchurch in the Isle of Sheppey. There seemed to be a good chance of taking advantage of McLean's offer, so I wrote to the secretary of the Aero Club putting my name up and duly became a member.

Members received a weekly copy of the club's paper *Flight* which I read carefully during the rest of the cruise. The *Dominion* came to Sheerness to give Christmas leave. At the first opportunity I took the Sheppey light railway to see the little village of Eastchurch and walked down the muddy cart track that led to a small cluster of sheds at the edge of the marshes, hoping to find Frank

McLean. He was not there, but I met a man in a dirty white sweater who told me that the Admiralty were taking over the two aeroplanes and were selecting the officers for flying instruction. He thought that Captain Murray Sueter of the Torpedo School Ship *Acteon* was in charge and that Lieutenant Gregory had been selected.

I had met Murray Sueter when he was captain of the cruiser *Barham* in the Mediterranean and also Gregory who had been his navigator. But as watchkeeper in a Home Fleet battleship already short of officers, it seemed very unlikely that I should have any chance of being selected if I applied. In the pages of *Flight* however I had seen advertisements of Grahame-White's Flying School at Hendon. I thought my best chance of learning to fly would be there, during my Easter leave. During Christmas leave I went to Grahame-White's office in Clifford Street and told him what I wanted.

He was very business-like, telling me it would cost me £50 with a further £25 deposit against damage, which he would return if I did not smash anything, and that there would be no charge for petrol. Fearing that most of the male population of the country would be wanting to learn to fly that spring, I closed with the offer and insisted on paying the cash there and then to make sure of a place in the class, though Grahame-White assured me it was quite unnecessary.

Flying was regarded as such a lunatic occupation in 1911 that I kept quiet about it. On my first day off after the *Dominion* returned to Sheerness, I travelled to Hendon. There Grahame-White employed one pilot and two mechanics. The pilot, who rated as instructor, was Clement Greswell and his job cannot have been easy. He was expected to instruct pupils as well as to take up joy-riders at a guinea a time. Of course he could not do both at once. The engine mechanic was Carr and the rigger Bill Hoare.

There were two aeroplanes, both original Farman 'Box-kites'. I always thought that the original Box-kite was a better aeroplane than the later ones, because there was no extension on the top plane, and with the smaller surface it had better speed and consequently more control, though it was more reluctant to leave the ground. A third aeroplane was added that week. It was called a 'Military' Farman and had the wing extensions and two seats for passengers, side by side, behind the pilot. I believe that it was called military because some had been ordered by the French War Office.

Flying, early in 1911, could only take place in a flat calm. The weather throughout that spring was bright and sunny but, as so often happens, a fresh north-east wind set in each morning and seldom died away before sunset. Consequently there was a lot of standing about and not much flying. My journeys from Chatham got me to Hendon about 4 p.m. where I stayed till twilight, hoping for a calm spell. Then I returned to London for dinner at the Junior Naval and Military Club and caught a late train back to Chatham. But I could only do that every other day. There were two other pupils: J. L. Travers, who later joined the R.N.A.S. and T. C. R. Higgins, a captain in an infantry regiment, who had started life in the Navy and served ashore in South Africa before transferring to the Army. We became good friends.

The pilot situation improved when Grahame-White made an arrangement with other qualified pilots whereby they could fly his aeroplanes provided they took up pupils as well. One of these was Hubert, a Frenchman, who later took part in the first air mail flight from Hendon to Windsor. Another was a South African named Patterson, a very good chap who, I believe, was the first South African to learn to fly. He resisted the urge to take up guinea joy-riders and insisted on taking pupils. He kept up a commentary on what he was doing and I think that my trips as passenger with him were about the only real instruction I had during that fortnight. Hubert however gave me some involuntary instruction when he took me up in the Military Farman. He stalled her on a turn and produced a spectacular side slip, only regaining control about twenty feet from the ground.

Higgins and Travers were living in what was called the mess, a lodging-house near Hendon where Greswell also lived. They were not too pleased with it as the landlady disliked people rising early, with the result that they missed the calm spell in the early morning. With the persistent wind in the middle of the day we were losing valuable time; so Higgins and I persuaded Grahame-White to let us trundle the school machine about on the ground to become used to rudder and engine control. The term 'taxiing' had not been invented then; we called it 'rolling'. The Box-kite Farman, with its big front elevator projecting forward on booms, was a ridiculous sight during this occupation; it looked just like a panic-stricken hen running with her neck stretched out.

In one of the side streets of Hendon, I saw a house with a 'Lodgings to Let' notice. The beautifully clean house was occupied by an L.C.C. tram-driver and his wife. When I inquired about terms, the woman said they had asked as much as half a crown a day, but added hastily that that, of course included breakfast and supper. I engaged the room for the first week of my leave on the understanding that she would leave a teapot and kettle and some bread and butter in her kitchen overnight so that I could get up early and make my own breakfast. In fact she always left an egg or some bacon as well and protested because I had my supper out.

Travers and Higgins had both succeeded in earning their Aero Club certificates before my leave started. When I arrived at Hendon I found there was a new pupil, Mrs Martin, the English wife of an American pilot. Martin was very keen that his wife should be the first Englishwoman to fly. He was teaching her and wanted to make use of the usual calm spell in the early morning; so did I. The keys of the aerodrome were kept by Carr, Grahame-White's engine mechanic who lodged in a house in Colindale Avenue. The Martins and I arranged to meet outside Carr's house at 6 a.m., waking him by throwing pebbles at his window. Then the four of us would push the school machine out of its shed, and Carr would start the engine for the Martins who would have the use of the machine for about half an hour while Carr could go home to breakfast. When Mrs Martin felt too cold to go on any longer (usually after about half an hour) I had the machine to myself. Martin having started the engine for me, they would go off to breakfast. I found that having bought an alarm clock and hired a bike the arrangements worked splendidly.

During the first morning I kept the machine on the ground running it up and down the aerodrome, but by the second day I felt confident I could get it into the air. After the Martins had gone I experimented and lifted her about ten feet off the ground. Nobody had told me anything about landing, but I concluded that if I cut the engine the machine was bound to return to earth. It worked all right and from about ten feet the resulting 'pancake' was comparatively gentle.

I was so pleased with myself that I went on making longer and longer hops for nearly an hour but not going more than about ten feet up. Then I saw Martin come back to the aerodrome and I determined to show him what I could do. I went up to about twenty feet and again cut the engine. From twenty feet, the resulting pancake was by no means gentle and I saw Martin start to run, waving his arms about. As he evidently had something to say, I rolled towards him. When he was near enough he shouted, 'You don't want to do it like that; don't ever cut that switch till you're right on the ground.' From then onwards I always put the plane firmly on the ground with the engine running full out.

The weather remained good for most of the week and I felt confident that I could pass the test for my Aero Club ticket. It involved flying two groups of five figures-of-eight, landing within fifty yards of a given spot and reaching a height of 300 feet. I had got as far as making circuits of the aerodrome with assurance but had not experimented with a right-hand turn. The pusher Box-kite with the rotary Gnome engine tended to turn to the left owing to torque, so a right-hand turn was considered more difficult. Before I could try it the weather turned bad and it was no good remaining at Hendon. I went to my uncle's house in Kent hoping that I might have a chance to come back if the weather improved. I did not want to tell my aunt and uncle about my efforts until I had the ticket, as I was afraid it might make them anxious.

Luck came my way as a married cousin was giving a dance in London to which both my adopted sister Kit and I had been invited. She was to stay in the house and it was suggested I should take a room at my club. The weather seemed to be mending so I took Kit into my confidence, telling her I meant to cut the dance. Of course she played up. I reached Hendon early in the afternoon. There was a flat calm, but standing in the middle of the aerodrome was the school machine with a damaged undercarriage. I found Grahame-White and told him if I could not have an aeroplane now to try for my certificate it would mean a postponement till August. He gave me the use of his exhibition machine. This was the newer of the two Farmans which he kept for his own use and no pupil had been allowed to fly it before, so I felt honoured.

I spent the rest of the afternoon practising right-hand turns. Meanwhile Grahame-White had arranged for the necessary observers to watch and certify to the test the next morning. One was Barber, the designer of the Valkyrie monoplane, the other a pilot named Ridley-Prentice. I made an early start, put in some more practice before they arrived and then passed the test without difficulty. Rather surprisingly they made no comment on my method of landing. My certificate was British Empire No. 90.

There were two events at Hendon that spring. The first was known as the Parliamentary Meeting when Grahame-White invited a number of M.P.s and staged an exhibition flying programme. One of the visitors was Sir Arthur Lee, then Civil Lord of the Admiralty to whom Grahame-White introduced me. As Lord Lee of Fareham, he later became First Lord and it was he who presented Chequers to the nation as the official residence for Prime Ministers. He told me that the Admiralty were considering buying aeroplanes but nothing definite had been settled.

The second event was the Circuit of Europe. Hendon was one of the controls and I watched some of the machines arrive. They were nearly all French monoplanes and it was evident that France was far ahead of England in aeroplane design in 1911.

The *Dominion* left Chatham after the leave period and we dropped down to Sheerness for a few days before starting the summer cruise. As Travers was at Eastchurch where he was trying to build himself an aeroplane, I went to see him and find out how the four original naval pilots were getting on. Samson, Gregory, Longmore and Gerrard were still on leave so I did not see them but they had all won their Aero Club tickets about a month before I did. I wrote a Service letter requesting that my name might be noted as an applicant if any more officers were required for aviation and Captain Morgan-Singer duly forwarded it to the Admiralty. The situation at the time was that the Royal Flying Corps had been established by the War Office, but no naval organization had yet been set up.

The *Dominion* left Sheerness for the summer cruise which

started with tactical exercises in the Channel, at the end of which the fleet was to anchor in Torbay. During the course of these we received a wireless signal from the Admiralty saying that I had been appointed to the armoured cruiser *Minotaur*, flagship of the China station. As this seemed to put an end to my chances of getting into aviation, it was a bad blow, but on the other hand, the China flagship was a much better job than a private battleship at home.

After some thought I decided to try and get out of it by arranging to exchange appointments with another of *Dominion*'s watch-keepers. I saw the captain who agreed to apply for the exchange; but when we anchored in Torbay my relief joined by the first boat. The captain said that as I had already been relieved, it would be no use for him to apply for the exchange but would give me a personal letter to the Naval Assistant to the Second Sea Lord supporting my hope of getting into aviation.

On arrival in London next morning, I went to the Admiralty and gave Morgan-Singer's letter to the Naval Assistant. He was Captain Lambert, who in 1918 became the first Personnel Member of the Air Council. He told me that there was no chance of any more officers being needed for flying, and that two years of hard work in the China flagship would do me far more good than any flying job could. As the China flagship usually had six or more officers available for watchkeeping, compared to the four in *Dominion*, I could not see where the hard work came in.

I was told to find my own way to Dalny (Dairen) in Manchuria via the Trans-Siberian Railway and to report the arrangements I made to the Admiralty. In conference with Thos. Cook & Son, I found that there was a train called the Nord Express which ran direct from Flushing to Moscow and on occasions synchronized with the arrival of the Trans-Siberian Express from St Petersburg. This could be managed if I waited about six days. If I left earlier, I should have a much longer and more complicated journey to Moscow, probably having to wait there for the Trans-Siberian train. Admiralty approval was given, which allowed me six days to do packing, arrange for a sea passage for heavy luggage and say my goodbyes.

In the course of the latter duties I went to see my uncle, Sir William Beale, in Whitehall Court and while talking to him, my aunt picked up the evening paper and exclaimed, 'Oh! Bill, Germany has gone into Morocco.' This was the first news of the Agadir Incident. For the next few days it seemed possible that there would be a European war and that my trip to China would be off. However, the Kaiser apparently was not ready for it and the Germans withdrew.

I started my long trip from Charing Cross in the evening, crossed from Queenborough to Flushing where I got into a very comfortable wagon-lit compartment and went to bed. Aboard the train was our ambassador to Japan, Sir Claude Macdonald, who had been Minister in Peking at the time of the Boxer Rebellion, and had taken command of the mixed force of Legation guards during the siege of the Legation Quarter. His company made the journey even more enjoyable.

We changed trains at Moscow and I then had a compartment to myself. The train, run by the Wagon-Lit Company, sported a bath car as well as the usual restaurant. One travelled therefore in considerable comfort. In marked contrast was the plight of the Siberian peasants one glimpsed from the windows of the train. The Russians ran occasional trains for emigrants, and peasant families who wanted to move to some other part trekked to a station with all their belongings; there they camped beside the line to wait for transport for perhaps as long as a week. They seemed quite apathetic, just squatting and doing nothing; it was very hot, yet the men wore a long buttoned-up garment like a dressing-gown and all that could be seen of them was a tangle of beard and hair and two slant eyes.

There was a wait of some hours at Harbin in Manchuria where the train was divided. The larger part, with the bath and dining cars, went on to Vladivostok, while the smaller part branched off to the Chinese Eastern Railway and Chang Chun. Harbin had been a Russian base during the Russo–Japanese war and had been extended in all directions by shacks made of flattened tins nailed on to wooden posts. By 1911, the shacks were in a state of collapse with the tins rusting away. The picture was about as dreary as can be imagined and was a pretty poor example of Russian municipality.

Here I said goodbye to the ambassador who was going to Vladivostok and on to Tokyo. Now, with no dining car, the train stopped at certain stations where we ate our meals. It came as a shock to look out one morning to find pig-tailed Chinese working in the fields. At Mukden we changed into carriages of the South Manchurian line, a Japanese railway running through Chinese territory. This train was just as luxurious as the Trans-Siberian and, the attendants being Chinese, it was kept perfectly clean.

In spite of a breakdown a few miles outside Dalny we arrived there only twenty minutes late. A petty officer and two sailors from one of our destroyers were waiting to take me and my luggage to the harbour and rickshaws had been engaged for the purpose. The destroyer, already under way when we arrived alongside, left for Weihaiwei at once, and there I joined the *Minotaur*, just twelve days and thirteen hours after leaving Charing Cross. Lockwood, the Governor, had done the same journey in thirteen days, not having had a destroyer to meet him, and I believe my trip was an all-time record until aircraft took to doing it. The copy of the *Daily Mail* which I still had with me was nearly six weeks more recent than the latest English paper in the ship.

Minotaur's captain was Cuthbert Cayley and she flew the flag of Vice-Admiral Sir James Winslow, the C-in-C. The latter's nickname in the service was 'Dismal Jimmy' but I think it was rather an unfair one. We did not see very much of him as he spent most of his time in *Alacrity*, the despatch vessel which was used as his yacht, and in her he toured the station. Cayley was big and genial and a very popular captain.

When I joined, *Minotaur* was in the middle of summer gunnery exercises and I soon discovered why the China Squadron always topped the list in gunnery. The weather could always be depended on. Firing areas were only just outside the harbour. Tugs and targets were ample and had no difficulty in keeping to programme; and, finally, there was no night leave and nowhere to get drinks except the club and canteen where the liquor was good. The gunnery period ran on oiled wheels. The regatta followed and by August there came a slack period before the fleet separated for the autumn cruise.

After the Agadir Incident there had been diplomatic rumblings on and off and apparently a war scare had flared up at that time. The situation was still not too good. The German squadron, consisting of the armoured cruisers *Gneisenau* and *Scharnhorst* with some light cruisers and destroyers, were at their base, Tsingtao, no doubt with full bunkers; but the British were scattered all over the station with bunkers half empty.

Minotaur returned to Weihaiwei at high speed and was joined there by the *Kent*. *Defence*, the only other heavy cruiser besides *Minotaur*, arrived a few days later also short of coal. *Monmouth*, the remaining cruiser, was in dock in Hong Kong. There was no collier at Weihaiwei where the dockyard had been closed and all coolies discharged. However, there was an emergency stock of coal in the dockyard sheds. The only thing that could be done was to land a party of sailors to fill coal bags at the dockyard sheds and carry them bag by bag on bamboo poles from sheds to pier and lower them into the ships' boats. It would have taken a week or more to complete with coal in that way. Luckily, the war scare subsided and a collier arrived from Hong Kong. Soon thereafter we moved to Hong Kong for the winter.

5
China Squadron

Chinese politics were on the move that autumn. Sun Yat-sen had returned to China and the rule of the Manchus was becoming shaky. The Manchu Viceroy of Kwang-tung had been presiding over meetings of Chinese notables in Canton, apparently in the hope of being able to sit on the fence.

One afternoon I was ordered to take a party of sailors from the *Minotaur* and commission one of the Reserve torpedo-boats which were laid up at Kowloon. We took over No. 037, an ancient vessel built in 1886; she was armed with a 3-pdr. gun forward, a .45-inch Maxim aft, which fired soft lead bullets, and three 14-inch torpedo-tubes. Her full speed was about 17 knots.

While we were completing with stores and coal I received orders to be ready to sail for Canton at daylight, calling alongside the Depot Ship *Tamar* to embark a Pearl River pilot. By 6 a.m. we were stopped near the *Tamar*, but after a little delay I was told that the only pilot available was considered unreliable. Asked if I was prepared to go up without one, I agreed and we went ahead. We passed the Bocca Tigris Forts, where the Imperial Dragon flag was still flying, and negotiated the second bar, the only difficult bit on the lower reaches, without much trouble. It was evening by the time we approached the Ho Shan Islands.

These are abreast of Canton city and divide the river into two channels. The normal approach is by the south channel of which the final approach is called the Back Reach. The north channel, narrower and rocky, is a bit shorter and its approach is called the Front Reach. The Front Reach is the main street and waterfront of Canton. It was near sunset and, not liking the idea of arriving after dark, I decided on the north channel. We negotiated that all right and passed the Dutch Folly, a lump of rock that marks the beginning of the Front Reach.

The channel in the reach is well marked by stone beacons painted black and red. Going up-stream black were left to port and red to starboard. The sun was just setting and there was a strong sunset glare straight in our eyes. I passed the first pair of beacons and looked for the next, but could see only a single black beacon ahead; I therefore steered to leave it close to port. As we came abreast of it, our bows rose out of the water and we slithered to a standstill on a smooth ledge of rock. We were just far enough past it to be able to see the illuminated side of the beacon: and that it was red not black. It was a grim moment. I had had an independent command for just twenty-four hours and had already run aground. The tide was ebbing and there was danger that the ship would fall over on her side at low water.

I had the *Minotaur*'s 'wash deck' bo'sun as second-in-command so sent him by sampan to report to the Senior Naval Officer. This was Commander Veale, captain of the *Clio*, sloop, which I knew was at Canton and moored off the island of Shameen only about a quarter of a mile up-stream. In the meantime, we unshackled the cable, got a turn round the base of the stone beacon and set it up taut. The ship was tending to list outwards and the cable held her well. Besides the *Clio*, the river gunboat *Moorhen* was off Shameen. Veale came on board, having given orders to *Moorhen* to bring spars in order to shore us up.

Moorhen was commanded by my old friend Georgie Leith. As she had not got steam, Georgie appeared in his sampan with a load of spars and a basket of bottles. He remarked to Veale, 'As we may be here all night, I thought I had better bring a few drinks to keep us going'. We laid an anchor out astern to hold us against the flood tide when it turned, and shored up as best we could. Everything held and we floated before high water early in the morning. Some of the bottom plating had been dished and water was seeping past rivet heads and along butts, but the leak was slight and easily kept under by the bilge pump. We moved up to Shameen and moored between *Clio* and *Moorhen*.

The situation that morning was that the city had definitely sided with Sun Yat-sen and the revolutionaries. Sun Yat-sen was anxious to keep on good terms with Europeans and wanted their property respected. The Canton mob however, no respecters of property, were out for loot, and the revolutionary leaders had no control over them. Shameen, the European concession, was an island separated from the city by a narrow creek spanned by several bridges. A volunteer defence force had been recruited from civilians of all nations and a small party of sailors was landed with Georgie in command. Their object was to hold the bridges. We landed our .45 Maxim to help. The three ships were moored so as to command the water-front.

By the afternoon looting was in full swing in the city, but no attack seemed to have been made on the Manchu Viceroy's *yamen*. Rumour said that the Viceroy was sick and in bed. Rumour also said that the mob had opened the gaols and let loose the convicts. Soon after dark there was a tapping on one of the windows of the British Consulate: it was the Viceroy disguised as a coolie.

The consul was very pleased that the old gentleman was safe; but he was a rather embarrassing guest. The mob was bound to sack the *yamen* and, when they found no Viceroy, would guess that he was on Shameen. The defence forces stood to all night. The *yamen* was sacked but Shameen was left alone.

At daylight, the destroyer *Handy* arrived with two companies, one of Marines and one of seamen, who took over the defence of the concession. The Viceroy was smuggled on board *Handy* and we were ordered to escort her to Hong Kong. There was just a possibility that the revolutionary leader might try to capture the Viceroy by blocking the river and we did not know on whose side the forts at Bocca Tigris would be. However, we had a peaceful trip and though the forts had hoisted the revolutionary flag they made no attempt to stop us.

No. 037 returned to the Kowloon basin and I was ordered to transfer to No. 036. I also had to face a court of enquiry into the stranding of H.M. Ship. I was very lucky in the court who took a lenient and almost sympathetic view of the matter, but I was admonished to be more careful in the future.

As piracy was increasing on the West River and in the Delta, two more torpedo-boats were commissioned. Our job was to organize convoy for the regular line of steamers running between

Hong Kong and Kong Mun, a port on the West River, and also occasional convoy between Kong Mun and Sam Shui, a town up-stream. There were a number of lines of river steamers entitled to fly the Red Ensign and nominally British owned. The companies were registered in Hong Kong but the bulk of the capital belonged to Hong Kong Chinese. There was also at that time a bad arrangement whereby Chinese owners in Canton, by paying a small premium, could obtain permission to fly the Red Ensign. General orders were to protect British shipping but not to interfere with Chinese unless caught red-handed in piracy. We took it in turns to escort the Hong Kong convoy, usually of two river steamers.

The Chinese river craft were fascinating. The usual passenger vessels which plied all over the river and through the Delta were the tow junks. They were large junks without engines, which were towed by small steam launches. The bows were very low and decorated with a sprawling dragon with open mouth through which the tow rope passed. The fo'c'sle, only a foot or two above water, was the third-class deck. Abaft it, a ladder led up to the waist deck. This was about four feet higher and was for second-class passengers. Abaft the waist another ladder led up to the poop deck for first-class passengers and there was good accommodation below it. Finally, right in the stern was the poop royal for the captain and helmsman. Poop and poop royal were surrounded with a forest of flagstaffs all bearing gaily coloured banners or streamers. In the Delta, these craft appeared to be sliding over the paddy fields, as the narrow waterway and small steam launch were hidden by the banks.

A cheaper form of passenger boat was the stern-wheeler. She had no engine but there was a treadmill amidships. The captain waited at a village until he had taken on enough passengers. He then mounted them on the treadmill and they walked the ship to the next village.

Fodder and brushwood came down-river in sailing junks. Four or more were lashed together with a platform of planks laid right across them. On this was built a large stack and all the junk masts were stepped on top of it. As the prevailing wind was up-stream they usually had to tack. It was a family affair. In each of the junks, mother manned the steering oar, father and offspring attended the sheets. The senior grandfather of the party stood on the stack and took charge. When it was time to tack, grandfather gave the order: all the steering oars came over together and the stack slowly came up into the wind and paid off on the other tack.

Timber was felled in the upper reaches and came down hundreds of miles in rafts. Six to ten logs were lashed together to form small rafts. The small rafts were lashed together to form large rafts, and when these reached the broad stretches of the river, three or four large rafts were lashed together to form huge structures. A small village of matting huts was built on them and there seemed always to be a farmyard of pigs, goats, chickens and ducks.

The skill with which these unwieldy craft were managed was wonderful. If they were approaching foul ground near the north bank, they would start to manœuvre perhaps ten miles above it. Small rafts were detached, carrying large wooden anchors weighted with stones and attached to stout grass hawsers. The small rafts were paddled towards the south bank and the anchors let go. The ends of the hawsers were then taken to strong posts built into the main raft. As the strain came on, the whole raft would be warped a few yards away from the north bank. Then the anchors were tripped, the small rafts paddled down-stream to overtake the main raft and the process was repeated. By the time they had drifted down to the foul ground, the raft had been warped well clear.

In the Delta there were duck junks. These were long, narrow craft with long, wicker cages containing the ducks, on either side. In summer while the rice was growing, the junks lay alongside the bank of the creek in the marshland, but when the rice harvest was over they were moved to a pitch near the paddy fields. In the morning, a little gang-plank was put out and the ducks marched ashore in single file to feed in the marsh or in the paddy. The owner walked slowly along the bund, keeping pace with the flock of ducks in the mud below. If two owners met, the flocks mingled but when they separated, the ducks sorted themselves out, each flock following its proper owner.

Strange craft were not the monopoly of the Chinese. The Standard Oil Co. of New York (Socony) had a lot of business on the river. One of their employees, a jovial American, travelled about in a house-boat loaded with tiny, tin paraffin lamps stained in brilliant colours. These he sold to the floating population at a price so ridiculously low that I could not see how he could make a profit. He explained that he was not interested in selling lamps; his job was to sell oil. If the Chinese were to buy oil they must have lamps. If he gave away the lamps the Chinese would think they were no good and would not use them. If he sold them very cheap, the Chinese would think they had made a grand bargain and would use them all the time.

The Chinese had some unfamiliar practices. The commodore at Hong Kong had sent up an interpreter to help us. He was an educated Chinese who dressed very smartly. Just after he joined us we had to go up to Sam Shui. We had not long been anchored when I heard a hullabaloo on deck and found the interpreter on his back with the A.B. who acted as cook, sitting on him and rubbing his face with something. Investigation showed that the great Chinese delicacy at Sam Shui was dried rats. The interpreter had bought one and taken it to the galley to be cooked for his dinner with this result. We returned the interpreter to Hong Kong and thereafter relied on Ah Sam, our cook, to do the interpreting.

To save face is an essential part of the Chinese code of conduct, and we encountered some fine examples of this. The first arose over the lighterage of coal. A contractor who had undertaken to carry the coal bags from the river steamer to us for a certain sum demanded double when the job was done. Drastic action was required lest this sort of thing became a habit. I called Ah Sam on deck and told him to make a speech at the top of his voice to the whole harbour and the world at large. He was to say, 'Look at this man, he has broken his contract. He has asked twice the money he is entitled to. Now he is going to be paid; let everyone see him paid the unjust money. Never, never, *never* again shall he work for an English war junk!'

Ah Sam loved it: he stood up on the berthing rails and screamed at everyone, soon gathering a host of sampans and a crowd on the bund. Before he had gone far with his speech, the contractor was begging not to be paid.

A further instance arose out of a visit from Commodore Ayres of Hong Kong. Being responsible for operations in the absence of the admiral he came to see for himself what the conditions were, intending to combine his inspection with a little snipe shooting. He had temporarily commissioned the old destroyer *Taku*, one of the three Chinese destroyers which had been boarded and captured by Roger Keyes during the Boxer trouble.

Neither the commodore nor the temporary captain of the *Taku* had been to Kong Mun before. They entered with a lot of way on, meaning to pass us and anchor farther up the harbour. But that end of the harbour was shallow with a stronger current and a bottom of hard sand over smooth rock. At our shout of warning they went astern, but were carried past and let go an anchor astern of us. The *Taku* started to swing, but when broadside on to the current, the anchor dragged and she drifted up harbour and grounded. In the course of her career, her stern had struck a cargo junk, smashing the big gang-plank used for embarking cargo. There was no other damage. We got the *Taku* off without much trouble and the commodore, who was in holiday mood, assumed all responsibility and offered to pay for the damaged gang-plank. But the junk master's demand was so extortionate that he refused to pay.

Having finished his inspection the commodore went off into the Delta to shoot snipe, leaving me to deal with the demands of the junk master. Kong Mun was the headquarters of the Imperial Chinese Customs for the lower river and the commissioner was Oliver Ready, a genial Irishman. Ready had long experience of dealing with Chinese, so on the first opportunity I consulted him. I found that the junk master was ahead of me. He had already sent a letter to the commissioner stating that his demand was a just estimate of the value of the gang-plank and that any shipwright in Kong Mun would confirm it. As there was only one shipwright, no doubt he had been squared.

But besides this it appeared that the junk master was a member of the Junk Guild, a powerful political body which had taken up the matter with the consul general in Canton who had also written to the commissioner. It looked like the beginning of an international mess. Ready advised that the best thing to do was to have a formal interview with the junk master in the commissioner's office and that he would tell me what to say. We duly met there: Ready, his Chinese secretary, the junk master and myself. The junk master was quite young, intelligent looking, dignified and soberly arrayed in dark-blue robes.

Primed by Ready, I stood up and made a flowery speech. I deeply regretted this accident and the resulting inconvenience. The English war junks were there to protect honest traders not to cause damage and delay. I was deeply impressed by the modesty of the captain's demand and of course I accepted his estimate of the cost of replacement. Many captains would also have asked for compensation for the delay in loading and for the inconvenience caused, but he had made no such demand. This I greatly appreciated. Further, as a sailor I admired the seamanlike ingenuity by which, in spite of the absence of a gang-plank, he had completed his loading and was now ready to sail for Hong Kong. My only wish now was to settle the matter without causing him further delay. With that object I proposed to write a letter to Hong Kong naval dockyard commanding that a new gang-plank be made and delivered to him without charge. He would carry the letter himself if he so wished.

All this was translated by the Chinese secretary. It worked like a charm, the junk master rose and made an even more flowery speech. He was fully conscious of the protection afforded to himself and honest sailors by the English war junks. He would never dream of demanding more than his just due. He was perfectly satisfied with the proposed settlement and would carry the letter himself. He also expressed gratification at the courteous manner in which he had been received. Of course he never delivered the letter: face had been saved.

Oliver Ready had a large staff of all nationalities including a number of educated Chinese. I had been lunching with him one day when he said that, as he was giving a dinner party that evening to his Chinese staff, he wanted to leave the bungalow for the afternoon so that his boys could get it ready. He suggested we should go for a walk after lunch. We returned to the bungalow late in the afternoon, when it was at once evident that a serious crisis had arisen. As always on such occasions the boys became completely dumb so that Ready could not discover what had happened. No. 1 boy and No. 1 cook were both absent and the angrier Ready became, the dumber became the boys. The storm was still raging when I left him and went back on board. He told me the full story a day or two later. The main dish for the dinner party was to have been a turkey. In hot climates it is not safe to kill turkeys and hang them for some days to grow tender. The alternative is to give the turkey a small tot of brandy just before it is killed. Apparently the cook had been too generous with the brandy or else the turkey had a weak head. At all events the turkey, feeling glorious within, had broken out of the compound and gone reeling across the paddy fields. At the moment of our return from the walk, No. 1 boy and the cook were in hot pursuit of it.

Piracy was frequent all that winter but the convoys were left alone, so we never had the satisfaction of catching a pirate. One day a telegram came fron Georgie Leith who, in *Moorhen*, was Senior Officer of the River, telling me to meet him that afternoon at a town called Kum Chuk. Another little channel through the Delta joined the West River there and the *Moorhen* often used it when coming from Canton. We had anchored off Kum Chuk and were awaiting *Moorhen* when rifle fire broke out on the far bank of the river.

An armed launch flying the revolutionary ensign was anchored near us and she started to take up her anchor. As orders allowed us to interfere with red-handed piracy, we weighed too. The river was about two miles wide with a shoal in the middle. We had to go some way up-stream to clear the shoal but the launch could cross it. It seemed that a battle was going on between a party on the shore and a party in some junks. The armed launch joined in, firing her ancient cannon, but I could not make out whose side she was on, as the projectiles were falling indiscriminately.

As soon as we were clear of the shoal we turned down-stream going full speed with guns manned and I hoped that we were looking fierce. When we drew near, the battle stopped. That was satisfactory, but while it seemed easy to stop a battle, it was not so easy to know what to do next. As everybody seemed to expect me to do something, I called Ah Sam on deck and told him to ask the captain of the armed launch what was happening. The captain replied vaguely that there were 'bad men'. That produced protestations from both sides that they were not bad men. We did not seem to be getting anywhere.

I instructed Ah Sam to tell the captain of the launch that the proper person to deal with the matter was the tao tai (magistrate) of Kum Chuk. He should tell the men on the shore to get on board the junks and then should tow the junks to Kum Chuk and report to the tao tai. To my amazement, everybody cheerfully did as they were told.

We went back and anchored off the town and shortly afterwards the *Moorhen*'s twin yellow funnels appeared amongst the houses and she emerged and anchored. Going on board, I told Georgie what had happened. He remarked, 'That's all right, old boy; I don't see what else you could have done. Of course you wouldn't know that the tao tai is the chap who runs all the piracy on this part of the river.'

Early in 1912, the Admiralty decided to put the torpedo-boats into permanent commission and officers were sent from England to relieve us. We stayed on board with our reliefs for a few days taking them round the lower river and Delta before returning to our proper ships.

The *Minotaur* was due to pay off and recommission in the spring of 1912, and as I had been only eight months abroad when I rejoined her, it seemed probable that I should be reappointed unless I did something about it. I was still very keen to get into aviation and, in spite of Captain Lambert's assurance, I had seen several appointments to the newly formed Naval Wing of the Royal Flying Corps. At the same time, if I applied to go home on paying off, I should run the risk of getting another Home Fleet ship. I concluded that the wisest thing was to do nothing until after recommissioning; then, if I were again in the China flagship, I could renew application without risk of being swallowed up by the Home Fleet. Recommissioning was to take place at Colombo.

The ship's final departure from Hong Kong was impressive. A vast number of yachts, launches, sampans and small craft had come to see us off. The ship's company were drawn up as usual for leaving harbour with guard and band on the quarter-deck. The long paying-off pendant was hoisted but with its end and bladder stopped to the after berthing rail.

We slipped from the buoy and, after exchanging the usual bugle salutes with the other ships present, gathered speed and drew away from the mass of small craft. At a pre-arranged signal, the whole upper deck was cleared of men except for the guard and band; the stops were cut and the paying-off pendant floated out astern; two sailors ran aloft and stood on the two trucks; the guard wheeled across the quarter-deck and faced aft and the band struck up 'Rolling Home': finally as we entered the Lye Mun Pass the tune changed to 'Auld Lang Syne'.

The new ship's company were coming out in the *Cressy*-class cruiser brought out of reserve to do the trooping trip. Both ships anchored outside Colombo harbour and the exchange was carried out by ships' boats. The only officers turning over to the new commission were the captain, another watchkeeper named Whitehead and myself. Officers' luggage and the men's bags and hammocks having been ferried across, both ships' companies got into the boats. Whitehead and I stood with the captain on the quarter-deck of a completely empty ship. The two long lines of boats were towed past each other with much cheering, and the new commission started. There followed the usual strenuous period of working up which was at once followed by the competitive gunnery exercises at Weihaiwei.

The Japanese Emperor Meiji died at about this time. His reign had begun while Japan was still a medieval state with the Shogun ruling over a feudal aristocracy, so the funeral was an event of more than ordinary significance to the Japanese. Ships of all nations assembled in Yokohama Bay and arrangements were made for foreign officers to watch the procession from the grounds of the Admiralty building in Tokyo. As the Anglo–Japanese treaty of alliance was still in force, *Minotaur* was invited to send an armed company of seamen to take part in the procession, though no other foreigners were invited.

The procession took place at night, starting from the Imperial Palace by torch-light. The first part consisted of Shinto Ritualists in their ancient robes. The hearse was a wooden vehicle drawn by white oxen and so constructed that the wheels gave out seven different melancholy creaks. After the nobility and politicians there followed a very long march past by the Army and Navy. The Japanese sailors, of small stature and with the very dark blue uniform and collars were not impressive as they marched to the monotonous funeral march played by their bands.

After them was a gap; the strains of Chopin's Funeral March were heard, beautifully played by our band, and then the *Minotaur*'s company appeared, looking huge after the Japanese, their light blue collars and cuffs showing up in the flickering torchlight. I was standing near a group of German naval officers and their comments of admiration were very comforting.

We paid another visit to Japan that autumn and I was able to go up to Nikko and Chusenji at the height of the maple season when the colours were literally unbelievable. This was confirmed by an American who was employed by a colour photography firm. He had a battery of cameras carried by a number of porters. He was very depressed when we met him and kept repeating, 'If I show these to the folks at home they'll call me a liar.'

A party of us went for a walk round the base of Fujiyama, staying in local inns. The inns were very clean and comfortable, as long as they were completely Japanese; but where there had been an attempt at Westernization, they were deplorable. We carried our food with us, except for eggs and tea which we could always obtain, and we did our own cooking over 'hibaskis', large earthenware pots full of sand with a little charcoal fire in the middle.

Soon after the *Minotaur* recommissioned, I had renewed my application to the Admiralty to be appointed to aviation and in the late summer I received an appointment to the Naval Flying School which had been established at Eastchurch. The appointment was accompanied by an order that I was to be relieved by the first supernumerary which occurred on the Station; but during the autumn none arose. We went back to Hong Kong for the winter and one day I received a letter from the Air Department of the Admiralty forwarded from my home address, asking why I had not taken up my appointment. I took it to the Admiral's Office and was at once ordered home.

6
Naval Flying School

On reaching London I reported to Captain Murray Sueter, Director of the Air Department at the Admiralty. The delay in sending me home had apparently been explained and, although a new batch of pilots was already under training at Eastchurch, he agreed to my taking a fortnight's leave.

The Aero Show was staged at Olympia early in February 1913 and I went there just before my leave ended. The chief exhibit was Cody's aeroplane with the famous Colonel Cody in attendance. On another stand was a tractor biplane exhibited by Tom Sopwith which was drawing a lot of attention. It was generally regarded as a big advance, being one of the earliest British designs in which a real effort at streamlining had been made. Subsequently bought by the Admiralty and given the number 33, it was followed by a long line of Sopwith naval aircraft.

I joined Eastchurch in mid-February 1913. The situation with regard to aviation at that time was that the Royal Flying Corps had been formed with an Army Wing, a Naval Wing and a Central Flying School. Officers in both wings retained their naval and military ranks but were graded flying officer, flight commander, squadron commander, etc. The Central Flying School at Upavon had been established to train officers for both wings and also to enter and train civilian volunteers for the special reserve. It was commanded by Captain Godfrey Paine, R.N., with Major Hugh Trenchard[1] as second-in-command.

The Admiralty however continued to maintain its own flying school at Eastchurch, with Acting-Commander Samson, one of

[1] Later Marshal of the Royal Air Force Lord Trenchard.

the four original naval pilots, in command. Another, Lieutenant Gregory, was first lieutenant. Eastchurch originated because Alec Ogilvie, a friend of the Wright Brothers, who had visited them at Dayton and bought a Wright aeroplane, owned a small estate at Leysdown at the east end of the Isle of Sheppey where he had erected the aeroplane. He had been joined by his friend Frank McLean, but the small marshy field at Leysdown proved unsuitable. McLean therefore bought the farm at Eastchurch, which he transferred to the Aero Club on sale or lease, but kept the little farmhouse which he used as a week-end cottage. Horace Short had also secured land alongside the aerodrome and had set up a small aeroplane factory.

Various members of the Aero Club had sheds on the aerodrome. Besides Ogilvie and McLean, Professor Huntingdon had one, and so had the Blair Atholl Syndicate. The Admiralty property bordered the Aero Club's aerodrome at the west end, and arrangements had been made with the club for its use. McLean, Ogilvie and Short were honorary members of the mess.

During 1912 the Admiralty had started to open coastal stations for seaplanes. By the beginning of 1913 Calshot and the Isle of Grain were in commission. Arthur Longmore,[1] another of the original naval team, had recently commissioned Cromarty seaplane station, while the fourth pioneer, Major Gerrard, R.M.L.I., had gone to the C.F.S. as instructor. The station on the Isle of Grain was commanded by John Seddon. Among the officers at Eastchurch besides Gregory, were Major Gordon, R.M.L.I., who was senior instructor, my two old friends from Greenwich days, Wildman-Lushington (Spot-White) and I. T. Courtney, both Marines, Lieutenant Sheppard, R.N., J. L. Travers, by then a sub-lieutenant in the R.N.V.R., and Byrne, a paymaster. The surgeon was Hardy-Wells, and E. F. Briggs was engineer officer as well as being a pilot. I was tacked on to them.

My first flight at Eastchurch was in naval aeroplane No. 1, one of the original machines which McLean had lent to the Admiralty in 1910. She was a Box-kite of the original Farman type, built by Short. The Admiralty was in the habit of buying aeroplanes of nearly every type produced in the early days. No doubt it was

[1] Later Air Chief Marshal Sir Arthur Longmore, Air C-in-C Middle East, 1940–41.

sound policy at a time when ideas as to how aircraft were to be used in naval war were entirely nebulous.

Horace Short had produced a number of machines of ingenious and varied design. They were given naval numbers and were also given nicknames. Two early ones known as the 'triple tractor' and 'triple twin' had already come to grief when I joined; both were twin-engined. Another twin-engined Short was deservedly known as the 'double dirty'. She was a monoplane of immense span with one tractor engine and one pusher. The pilot sat between them in a constant bath of black lubricating oil.

Another of Short's early efforts was known as the 'little dirty'. She was a single-engined monoplane rather like a Bleriot, but something was wrong with the tail design with the result that if the engine was cut, her tail dropped. She would go up but would only come down either with engine full on or tail first. Short wanted to take her back but we had kept her for instruction on the anatomy of the aeroplane.

No. 10 had been the first seaplane Short built for the Navy. As such she had a 14-cylinder 100-h.p. Gnome engine. By 1913 Short was producing a better wing design for his seaplanes, so No. 10's floats had been replaced by a land undercarriage. French design was still ahead of British in 1913 but the French were mainly interested in monoplanes without much weight-carrying capacity. Probably the best aeroplane at Eastchurch at that time was a French-built Deperdussin monoplane.

I found that the two years which had passed since I left the Grahame-White School at Hendon had not made much difference. I was able to start again where I had left off and, under Gordon's instruction, soon achieved a less violent method of landing. Besides No. 1, there was a Bristol Box-kite available for pupils and, after about a week, I was passed on to a Maurice Farman, thence to a Short (known as a 'bicycle') and an Avro. The qualification for the grade of Flying Officer, R.F.C., was not strictly laid down. It depended on the recommendation of the commanding officer, but it normally involved 100 hours as pilot and making at least two cross-country flights satisfactorily. It was the second half of April by the time I had qualified and was graded Flying Officer.

No. 27 was the first Sopwith aeroplane the Navy possessed and must have been one of the earliest that firm produced. It was a tractor biplane with Wright-type wings in which lateral control was achieved by warping. It had been allotted to Courtney, and during my training, I persuaded him and Travers to take me as passenger in it as often as possible. This was fortunate as early in the year the Sopwith No. 33 (see illustration facing p. 118), seen at Olympia was delivered to Eastchurch by Hawker, and Samson allotted it to me.

No. 33 also depended on wing-warping for lateral stability, but in her case it was only the outer bay which could be warped. The inner one was rigid. Lateral control by control wheel was thus very slight; but she was very sensitive to rudder. The slightest kick on the rudder-bar would throw her into a steep bank. She suffered from a constant tendency to drop the left wing, to correct which entailed holding on full warp. This brought a constant strain on the arms which soon began to ache badly. I found I could relieve the strain by frequent kicks with the right foot but that interfered with keeping a steady course.

I spent a lot of time trying without success to find the cause of this trouble, which I assumed must be due to the aircraft being out of truth somewhere. It was only after several months that it dawned on me that it was really due to the torque of the rotary engine, which with aileron control would be unnoticeable. I overcame the difficulty by drilling one of the spokes of the control wheel and attaching a piece of Sandow elastic. By putting tension on the elastic, I could make it do the work of my arms.

Soon after I qualified, the seaplane stations at Great Yarmouth and Felixstowe became ready for use. Gregory was appointed to command Yarmouth and Captain Risk, R.M.L.I., Felixstowe. This left the first lieutenant's job vacant and I knew that Samson wanted to give it to Courtney. However, after visiting the Admiralty, he issued written orders making me first lieutenant, and Courtney and Wildman-Lushington instructors. I felt badly about it as the others all had far more flying experience than I, and I feared things might be a bit difficult. However Wildman-Lushington told me he had been talking to the others who wanted me to know that they would back me up for all they were worth. It was typical of him and I felt most grateful.

The commissioning of the new seaplane stations left Eastchurch short of officers for a time, but soon afterwards a fresh batch of pilots came from the C.F.S. They included Bowhill,[1] Vernon, Bigsworth, Marix, Rainey and Littleton. When the old cruiser *Hermes* was fitted with a flying-off deck over her fo'c'sle, Bowhill was appointed to her, starting off her career with a number of Caudron amphibians.

It was early in 1913 that we became possessed of another aeroplane which achieved fame in her day. This was 'Rickety Anne' which had been designed by A. V. Roe as a seaplane with a central float. Her naval number was 16. As a seaplane she was not a success, Roe having gone in for strength to such an extent that she was too heavy to leave the water. The Admiralty agreed to accept her as a land-plane provided she could pass acceptance trials, which involved among other things reaching a height of 3,000 feet in the course of half an hour.

Roe had designed a land undercarriage which consisted of a central skid where the float had been, with a short axle across it carrying two wheels which for some reason had very narrow-tread tyres. The undercarriage being too narrow to support her in a vertical position when stationary, he had fitted wing-tip skids. At rest she put one wing tip on the ground and raised the other high in the air, which gave her an appearance of drunken abandon. She had no tail skid but the rudder was sprung and the lower part was clad in steel.

Roe and his chief pilot, Rainham, came to put her through acceptance trials; but nothing that Rainham could do would lift her to 3,000 feet. Roe sent for a number of airscrews of different makes. He and Rainham spent several days pulling bits off her and finally she was accepted. We came to know A. V. Roe and Rainham very well during those days.

Rickety Anne's chief claim to fame rested on a visit she made to C.F.S. I think Vernon was the pilot. Unknown to him, the day he chose was also the day that H.M. King George V had decided to inspect the C.F.S. All the aircraft were ranged in lines and all officers and men arrayed in their Sunday best when Rickety Anne descended. The turf was fairly soft and she made her usual landing; that is to say the narrow-tread wheels bit into the turf, which produced a sharp braking effect and caused her

[1] Later Air Marshal Sir F. W. Bowhill, C-in-C Coastal Command during World War II.

long tail to rise high into the air, the nose of the central skid prodded into the ground bringing her to an abrupt halt, the tail with its steel-clad rudder then came down like an executioner's axe, she tipped up on one wing and lay there, dripping black oil. Trenchard at once gave orders to have the eyesore removed, but everyone was in their best clothes and to touch Rickety Anne meant being smothered in oil. At that moment the King arrived.

At Eastchurch, Charles Rumney Samson, our C.O. and the best-known naval pilot of those early days, was a very strong personality. I have heard it said of him that nobody who had served with him under six months ever had a good word to say for him, but that nobody who had served with him over six months had a bad word to say of him. His outstanding quality was guts. Always keen to try out any new experiment, he had made the first flight from a platform built over a battleship's bows, and on a moonless night. His manners were brusque, he was quite frequently rude and had no tact, but as a friend he was absolutely loyal.

He was unpopular with many of his naval contemporaries who believed that he courted publicity in the Press. I don't think that he did and he was certainly often rude to newspaper reporters. But his performance in the air together with his truculent, black-bearded, piratical appearance combined to make him good copy and I don't suppose he objected to seeing his name in the papers. Having started in the days when it was considered dangerous to fly in anything but a flat calm, he delighted in rough weather and had no use for anyone whom he considered a fair-weather pilot.

He had reserved the Short No. 10 for his own use, but when in 1913 two BE 2's were supplied to Eastchurch Aircraft Factory he substituted one of them, No. 50, for No. 10 which was returned to Short's for repair. The practice of sending back aircraft to the makers for repair was common in pre-war days. It arose from the fact that money for new aircraft had to appear in the Naval Estimates as a separate item, whereas a lump sum covered unspecified repairs. When an old aircraft was returned for repair, the contractor was enabled to design an entirely new aircraft, though he was supposed to incorporate something of the old one.

The torpedo-man attached to Eastchurch when I joined was Raymond Fitzmaurice and he was mainly concerned in developing a spark wireless set for use in aircraft. Later he was relieved by Ireland. The gunnery officer was Robert Clarke-Hall who was experimenting with bomb dropping and also with the possibility of installing a machine-gun in aircraft. But the only machine-gun then available was the water-cooled Maxim. Towards the end of 1913 Short produced a pusher biplane, No. 66, specially designed to carry a Maxim gun on a swivel mounting. It had a long coffin-shaped nacelle. The pilot sat at the after end while the gun operator had the use of the bows. Clarke-Hall spent a lot of time experimenting and we insisted on chaining him to the mounting as, the gunwale being very low, there was every possibility of his falling overboard. This type proved a failure as a fighter because she was much too slow.

There was no navigator attached in 1913 but we were all interested in air navigation. The flat card, liquid compasses marked in points and degrees, which were fitted in aircraft, were good though rather clumsy. Gregory, having been a navigator, had laid out a compass-swinging platform so that a deviation table could be made out for each aircraft. Constructors at that time did not worry much about the magnetic field of aircraft and I found several cases in which the tubular steel of the control column was highly magnetized. We surmounted that by obtaining corrector magnets from the dockyard and securing them, reverse-pole-up, to the control column with insulating tape.

There was no means of obtaining upper wind speeds, but we could estimate the speed at ground level with the aid of a hand anemometer and then we added a bit for luck. Hardy-Wells, the surgeon, acted as meteorological officer and we got synoptic charts every day from the Admiralty. I used to help him in forecasting and our results were not too bad.

Instrumented aids to flying were still very crude. Since 1911, revolution counters had become more or less universal. Various forms of air-speed indicators were under trial. Farnborough had produced one which was operated by pitot tube. The indicator consisted of a column of purple liquid which rose and fell in a tube which had a scale of miles alongside it. I had one of these in No. 33 but it always registered 20 miles an hour on the ground;

in the air it slowly rose to 45 m.p.h. and stayed there, although 33's normal speed was about 60 m.p.h. Once when I landed at Farnborough, Edward Busk said he would have it adjusted for me. After that the column of liquid sank out of sight and was never seen again.

The air-speed indicator which functioned by pitot tube affecting a diaphragm was invented by Alec Ogilvie. It came into general use in 1914.

Aneroid height indicators were good and reliable. The instrument to which we all attached great importance was another invention of Alec Ogilvie's and consisted of a piece of string and nothing else. The string was attached to the aeroplane in front of the pilot and in the full air stream. In normal flight or during a correctly banked turn the string pointed at the pilot's nose, but if there was any side-slip the string was deflected. For blind flying in a cloud it was most useful, particularly as most early aeroplanes were directionally unstable.

Practically every engine at Eastchurch in 1913 was of French make. Gnomes predominated, though Maurice Farmans and BE 2's had Renault engines, two Deperdussin monoplanes had Anzani, and a Breguet had a Canton-Unné. Short was concentrating more and more on seaplanes and his difficulty was to generate enough power to lift them off the water. The Gnome company had just produced an engine of nominally 160 h.p. It consisted of two 80-h.p. engine units on a single crankshaft and was, I think, the biggest rotary engine ever produced. When I first saw one of these engines in Short's works it gave me a bright idea; at least I thought so.

I sought out Horace Short and asked him if he would design a new tail unit for the little dirty so as to produce a normal method of descent. Any mention of the little dirty always aroused Short's suspicion as he was determined that she should stay on the ground. He at once demanded what I proposed to do with her. I told him that I wanted to fit the 160-h.p. Gnome and have a shot at the British speed record. There came the deep rumbling sound which did duty for laughter with Horace and he asked, 'Do you know what will happen if you do that?'

'No, what?'

'Why, when you start that engine, the airscrew will stay still and the little dirty will go round and round and round like a tee-to-tum.'

I did not try for the speed record.

The Sunbeam Company were experimenting with an aircraft engine of the stationary, water-cooled type and had fitted it into a Maurice Farman. They engaged John Alcock[1] to demonstrate it and to discover its teething troubles of which there were many. When he had it running satisfactorily he usually demonstrated it at Hendon or Brooklands, but when it showed signs of trouble he brought it to Eastchurch for an abdominal operation. We made Alcock an honorary member of the mess, but he did not use it much. He was usually fully occupied with his engine and sought the company of our senior engine mechanic, Chief Petty Officer Susans, who was best able to give him help.

[1] Later Sir John Alcock who with Sir Arthur Whitten-Brown made the first non-stop transatlantic flight.

7

Flying Organization and Vicissitudes

Soon after taking over the executive job I was graded flight commander. I certainly had not much flying experience at the time, so I suppose that promotion was the result of getting the job. The Air Department encouraged cross-country flying, allowing naval aircraft to be used for week-end trips, and we all took full advantage of this. My friend of Hendon days, T. C. Higgins, had been seconded to the King's African Rifles for the last two years so had not joined the R.F.C. He was now back with his own regiment, stationed at Dover where, as there was good landing on the downs, I visited him several times. Eastbourne had a small aerodrome and was a favourite place for week-end visits.

In the meantime, Parker and I decided to visit the two newly established seaplane stations at Felixstowe and Great Yarmouth. I went in No. 33 taking the chief boatswain's mate, P.O. Andrews, as passenger. Parker took his own machine, a Short bicycle. We spent the night at Felixstowe and started for Yarmouth the next morning. Soon after taking off, the petrol pipe in 33 broke.

We were at about 2,000 feet over that queer belt of poor land in Suffolk which is largely wooded. Beyond the woodland area there were small fields mostly with growing crops, but just alongside the wood there seemed to be a strip of grass. I made for that but when I drew near and was too low to change I realized that it was bracken. Though I put 33 down as slowly as I could the bracken was too tough for the undercarriage which collapsed. That was the only damage; but 33 had to go home by rail.

Andrews and I decided that the first thing to do was to get some lunch; as there was no village near we went to the nearest farm.

The farmer and his wife were away but the girl in charge of the house at once set about producing food, keeping up a commentary in the East Anglian dialect which I had not heard since I left prep school in Suffolk.

When the farmer turned up he said he could produce a hay wain which could contain 33 and he was very helpful in stripping her down. Having got her to the nearest station I asked the farmer to make out a bill for his help, hire of wain and for lunch but he replied, 'I ain't schollared, more's the pity.' It seemed extraordinary that there should still be men in England in 1913 who could not read or write. He said that Fred in the signal-box was schollared, so we all repaired to the signal-box. I wrote out the bill and paid it, and then wrote 'paid' on it; Fred wrote the farmer's name and the farmer made his mark. He had protested against being given any money, particularly for the lunch, until I told him that the Government would be paying.

It was while 33 was still having a new undercarriage made that Parker and I decided to spend a week-end in London, going to Hendon on Saturday in his Short bicycle. On Monday morning we found a strong east wind blowing. We had gone to Hendon reasonably early, but it was about 11 a.m. by the time we had filled up with petrol and were ready to start back. It was quite evident that we could not make Eastchurch against the wind without coming down for petrol. Worse still we could not get there for lunch. So we decided if we saw a hospitable-looking country house about lunch-time, we would come down for lunch and petrol.

After starting, the wind seemed to grow colder and stronger and the Short was appallingly slow and draughty. At 12.30 p.m., Tilbury was still a long way ahead, so being the passenger I started to look for country houses. There are not many in the Tilbury district and it was some time before I saw a possible starter. It was a large brick building standing in the middle of a park. I pointed it out to Parker who started down. The park had a good many trees in it but there was plenty of good open turf as well: a cricket match was in progress near the house. Selecting a stretch of turf clear of the cricket match, but close to the drive which ran through the park, we duly landed.

The cricketers all came streaming towards us and we inquired about petrol and lunch. They told us that we could find petrol in the village of Grays, quite near, and a pub there where we might get bread and cheese. That was not our idea at all. To our delight, Mrs Stead who with her husband occupied the house, on hearing that we were distressed naval aviators, at once invited us to lunch.

The house was Belhus Park. Built in Tudor times, Elizabeth I had stayed there when she reviewed the troops at Tilbury in 1588. Our unexpected visit was a piece of good fortune because not only did we enjoy an excellent lunch in a lovely setting, but the encounter paid handsome future dividends in pleasure.

During lunch, Parker discovered that Mrs Stead was desperately keen to go up in an aeroplane. Having filled up with petrol, he offered to give her a flight. Taxiing for a long take-off, he crossed the drive and unfortunately the jerk as the aeroplane dropped off the grass verge on to the gravel cracked one of the landing struts. We telephoned to Eastchurch, whence Bigsworth and Rathbone brought a spare strut to us in another Short bicycle.

Taking off for the return flight, Bigsworth, failing to allow himself a long enough take-off run, found himself airborne just short of a line of tall elms which stood in the park. There was no way round or through. He had to go over. The Short just did it in a badly stalled attitude, dragging her tail through the upper branches. It was a narrow shave and Bigsworth landed at Eastchurch with a fair-sized elm branch hanging from the tail. It was nailed to one of the shed doors to serve as a warning. Parker and I shifted our landing strut and invited the Steads to come to tea at Eastchurch where we could give Mrs Stead her flight well clear of elm trees and gravel drives.

The Army manœuvres took place in the first half of September and Eastchurch was invited to make up a half flight and join the Military Wing. Samson being in command of the station could not come; Wildman-Lushington being senior instructor also had to remain: I. T. Courtney (Captain, R.M.), the senior flight commander, therefore took charge and we made up a party of six.

The R.F.C. had selected as the headquarters aerodrome for the manœuvres a meadow near Coventry to which we flew independently. I took 33 with P. O. Andrews as passenger, leaving Eastchurch at 3 p.m. and landing at 4.55 p.m. There must have been a fresh southerly wind that day.

The naval party joined up with a half flight of the R.F.C., the combined flight being commanded by Captain Geoffrey de Havilland and attached to the squadron of Major John Higgins. As we had no military training, Army observers were lent to us. Mine was Captain Furse who had recently graduated at the Staff College, but I don't think he had had any air experience before. On our first reconnaissance of some roads south of Oxford, we ran into hazy weather and lost ourselves. I proposed to land and find out where we were. Furse was conscientious and protested that we were over enemy territory and should be taken prisoner if we landed. My persuasion proved effective so we landed, found out what we wanted and evading capture took off again.

After that we got on quite well until Furse, leaning over the side with his binoculars, put his knee against the main petrol pipe and broke a connection. There was plenty of grassland about, but it was all ridge and furrow with the wind blowing across the ridges. No. 33 made a series of kangaroo-like leaps from ridge to ridge and when we climbed out, I found that one of the landing struts was sprung. As we were still in enemy territory, Furse felt it his duty to escape with the information he had obtained, which he did very comfortably by train. I found a village wheelwright who did not know that he was an enemy, and got him to make a pair of oak splints to fit the sprung struts. A hospitable retired colonel gave me dinner and a bed; I 'fished' the strut and flew back next morning.

The R.F.C. had proved the value of aircraft in land war during 1912 manœuvres and the lesson was confirmed by those of 1913. They lasted about a week during which we got to know most of the officers of the Military Wing, including Colonel Sykes. At the conclusion, H.M. King George V inspected the squadrons.

Back at Eastchurch, at the end of September we heard that the First Lord, Mr Winston Churchill, was taking a great interest in aviation and had sent the Admiralty yacht *Enchantress* to Sheerness so that he could live in her when he came down. He usually came to Sheerness for the week-end and he spent several Saturdays at Eastchurch learning to fly in No. 1 Short with Samson as instructor. He also took a great interest in the seaplanes at the station in the Isle of Grain.

Up to this time, aeroplanes on floats had been called hydro-aeroplanes, but I heard Winston Churchill say, 'That's a beastly word. Let's give them a better name; let's call them seaplanes.' And seaplanes they have been ever since.

John Seddon who was in command at Grain, invited the First Lord to lunch in the mess. Taking a seaplane out over the Thames Estuary for a duck hunt, he succeeded in shooting a couple of mallard which were duly cooked for the lunch party. Seddon's performance in providing wild duck for the First Lord called for an effort from Eastchurch. Gordon-Bell was then pilot for the Martin Handasyde monoplane. He was an honorary member of the mess and spent a lot of time at Eastchurch. Hearing that we wanted to produce something to rival Seddon's mallard for the First Lord's lunch, he said that he knew a farmer near Whitstable who was mad about aeroplanes. The farmer had been constantly begging him to land an aeroplane in his big hay meadow, and Gordon-Bell had promised to do so one day on one condition: when the farmer saw the aeroplane circling the meadow he should send his boy on a bike into Whitstable to buy a barrel of oysters. Gordon-Bell suggested that Whitstable oysters would be a suitable corollary to Seddon's ducks, a proposal which was unanimously agreed to in the Eastchurch mess.

The First Lord had come to Sheerness on a Friday, inviting all of us to dine in *Enchantress* that night. He was to lunch at Eastchurch on the Saturday. It was well on in the afternoon of Friday that the oyster expedition was agreed on and I took Gordon-Bell over the Swale in No. 33. I circled the meadow which he pointed out. Very soon a small figure appeared pedalling energetically in the direction of Whitstable; G-B then signalled to me to land, which I did, and we were given a most enthusiastic reception by the farmer. Presently the small boy returned puffing and panting, with a barrel of oysters strapped on the back of his bike. We transferred the oysters and took a cordial farewell of the farmer.

G-B had the bad habit of flying across country at tree-top height for which I had abused him, but he maintained it was much more interesting. As we climbed into 33, he remarked, 'None of your 5,000-feet stuff this time.' As there was a strong head wind and it was getting late I agreed and told him that if he wanted to hedge-hop we would. We crossed the Swale at about twenty feet, skimming on over the Sheppey marshes at the same height. We were well into the marshes when an inlet valve broke. When that happened in a Gnome engine, the whole gas contents of the crankcase discharged itself in a sheet of blue flame into the passenger seat. G-B was wearing a smart suit of tweed plus fours with hand-knitted stockings provided by his lady friends. There came a strong smell of singed wool.

The Sheppey marshes were cut up into very small paddocks by deep drainage dykes filled with mud always covered in green slime. To make matters worse there was an immense mole population, each little bit of firm ground being covered in mole-hills. I kept 33 in the air till nearly all flying speed had gone, just cleared a scum-covered dyke and dropped on to a tiny patch of grassland. The molehills functioned as an arrester gear and the plane pulled up on the verge of the next dyke.

Even so it was a grim situation. Darkness was setting in. I was determined to get back to the station in time to dress for dinner in *Enchantress*. There was no way of crossing the slimy dykes except by wading, and we had a barrel of oysters to carry. That journey was a nightmare. Taking turns with the barrel, we made straight for the nearest firm ground. It was quite dark by the time we reached it, but we could just make out a cart track leading towards the main road. As we were floundering along, we saw the head-lights of a car on the main road. It could only be the station car since there was no other in the neighbourhood. With the last of our breath we produced such a banshee yell that the driver heard us and stopped. I arrived in time for dinner in the *Enchantress*, and Mr Churchill had oysters for lunch; but G-B's stockings and suit were never quite the same again.

It was during one of these week-end visits of the First Lord that we first met General Sir Ian Hamilton. Winston Churchill had served with him in South Africa and held him in admiration. I suppose it was on Churchill's suggestion that he visited East-church. He brought a small party with him, none of whom had been in the air before. As Samson was instructing the First Lord, it fell to me to take up the General and some of his friends. Sir Ian Hamilton never forgot his first flight and was always very kind to me afterwards.

When we were lunching on board the *Enchantress* after this visit, the First Lord asked me if it was I who had taken up Sir Ian of whom he spoke very warmly. He then asked me who was the second member of the party who had flown in 33. I replied that I had not caught his name, but that he was a tough-looking elderly man. The First Lord considered that for a moment and then exclaimed, 'Percy Girouard, of course. "A tough-looking elderly man." I call that a jolly good description.' Sir Percy Girouard was the French-Canadian railway engineer who, after being concerned in the C.P.R., had constructed the military railway lines both in the Sudan and in South Africa. He had also been Governor of Nigeria.

These visits of the First Lord had coincided with the crisis of the Irish Home Rule controversy, including the 'mutiny' at the Curragh when British officers had resigned their commissions rather than accept orders to coerce Ulster. The 3rd Battle Squadron had been suddenly ordered to Lamlash in the Firth of Clyde on Churchill's sole responsibility. There had been uproar in Parliament during all-night sittings. Winston Churchill had been one of the chief targets for abuse and must have been under heavy strain all through the weeks. Yet at the week-ends he had been able to appear carefree and happy, displaying a kind of schoolboy humour and entertaining us on board *Enchantress* as though the only thing he was interested in was naval aviation.

During the late autumn I received several invitations to shoot at Belhus Park. I would take Wildman-Lushington with me and he soon became a firm friend of the Steads. We both thoroughly enjoyed the Saturday partridge shoots and we usually stayed the night at Belhus, driving back to Eastchurch on Sunday.

During the winter of that year we carried out several exercises with submarines working in the Thames Estuary. Not much was learned though the exercises confirmed the fact that submerged submarines in home waters were no more visible from the air than they were from surface ships.

Our other air activities that winter included experiments to increase the range of existing aircraft with additional fuel tanks. We also experimented with air interception and discovered for the first time how difficult it is to sight another aeroplane when in the air. We reached the conclusion that unless some way could be devised of giving help and direction from the ground to defending fighters, the defending force would have to be concentrated over the target area. We also experimented with flying in company and found that the V formation was the most satisfactory both for forming up and for avoidance of collision. Most of us went over to the Isle of Grain station from time to time to get practice in flying seaplanes.

It was during that winter that Eastchurch held for a few weeks the British height record, E. T. Briggs, the engine officer, having succeeded in taking his 80-h.p. Gnome-engined Bleriot to a height of 15,000 feet. Briggs's nickname in the service was 'Skully' because of his very lean face; but in the course of this effort he suffered superficial frost-bite all over his face which swelled like a football.

Early in 1914 rumours reached us of a reorganization. It had become clear that the number of Special Reserve officers who could be trained would all be needed by the Military Wing in the event of war. The Admiralty wanted to expand the Naval Wing but could not afford to appoint many more regular naval officers: the same applied to the trained Reserve officers, both R.N.R. and R.N.V.R. The only solution was to enter candidates from civil life and train them. Expansion of ground crew personnel was also needed.

Samson was asked to make proposals on the latter subject and he referred the matter of engine mechanics to Briggs and of airframe ratings to me. We both believed that the best solution was to expand the normal naval intake and, after basic training, to superimpose a specialist course. This would have involved introducing a non-substantive rating for artificers and artisans. Our scheme was never adopted, because the vast expansion following the outbreak of war made it impracticable. One interesting point arose out of it: airframes were practically all wood; there were two categories of naval tradesmen who could work in wood – shipwrights and joiners; the basic rate of pay for shipwrights was higher than that for joiners, so the economical mind of the Treasury would probably insist on the intake of joiners being increased, not that of shipwrights. It was foreseen however that before very long, airframes would be made of metal not wood. Under trade union law metal must be handled by a fitter not a joiner, so that when the change came along the Navy would be at loggerheads with the T.U.C. Fortunately it turned out that since time immemorial craftsmen of three trades in Great Britain had traditionally worked in both wood and metal. They were the mill-wrights, the wheelwrights and the shipwrights. By expanding the shipwright intake we would be able to keep the peace with that staunchly conservative body, the Trades Union Congress.

I had been graded squadron commander at the New Year and again I think it was because Eastchurch was expanding and the first lieutenant's job was held to justify it. We were still ignorant of what form the reorganization was to take when, one day, orders were received that all squadron commanders were to assemble at the Admiralty for a meeting to discuss uniform. My ideas at the time were nebulous, but the one thing which I held clearly in mind was that naval aviation ought to be an integral part of the Navy and on that point I knew Samson felt as I did.

When we assembled we were not a full muster. Gregory could not come; Spencer-Grey, having had a bad crash, was in hospital. Besides myself there were Longmore, Gerrard, Seddon, and L'Estrange–Malone. Lambert, by this time a rear-admiral, was Naval Secretary to the First Lord. He called us into his office to explain that Winston Churchill wanted our views on what the uniform for the new organization was to be. The intention was that all officers should have the same, naval (executive and engineering), Marine, R.N.R. and R.N.V.R., as well as for the new entry from civil life. We had no chance to discuss it amongst ourselves as almost at once we were shown into the First Lord's office.

Longmore was looking very ill. In the few moments that we were in Lambert's office he told me that he did not think he would be able to last out the meeting but added 'One thing I'm sure of is that if we agree to letting all the new entry get into our uniform, the rest of the lieutenants will never speak to us again.' I agreed. The First Lord told us that the choice lay between a non-executive uniform, i.e. one without the executive curl on the stripes, an eagle badge being substituted for it, or an executive uniform, but with an eagle in place of the foul anchor on cap-badges and buttons. In 1914, the curl on the stripes was limited to the executive branch and, no doubt we were all snobs where that was concerned. The foul-anchor badge on the other hand was common to all ranks and ratings from cook's mate to admiral of the fleet. Having put the matter before us Winston Churchill asked for our views. Gerrard put in a plea for the moustaches of the Marines and was promptly overruled. I spoke up badly in favour of the foul anchor and was told I was very stupid. Then the First Lord withdrew and left Lambert to take the chair. We wrangled about it for a bit, Lambert being strongly in favour of the executive type uniform with the eagle replacing the foul anchor. Eventually he said he would leave us to talk it out and would report the result.

When we were left alone I found that Seddon agreed with me. Gerrard, having lost the battle of the moustaches, had an open mind, while L'Estrange-Malone said that, having been a long time at the Admiralty, he considered himself out of touch and would not give an opinion. So we duly reported that we favoured the non-executive uniform with foul-anchor badges. Perhaps I attached more importance to the uniform question than it deserved, but it seemed to me to indicate whether naval aviation was a branch of the Navy or an auxiliary Service. In the end, the Admiralty wisely decided that regular officers, both Naval and Marine, might continue to wear their own uniform with the addition of an eagle badge on the sleeve. Direct entry officers were to wear the executive uniform with the eagle substituted for the foul anchor. I suspect that the wisdom came from Murray Sueter.

The spring of 1914 saw the last of pre-war Eastchurch for me. There can seldom have been a naval establishment where the general atmosphere was so happy. The main reason was that everyone, ratings as well as officers, was intensely interested in his job. There were literally no defaulters. We kept an open gangway and allowed beer in the messes and there was no drunkenness. Working-hours in summer and winter lasted throughout daylight and at 'close sheds' in the evenings, officers, petty officers and ratings all worked together as a team with Petty Officer Andrews in charge. No night leave was given except on request, but long week-ends, Friday evening till Monday morning, were given regularly except to duty officers and the duty part of the watch.

Our time at Eastchurch had been saddened however, by two fatalities. Byrne, the paymaster, was killed by a propeller and my great friend Wildman-Lushington was killed in a crash. These were, I think, the only two fatal casualties in naval aviation before the outbreak of the first German War.

In April I happened to meet Boothby of the Airship Section at the club and we lunched together. He told me that the Admiralty were considering using airships in Somaliland to assist the Camel Corps in suppressing the Mad Mullah. While it had been definitely decided that it must be an airship show, Boothby had suggested that an aeroplane pilot should accompany him to report on possibilities generally in that country. He offered to ask for me. It sounded interesting and I agreed.

We travelled out by the Indian Mail route: train to Brindisi and thence by the small, fast, turbine-driven P. & O. ship which took the mail to Port Said for transfer to the regular liner for India. On arrival at Aden we embarked in a clean and comfortable little cattle-boat for Berbera.

While waiting there for arrangements to be made for us to join the Governor, who was inland at a place called Lower Sheik, we suffered the discomforts of the karief, the dry, scorching south wind which gets up early in the morning to reach full force by midday, when the temperature reaches more than 120°F. About 4 p.m. it dies away to be succeeded by a damp northerly breeze which, though it brings the temperature down to the 90s, leaves one continuously bathed in sweat. These conditions called for a strange routine by night.

All bungalows at Berbera were built round a square compound with the veranda inside the compound, on to which the windows of all the rooms opened. Everyone had three camp beds. Bed No. 1 was in the compound under the open sky; bed No. 2 under the corrugated-iron roof of the veranda; bed No. 3 inside the bungalow. You started in bed No. 1 while the moist north breeze was blowing, and lay bathed in sweat. About 1 a.m. the north wind dropped, the air dried up and you fell asleep. When the karief started at about 3 a.m., sand and small bits of coral were blown around so you shifted to bed No. 2 on the veranda. By 4.30 or 5 a.m., by which time lumps of coral were rattling against the veranda roof and the air was full of sand, you had to move to bed No. 3, having shut fast all doors and windows to keep out the sand. When you tired of bed No. 3 you decided to have a bath, the water supply coming boiling hot from a volcanic spring.

Arrangements having been made for us to join the Governor at Lower Sheik, we set out on trotting camels with our Somali boy and two Somali soldiers of the Camel Corps as escort. Of all ways of travelling, a trotting camel is about the worst. If you try to ride him like a horse, rising in your stirrups, about every third trot the camel is going up when you are coming down and the resulting jar is violent. The only way to deal with the situation is to lean well back and just jog; but until you get inured, this produces more muscular aches than any other form of exercise.

There were no roads and we followed a dry water course. At intervals of several miles, wells scooped in the sand provided drinkable water. (Rivers in Somaliland only reach the sea if there is a cloudburst in the hills.) We started in the evening and spent a few hours in a thorn hut near one of the wells, arriving at Sheik the following morning.

The Mad Mullah was a problem of long standing. With a force of dervishes he constantly raided the unfortunate Somalis from his strongholds in Ethiopia and Italian Somaliland. The Indian Government, which until recently had administered British Somaliland, had repeatedly sent troops in efforts to catch him, but his pony-mounted dervishes had always slipped away across the border. An enterprising journalist, who succeeded in entering British Somaliland from Ethiopia and touring the interior, wrote such a harrowing report on the sufferings of the Somali tribes that the British conscience was aroused.

The Colonial Office had meanwhile taken over administration and had set out to form a Somali Camel Corps which it was expected would eventually become strong enough to deal with the Mullah. By 1913 it was in control of the maritime plain, but an advance into the interior had resulted in a bloody battle at a place called Dul Madobah in which, though the Mullah was forced to withdraw, the Camel Corps suffered heavy casualties, including the commanding officer killed.

As a result, it had been decided both to strengthen the Camel Corps and to use airships to reconnoitre and so avoid surprise by the Mullah's forces. Airships had been chosen instead of aeroplanes at that time because aero engines were so unreliable. Failure in the latter would mean a forced landing which the Mullah would claim to be a result of his magical powers.

The outbreak of the German War in 1914 put a stop to our operations in Somaliland, but when they were resumed in 1919, the elimination of the Mad Mullah was finally brought about almost entirely by air operations of the Royal Air Force.

We spent a week at Sheik as guests of Archer, the Governor, discussing possibilities and then returned to Berbera. The return journey was worse than before as we rode all day in a shade temperature of 126°F. My camel was independent-minded and decided to follow a different track to that followed by Boothby and the Somalis. We were out of sight of them, when it fell down and pitched me into a thorn bush. By the time I had extricated myself it was standing up again. The problem was how to get on to its back. Grasping its head rope, I made a noise like a sneeze. At first nothing happened so I sneezed again, hard. Then the camel began to wag its head and grumble. Encouraged by that I went on sneezing until eventually it folded up in front and then behind and I was able to mount.

On my return home I rejoined Eastchurch. Courtney had been acting as executive officer while I was away and was making out the arrangements for our part in the Naval Review which was to take place in July. During my absence the Air Department had engaged a number of slide-rule experts (boffins) to vet the aircraft which the Navy possessed and to pass or fail them for air worthiness. To my intense indignation No. 33 had been condemned as unfit to fly. She had been stripped of engine and wings and stowed away to await possible rebuilding.

Samson had decided to let Courtney carry on with the executive job until the start of the Naval Review. We were to be organized as a mobile squadron with make-shift transport, going to Portsmouth to fly during the review, and then to make a squadron tour of the west country. Courtney was to remain at Eastchurch in command; I was to take over as executive officer of the squadron when we left. The only unallotted aeroplane available being a 50-h.p. Gnome Avro, I took that over for the review and spent the short time before we left getting used to it. The squadron left Eastchurch on 13 July.

91

I had not been feeling well for some days and soon after taking off for Portsmouth, I felt thoroughly ill. Knowing there was a small landing ground at Shoreham which possessed a clubhouse, I landed there and stood myself a stiff brandy and soda. That did some good and I went on to Portsmouth. The ground that Samson had chosen for an aerodrome was that by Fort George, which is now the Municipal Airport. Fort George was still in military occupation and while we were made honorary members of the officers' mess, we were to sleep at the naval barracks. When I reached the barracks that evening I reported to the sick bay where the doctor took my temperature, told me I had jaundice, and sent me to bed. The next morning I was put into an ambulance and sent to Haslar.

It was a very different Haslar from the hospital of 1903. The new officers block had been built and there I had a comfortable cabin to myself. There were no more messengers but instead a sick-berth attendant was permanently on duty in each corridor and a nursing sister day and night in the block. Meals were regular and good: not that meals mattered much to me for the next week as jaundice is a beastly complaint.

The review passed off quite well without my assistance, and by the time I was able to take an interest in newspapers again they were full of the murder of the Archduke Ferdinand at Sarajevo. I was sent off on sick leave at the end of July by which time the possibility of war was beginning to dawn on everyone. I wrote to Samson telling him I was on sick leave but quite ready to come back if he wanted me. He replied that Courtney had been sent to Killingholme on the Humber with two other pilots as a precaution against possible Zeppelin attack on the Admiralty oil fuel depot, but that there was no probability of any other emergency and that I should stay on leave. I had hardly finished reading the letter when a telegram arrived from him calling me back.

No appointment came for me so that, as far as I know, I shall remain permanently and officially on sick leave from Haslar. When arrived at Eastchurch I found that Christopher Draper,[1] who had taken over my Avro when I went sick, had had a forced landing and had written it off, leaving me without an aeroplane. However the carcass of No. 33 was still in the crock's shed so I

[1] Later famous for his exploits as the 'Mad Major'.

took her out. Her planes were intact and had been slung up over-head, but the shed being inhabited by a large number of sparrows, everything was in a shocking mess. As all the mechanics were already fully employed, I roped in a number of newly trained officers who had joined from the C.F.S. to reassemble No. 33. Years after when Lancelot Tomkinson was assistant to the Deputy Chief of the Air Staff, he reminded me that the first responsible duty he had to perform after qualifying as a flying officer was to scrub sparrow droppings off the wings of my aeroplane. No. 33 was completed and on 4 August I took her up for a trial flight. At midnight war was declared.

8

France 1914 and Zeebrugge

The last few days of peace had been full of rumours: spies, Zeppelins and mysterious ships were reported everywhere. My first war-time flight was as observer with Samson over the Thames Estuary and the Medway. Of course we saw nothing. On 8 August 1914 Samson was called to the Admiralty, returning to announce that we were to form a mobile squadron and move north to Killingholme on the Humber. The hired transport used on the west country cruise had been dispersed so we collected transport by the simple process of stopping the buses which plied between Sittingbourne and Sheerness when they reached Sheerness and driving them off to Eastchurch.

We left on the 9th, a mixed unit of six aircraft; two B.E.2's, one Bristol, one Bleriot, one Short pusher armed with a Maxim, and No. 33 Sopwith. Besides the Maxim gun, we each had an automatic pistol and there was a small supply of hand grenades. I took P.O. Andrews as passenger in No. 33 and after about two hours we started having trouble. The engine cut out when we were near Lincoln and we landed on plough.

We found that the supply pipe from the reserve to the gravity tank was nearly choked and the engine was being starved of petrol. After putting that right and pumping up petrol we got the engine to run but not at full power. It was Andrews who eventually diagnosed the trouble. He said that when he filled up at Eastchurch he noticed that the reserve tank was already half full. that meant that since April the tank had been lying half full of petrol slowly evaporating; so we drained the whole system down and filled up with fresh petrol.

By that time it was late evening and pouring with rain. I was still suspicious of the engine and doubtful if the plane would get off the sodden plough with a passenger, so telling Andrews to find his way to Killingholme as best he could, I went on alone. The rain grew worse, and I lost myself somewhere in North Lincolnshire; it was by then nearly dark, so I found a good grass field where I landed for the night and took shelter in a farm. Early next day, the rain having stopped, I flew on to Killingholme where Courtney had arrived with his three aircraft and had fixed up a camp of sorts on a field next to the Admiralty oil fuel tanks on the bank of the Humber, a mile or so from Immingham.

Samson's orders were to institute a reconnaissance patrol along the coast south of the Humber to connect with the seaplane patrols from Yarmouth. Selecting Skegness as a base, we shifted there and rigged up a camp. That coastal patrol continued until 24 August when we were ordered to return to Eastchurch. On the return journey I was again forced down, this time by and near Great Warley.

To telephone to Eastchurch for a spare engine I went into Warley Barracks, depot for the Essex Regiment. Reservists were still pouring into the barracks and orders had just been received from the War Office to enter 100,000 recruits. The senior officer, a major just recalled from retirement, was trying to imagine how the recruits could be trained when all the regular N.C.O.s were in Flanders. He sought comfort in his belief that Kitchener was sure to have it all planned. I was put up for the night, the spare engine arriving next morning and I reached Eastchurch about noon.

A brigade of Marines had been ordered to occupy Ostend and our Squadron was to co-operate with them. We found Samson's brother Felix, who was acting as transport officer, had collected a mixed lot of cars and lorries and had also entered transport drivers who came from every strata of society and were all, of course, volunteers. They proved to be a remarkably fine lot, remaining with us until the evacuation of Gallipoli in January 1916 when the squadron was dispersed.

We crossed on 27 August, flying via Dover and Calais in rain and low cloud. I saw that the Ostend race-course was marked as a landing ground – Samson and some others had already arrived – but, on gliding in to land, I was received by volleys of rifle fire

from our war-like Marines. Soon after landing, I saw my old shipmate Hatton (once the guest of Riff brigands) approaching and
thought it civil of the Marines to send an officer to apologize for
their rude reception. But I was wrong; all Hatton had come for
was to find out how many hits they had scored.

I have referred to our party as a squadron but in fact it was
some weeks before we were officially designated No. 3 Squadron
R.N.A.S. Until then we were referred to as Samson's aeroplane
party, which had a pleasant seventeenth-century sound about it.
After all the Coldstream Guards were originally Monk's Foot.
Shifting to a better landing ground east of the town, we took up
residence in and around a ruined fort.

The marine brigade's visit to Ostend lasted only three days
when they, and we, were recalled to England. Samson, determined
to stay on the Continent, decided that there was going to be a bad
fog in the Channel which would force us to land at Dunkirk. A
suitable landing ground just west of the town near the suburb of
Saint Pol had been selected and there we duly landed. The general
commanding the garrison, having been persuaded by Samson that
we could be some use to him, gave us the use of the ground and of
the buildings of a disused hospital beside it; so we settled in.

It was very difficult at the end of August 1914 to get an idea of
what was happening at the front, or even where it was. We knew
vaguely that the main German thrust was aimed at Paris and that
the Allies were in retreat, but nobody knew what was taking
place on the flank north of the main German advance. The
Germans were probably worried about that open flank towards
the sea and their cavalry patrols appeared from time to time,
presumably on reconnaissance.

Samson at once realized the possibilities of using armed cars. He
threw himself with all his usual energy into the task of producing
them and was very successful in operating them, getting into
action with German patrols on several occasions. I went with
him on these trips once or twice, but as he had his hands so full
with the cars, I had to concentrate on the aeroplanes. These were
used on reconnaissance to the south to watch for any movement of
German troops in the general area of Lille, Douai, Cambrai,
Amiens and Arras.

One evening, a major and a captain of the R.A.M.C. came into our mess in the old hospital. From them we heard something of the war situation. They themselves had had a comical experience. Left in charge of a casualty station near le Cateau when the B.E.F. fell back, they had handed their wounded over to German doctors and then, as nobody had seemed interested in them, had walked out. They walked north, nobody stopping them. Coming to a level crossing guarded by a German sentry, they stopped to consider; at that moment a train carrying German wounded passed the level crossing and pulled up at a little station just beyond. When the sentry went off to talk to the German wounded, they walked on. The sentry was thus some way off when he saw them on the crossing. He stared at them, recognized them to be officers and saluted. Returning his salute they walked on. Eventually they got a lift on a lorry and reached Dunkirk.

On 10 September I took No. 33 on reconnaissance over Tournai, Roubaix and Oudenaarde. On the way back, near Roulers, the engines failed. I landed in a grass field after dodging a lot of poplar trees, to find that the spring of the magneto was broken. The oil pump had also given up the ghost. Magneto springs could probably be replaced by a local garage, but the oil pump could not and I should have to get a spare from Dunkirk.

I was given a lift into Roulers where I went to the police station. The helpful Belgian police put me through by telephone to the Dunkirk aerodrome and I arranged for a car to bring out an oil pump. They then took me to a garage which undertook to replace the broken spring of the magneto. Being pretty late by that time, I arranged to spend the night at the best (and only) hotel in Roulers.

Early next morning the car with the oil pump arrived from Dunkirk. About the same time there was a message from the police station to say that a large force of German cavalry was approaching Roulers and that I was advised to lie low and prepare to evacuate northwards. Filling up the Dunkirk car with petrol we stationed ourselves near the police station to await further intelligence. I did not feel worried about No. 33 as it did not seem likely that German cavalry could get much use out of an obsolete British aeroplane without a magneto or oil pump. Eventually news came by telephone that the German patrol was moving southward again, so all was well.

When we reached No. 33 again we found that patriotic peasants had started to saw the wings off, presumably to prevent the German cavalry from flying off in her. We stripped her of what was left of the wings and, with help from the locals, got her on to the road. Setting the tail skid on the back of the car we started to tow her, stern first, back to Dunkirk. The outskirts of the little village of Pervyse had been reached when the undercarriage started to collapse and it was decided that it would be necessary to lift the plane into a lorry. The driver of the car and the mechanic from Dunkirk were left to look after her and prevent traffic collisions while I went into Pervyse to find a telephone.

Back in Pervyse I was taken to the mayor's small villa and arranged by telephone for a lorry to be sent. The mayor then said that we must go to the village hall or commune, because the people wanted to hear all about the war, and on learning that the driver and mechanic were guarding the remains of No. 33, he announced that this duty must be carried out by the constable, or *garde-champêtre*, so that my two men could join us in the commune.

After sending a number of villagers off to take beer to the commune, he and I and most of the rest of the inhabitants repaired to the constable's house. That worthy must have weighed about eighteen stone, and was fast asleep when the deputation arrived; but at the call of duty he arose, arrayed himself in a huge, blue great-coat which had about three capes attached, armed himself with a cudgel and a large candle lantern and set off to mount guard. We all then went to the commune to discuss the war and drink beer. Although discussion in three languages was a bit difficult, I gathered that the general opinion was that the Germans would never take Pervyse.

It was well after dark when the lorry arrived. With the help of the villagers, the remains of No. 33 were loaded into it and we said goodbye to our kind and genial hosts. When last seen, the *garde-champêtre*, looking a bit blue about the gills from the cold, was being escorted to the commune to finish the beer. Luckily another Sopwith (No. 103) was available, an improved version of the original, with aileron control instead of wing warping, and I took it over. No. 33 was sent back to England, but was never repaired.

Shortly after this incident, Samson set out with all the armed cars on a Uhlan-hunting expedition. That evening after his departure a telegram arrived from the Admiralty to say that an inspecting officer would arrive at Dunkirk Harbour at dawn next day. Only one reliable car was available, a small four-seater tourer, all the rest being with Samson. Setting off in it, I reached the long mole of Dunkirk harbour at 5.30 a.m. to find the harbour master waiting there. I asked him what information he had and he replied that he had been told that *un personnage* would be arriving, but he did not know who. Soon a light cruiser, looming out of the mist, stopped off the entrance. A boat put off from her and came in to the steps of the mole, and out of it climbed Winston Churchill (First Lord of the Admiralty), Admiral Hood (Commanding Dover Patrol), Admiral Lambert (Naval Secretary) and Commodore Murray Sueter (Director of the Air Division).

There seemed to be rather too many *personnages* for the car, but we arranged matters by putting the First Lord in front with the driver, the two admirals in the back, the commodore on one running board and myself on the other. After a quick look round the landing ground and the old hospital buildings, the First Lord decided to visit General Bidon, commanding the garrison. The general was apparently caught still in bed, for he came into his office buttoning up his tunic over his pyjamas. After giving an explanation of the Dunkirk defences, he produced more suitable cars and took us round the defence perimeter. After that I left the party which in due course was returned to the harbour to board the light cruiser.

As a result of this visit, the armed-car party was strengthened by the addition of a small force of Royal Marines. They were mostly reservists and among their officers were Graham (afterwards Mayor of Gosport) and Wilding, the tennis champion, the latter having a temporary commission. A little later the Marine brigade was landed at Dunkirk.

During September, reconnaissance both by air and car was being pushed farther afield, Samson establishing an advanced landing ground and headquarters at Morbecque. When on 1 October the Marines decided to occupy Lille, I was sent with two other aircraft to co-operate with them. There was an aerodrome at Lille where we had a telephone installed in one of the sheds, which enabled us to talk to the Marine H.Q. The Marine battalion at Lille was commanded by Lieutenant-Colonel Luard.

Up to that time, although we had sighted small bodies of German troops from the air and Samson had had several encounters with cavalry in his cars, we were still vague as to what towns were being held in force. Leaving Lille on reconnaissance to the eastward on the afternoon of 1 October, I found German troops in force in both Leuze and Ath. In the early stages of the war the German soldier could not resist firing off his rifle whenever he saw an aeroplane, so that it was fairly easy to find out if a town or village was occupied. It was only necessary to cut the engine and listen. The roar of rifle fire from Leuze and Ath left no doubt. The method had its defects however. When I sent another machine, flown by Rainey, on a line farther to the north to see if any movement was taking place in that direction, he flew too close to Ath at too low a height and was brought down by rifle fire. He was unhurt and returned after some adventures; but we lost the aircraft.

During the following day all sorts of rumours were coming into Lille and we were kept constantly on reconnaissance. Fighting was going on around Douai, but it was not until later that we heard that Samson and his cars together with a French force had been heavily engaged and had had a narrow squeak. It was thanks to Samson that they were not cut off and overwhelmed.

Just before dark, I received a message from Marine H.Q. that they had been informed that a strong German force was approaching Cambrai. Refugees crowded the roads which were bordered by poplar trees so that it was not easy to see from above if troops were mingled with the refugees. The only way to make sure was to fly low beside the roads and outside the lines of poplars. In this way I made a thorough search of all roads in the suspected district and on getting back rang up Marine H.Q. I found Colonel Luard himself on the line and was able to give him a detailed report. He finished the conversation by saying, 'I hope it will be some satisfaction to you to know that the only reliable information I have had all day has been what I got from the air.'

Telephone calls kept coming in all night and it was clear that some big move was on. Before morning the Marines and we were ordered back to Dunkirk. We landed there on the morning of 3 October to find Samson and his party back from their adventures at Douai. News was received that the Naval Division was to go to

Antwerp with the Marine brigade as part of it. Our squadron was to move there as soon as possible. London omnibuses in large numbers were being landed at Dunkirk.

The next two days were hectic. Not knowing how long we should be at Antwerp or what sort of supplies we could get, we decided to take most of our spare engines and aircraft spares and also a big supply of petrol and lubricating oil. Rail transport was available so we loaded most of this into goods wagons. As Samson was taking his armed-car party and was also responsible for organizing the convoy of London omnibuses, I had to concentrate on the aeroplane side of the affair. I don't know what the combatant status of the drivers and conductors of those buses was. They were still in the uniform of the London General Omnibus Co.

The squadron reached Antwerp on 5 October to find the Germans already attacking the outer defences and the Belgian Field Army and naval division heavily engaged. One aircraft failed to arrive; it was a Bleriot flown by Lord Edward Grosvenor, the Duke of Westminster's uncle, who had joined the R.N.A.S. as sub-lieutenant at the outbreak of war. A Belgian air unit was using the aerodrome but I arranged with them to keep one of our men at the telephone in the sheds to take English messages. Soon after landing, the telephone orderly reported he was receiving a message in English but that the line was so bad he could only make out that it was from Dunkirk. I tried to take the message but could make nothing of it and had to ring off. A few minutes later there came another ring. Again it was from Dunkirk, but I could hear no better than before. Suddenly a girl's very English voice broke in and said quite clearly, 'It's *frightfully* important. You've got to hear it.' I asked 'Who are you?' She replied, 'I'm a telephone girl in London. It's most important. Keep on the line and I'll try to get the message and pass it on to you.' She eventually succeeded and I learnt that Grosvenor had had engine failure near Bruges, that he was all right though his Bleriot was written off and that a car from Dunkirk had gone to collect him.

Aeroplanes were not really much use at Antwerp. No reconnaissance was called for as it was only too obvious where the Germans were. We dropped some bombs on the German batteries but that was about all we could do. Samson, on the other hand, had taken his armed cars to the front where they had been in close action, Samson himself getting a shrapnel bullet across his shoulders, luckily not a serious wound.

During the afternoon of 6 October it became clear that Antwerp could not be held and that the Belgian Field Army intended to withdraw to the coast. The unloading of our stores which, between flights, had been my principal preoccupation had now to be reversed. I took a car back to the goods yard to arrange for the trucks with all our spare engines and fuel to be sent back to Ostend. Leaving a petty officer there with instructions to get them to Ostend somehow, I returned to the aerodrome where I found Samson and the rest of the party reloading all the motor transport.

Samson had organized a flight to attack the Zeppelin shed at Düsseldorf which could be reached from Antwerp. Reggie Marix had been selected to undertake the mission, flying his single-seater Sopwith 'Tabloid', so he was to remain behind with one car. Working all night, we started the cars off at daylight and then got the aircraft away. I took No. 103 Sopwith and had a last look at Antwerp as I climbed away. It was a dismal sight. Everything on the perimeter seemed to be on fire. The Belgian garrison was still holding up the Germans and covering the retreat, but they and the city were bound to be in German hands in a few days.

It was a lovely morning with a clear blue sky, but as I gained height two little white clouds appeared low down to the north; after a little while I realized they were the Dover cliffs. They looked so clean and peaceful compared to Antwerp. We landed at Ostend at about 7 a.m. on 7 October. Reggie Marix was completely successful in his attack on the Zeppelin sheds at Düsseldorf, sending airship and shed up in a sheet of flame. Running out of petrol on the return flight, he had an adventurous time reaching Antwerp, partly by railway locomotive. He escaped in the solitary car left there for him, having to pass between blazing oil tanks and store sheds.

At Ostend, the 7th Division under General Sir Harry Rawlinson was being disembarked. It consisted of troops who had been on service overseas at the outbreak of war, mainly in India. Rawlinson established his H.Q. in the Hotel Terminus which had a door into the railway station. As we had an office in one of the station buildings where there was a telephone, I frequently passed through the hall of the hotel. I was doing so, soon after arriving at Ostend when, from the crowd of staff officers thronging the hall, someone called 'Hey, what have you done with uncle?' The speaker was a major with staff tabs on his collar.

Thinking it was a leg haul of sorts, I replied, 'I haven't got your ruddy uncle.'

He retorted, 'Well you ought to have; you're Davies, aren't you?' I admitted it and he continued, 'I'm Westminster and Ned Grosvenor is my uncle. What have you done with him?'

I was able to tell the Duke of Westminster in Ostend what the telephone girl in London had told me at Antwerp about what somebody in Dunkirk said had happened to Grosvenor at Bruges. The Duke seemed to find it a bit complicated but was glad to hear that his uncle was all right.

Our trucks with the spares and fuel duly arrived, but the congestion on the railways was such that they could not be got at. I had to convince the station master that the whole Allied war effort depended on our being able to unload them. Eventually he believed me and the trucks were shunted clear of the tangle.

Reconnaissance for the 7th Division from Ostend was mainly over the Ypres and Poperinghe areas which appeared to be occupied by Germans. By 10 October it was clear that the division was going to move south and that Ostend would probably be overrun by the Germans. The population began to leave and there was much confusion. Samson told me that the Army base was to be shifted to Havre and that our stores would go back to Dunkirk. We had not enough motor transport, so I went to the docks and found a small British coaster, the skipper of which I persuaded to undertake the job. The last day at Ostend was a nightmare with the population really panicking, the station besieged by a mob trying to flee by train, while every road was crowded with refugees.

The arrangements for feeding our men had been by requisition on a little *estaminet* near the landing ground. It had worked well and each day the proprietress, a big Flemish woman with a face like a horse, had brought me the requisition forms to sign, certifying the number of meals supplied. On this last day she said that she would not remain in Ostend under German occupation but intended to go to England, and asked if I could give her a little English money in exchange for some of the certificates. I tried to dissuade her, pointing out that it would mean the loss of her business and all her stock, but she was quite determined and kept repeating that she was strong and could work in England. We had a contingency fund consisting of a bag of golden sovereigns, so I gave her five, upon which she tore up all her certificates; there must have been £20 worth.

There were by this time only four serviceable aeroplanes left. Briggs had a Bleriot, Peirse a B.E., Marix had taken over Samson's B.E. and I had a Sopwith. On 13 October, Samson took the armed cars to Roulers as well as the squadron's light transport and I had a busy time getting the odds and ends away, particularly the members of the office staff; to force them and their belongings through the mob in the station was almost a military operation. We were finally left with one small car to carry the party who started up the aircraft and saw us off.

We took off about 2.30 p.m. in the rain. Briggs's engine failed as soon as he was airborne and though he came down without hurting himself, the Bleriot was a write-off. He and the starting party rescued the engine and the instruments. These they put into their small car which, very overloaded, reached Roulers that evening. Peirse, Marix and I reached Roulers in the rain to find that the advance party had marked a small grass field as a landing ground. Samson and his people had taken possession of an empty house, while we were billeted about the town. About 4 a.m. we were aroused by messengers from Samson with news that the Army was falling back to Ypres and that we must start at dawn. General Rawlinson had a letter to be taken to Sir John French's H.Q. at St Omer.

As I had found before, the Roulers district was a bad one for aircraft, not only on account of the many tall poplar trees but because so much of the land was under a crop of sugar beet. Our small grass field was bordered by a strip of this, separated from it by a drainage ditch. There had been rain all night. The ground was sodden; so were our aircraft. It seemed very unlikely that they could take off on the very short run over the turf.

We decided to fill in the ditch and take a chance among the

sugar beet. Fortunately the car carrying the starting party also carried four Marines. We had no tools to help in filling the ditch, but the Marines have always been famous for their boots. By dint of kicking up sugar beets, we soon filled in a length of ditch. The Sopwith had fat tyres on her wheels, but the two B.E.s had narrow treads. As I had the best chance of getting up, therefore, I said I would take General Rawlinson's letter and have first shot at taking off.

The Sopwith squelched across the grass and over the ditch and then bounded about amongst the beet. A particularly fat one must have bumped the plane into the air, and as soon as I was above the poplar trees I headed for St Omer, trusting that the other two would get off somehow, which they did.

On arrival at the St Omer aerodrome I found it occupied by the R.F.C. and was greeted by 'Ginger' Mitchell. As it was the first contact we had had with the R.F.C., I was very anxious to hear all their news, but before I had any time to talk to Mitchell, Colonel Sykes appeared.

When I told him I had a letter from General Rawlinson to the C-in-C, he took me off by car to French's H.Q. where I gave the letter to General Sir Archibald Murray, French's Chief of Staff. The conversation showed how little the air was in the minds of senior officers in 1914. Sykes merely said that I had brought a letter from General Rawlinson from Roulers.

'Have you come from Roulers this morning?' the general asked.

'Yes, sir.'

'But how on earth did you get through?'

'By air, sir.'

'Oh, of course.'

He took the note to the C-in-C and on return said that French would not trust anything to writing, but that I was to tell Rawlinson that reinforcements were being sent. French hoped that Rawlinson would be able to hold on to Menin. Sykes took me to R.F.C. H.Q. for breakfast where I met General Henderson, commanding the R.F.C. in France, after which we went back to the aerodrome. I still hoped to hear some details of the R.F.C.'s doings from Mitchell but Sykes very properly bundled me off.

It was still raining and visibility was bad. When I reached

Ypres, unable to see either of the other two aircraft or any marked field, I came down on a grass field just west of the town. Walking in, I found that General Rawlinson's headquarters was established in the Cloth Hall where I reported to him that his letter had been delivered and gave him the return message. He gave a wry grin when I mentioned Menin.

During my absence things had been happening at Ypres. First a German aeroplane had flown low over the town and landed. Everyone had shot at it and everyone claimed to have brought it down. When examined, it proved to be quite unharmed and there seemed to be no reason why it should have come down at all.

Then Reggie Marix, whose B.E. was in a field south of the town with a troublesome engine, discovered that there were Uhlans in a farm nearby. He collected a party, mainly of Marine reservists, and advanced on the farm; but before they reached it, the Germans made off. However as there was one horse without a rider, there had also to be a rider without a horse. He proved to be the officer in command, who started to run after his men. Reggie ran after him and the reservists ran after Reggie. The Marines were stout of heart but being elderly were also inclined to be stout of body. They began to lag behind. Then the German produced a pistol and started to shoot at Reggie; Reggie produced his and shot back. Nobody was hit. Then some of the Marines, short of breath, stopped running, lay down, and started to shoot at the German. That settled it and he surrendered. Reggie disarmed him and took him into the town, Reggie being then armed with two pistols and a cavalry sabre.

After leaving the Cloth Hall, I found out where the field selected as a landing ground lay. It was outside the town to the north-east. Peirse had already taken his B.E. there, but Reggie Marix's B.E. was still grounded with engine trouble near the late 'battlefield'. Collecting a car and starting party, I drove out to get the Sopwith, then round a corner outside Ypres we almost ran into a column of grey-clad cavalry. I shouted, 'Go astern.' The driver slipped into reverse and we shot backwards round the corner again. As we did so there came a burst of laughter and shouts in French. The horsemen were cuirassiers with their blue uniforms hidden under long grey rain cloaks.

I took the Sopwith over to the selected landing ground where Peirse and I together viewed the situation. We had been able to acquire army rations and found a large barn in which the handling party could sleep. There was a road leading past the field to Roulers and a muddy lane led from the landing field to the road. A small *estaminet* nearly opposite the entrance to the lane was selected as our quarters.

All morning infantry were passing into Ypres along the road, and in the afternoon infantry gave place to cavalry. We began to wonder what troops there could be between us and the Germans. By evening when the cavalry were thinning out, I asked an officer in one troop if he knew what troops were behind him. He thought that there was a company of cyclists. Soon after that the cyclists appeared and when I asked an N.C.O. the same question, he said that there were two chaps with punctures half a mile behind. Peirse and I decided that two chaps with punctures were not an adequate safeguard against the German Army.

Peirse took a car up the road almost to Roulers without meeting anyone, British or German. As it appeared that we were the advanced post of the Army, we took precautions. Moving a car which had powerful headlights some hundred yards up the road towards Roulers, we arranged for sentries on it throughout the night. Upon hearing anything, the sentry was to switch on the headlights, jump into the ditch, and then if necessary open fire with his rifle. We also arranged for a guard on the aeroplanes who could lie under tarpaulins on the field. The rest of the aircraft-handling party were to sleep in the barn with their rifles handy and on any alarm to muster in the road.

Peirse and I retired to the *estaminet* where the owner insisted on taking us up to the spotlessly clean bedroom while he himself sat on a chair at the foot of the ladder leading to it, with a shot-gun beside him. It was nearly midnight when we were awakened by an outburst of rifle fire from the field. Peirse and I slid down the ladder and out, to find the handling party mustering in the road with their rifles. As the firing stopped, we divided the handling party into two and he and I led them up the lane keeping in the ditches at the side.

Presently we heard a sound of swearing in the lane. A Flemish peasant appeared being driven by two sailors with fixed bayonets.

Investigation showed that he had set off that morning to sell a pig in Ypres. He had not noticed any military activity and had obtained a good price for the pig. After a meal at his favourite *estaminet* he had gone to sleep, waking some time in the afternoon to spend the rest of the day drinking. Turned out at closing time in a fuddled condition by the landlord he had started to walk home across the fields, had blundered into our aeroplanes and narrowly escaped being shot.

The next day, on aerial reconnaissance, we saw that all roads were full of German transport. Passing over Menin I realized why Sir Harry Rawlinson had grinned at the suggestion of holding it. As our Army was digging in round Ypres, and it was clear that our field would be very near the front line, we moved back in the afternoon to a field outside Poperinghe where we found an R.F.C. squadron in process of forming. During the next few days we were used mostly for reconnaissance towards the coast as the situation there was sticky. With the Belgian Army retreating towards Nieuport, a gap opened in the Allied line which was hastily filled by a force of French Marines commanded by an admiral.

Once the front became stabilized in trenches we were of less value to the Army, the R.F.C. squadron being much better equipped for the work than we were. In fact if it had not been for Collet we should have been pretty useless, A regular Marine, he had a photographic memory and was one of the few people who can play chess blindfolded and usually win. The reconnaissance task was now no longer a matter of finding where the Germans were but of pin-pointing on a map the position of the German guns. I found this extremely hard to do as did Peirse and Marix, but Collet had no difficulty at all. He was able to give the gunners an accurate picture of the German batteries, so we used him as an observer.

He was up with me one morning when I saw a German aeroplane ahead and gave chase. The German failing to see us I got close on his tail, but Collet did nothing. I roared at him, 'Shoot, you bloody fool. Why the hell don't you shoot?' Collet was liable to stammer in moments of excitement and he shouted back, 'I h-h-haven't got a bloody g-g-gun, you ass.' The German departed unhurt.

The Belgian Army had dug in along the Yser and the front extended from Ypres to the sea. The German batteries opened up all along the front so that it was possible to see the whole line clearly marked by the smoke of bursting shells. My friendly little village of Pervyse, still in Belgian hands, was being steadily pounded into a heap of rubble.

By 17 October, British ships were in action off the coast. They included the ancient gunboat *Excellent*, name ship of Whale Island gunnery school, and were firing on the German supply lines on the coastal road. The Belgian lines were gradually pushed back until they were holding the line of a railway embankment west of the Yser. Then one morning the war seemed to have completely stopped towards the coast. Where the trench lines and batteries had been was one great lake. The Belgians had opened the sluices at Nieuport at high tide.

Throughout the rest of October we continued to work for what had now become the 4th Corps. Samson and the armed-car party had remained based on Ypres and until the front settled into trench war, they had been able to do good work. The aeroplane party were billeted in Poperinghe where we fixed up a camp of sorts in a field next to the landing ground and meals made up from army rations were cooked there. My billet, which Peirse and Collet shared, was over a blanket shop. The owner and his wife were a splendid couple who insisted on supplying us with lots of blankets. They remained for the first week but then decided to go to relatives in France and we were able to help them get away.

We generally had breakfast and supper in an *estaminet* on the main square, where the proprietress gave us the use of a small room to ourselves. One morning I saw two officers in the Black Watch, a major and a captain, standing in the square, looking rather lost. Learning that they were looking for a place for breakfast, I took them into our *estaminet*. They belonged to a battalion which had been serving in India and they had just arrived in Flanders, having travelled to Bombay in first-class sleepers, then in first-class saloon by P. & O. to Havre, where they had come to Poperinghe in first-class wagons-lits. 'And now we are to get into a trench this afternoon and try to kill Germans,' the major said. 'I just can't believe it.'

No doubt they quickly overcame that difficulty, for a few days later the Germans delivered a very heavy attack at Ypres and nearly broke through.

A number of lightly wounded men of the Black Watch, in charge of a sergeant, appeared at Poperinghe and we took them into the *estaminet* and stood them beer. The sergeant was vague about what had happened but said they had been in a trench in a wood and Germans had invaded the trench. 'What happened then?' I asked. 'We turned 'em oot. Jock here, he hit yin o' 'em i' the face wi' his pack.' There was a chorus from the rest, 'Ay, hit yin i' the face wi' his pack he did.' Evidently Jock's pack had saved Ypres.

By November the R.F.C. squadron was operating at full strength. Opportunities for Samson's armed cars were becoming scarce. Samson had to return to England to confer with the Air Department. Soon after he left, I received a polite note from General Rawlinson thanking us for our work and saying that as he now had air support from the R.F.C. he did not feel justified in holding on to a naval squadron. So on 7 November I sent the armed cars and transport back to Dunkirk and we followed with the aircraft.

I had been expecting that message from the Army for some time, but felt pretty sure that it would be a bad blow to Samson. When he returned a day or two later he was furious. We had been kicked out of the war and it was all my fault. When Samson really went off the deep end it was no good arguing with him, so like Brer Terrapin 'I sot and tuk it'. The next morning when the storm had subsided he told me that the Air Department had a chance to acquire some new aircraft, Farmans and Nieuports from France, but wanted a report on the machines before placing an order. They could be inspected in Paris and as he could not go himself he would send Peirse and me. Since Wilding had been driving a new Vauxhall car it was arranged that he should take us to Paris. Also the Ritz Hotel was putting up officers on duty free of charge, so rooms there would be reserved for us.

We reached the Ritz late in the evening. Though it was housing us free, it was not feeding us, so we went out for supper somewhere cheaper. When we arrived back at the hotel we found the lounge full of French tennis fans, the news of Wilding's arrival having spread. They demanded that he play some exhibition matches next day. Wilding was annoyed, saying he had come to France to fight Germans and not to play tennis. He wanted to refuse but Peirse and I urged him to agree for the sake of the Entente Cordiale. Eventually he did, on condition that he played against Peirse and not any of the fans. Peirse's tennis was good but he found it embarrassing playing in borrowed flannels against the champion before a large crowd of spectators.

Having inspected and reported in favour of the aircraft we drove back to Dunkirk. We were joined there for a short time by a French squadron, one of whose pilots was Roland Garos, generally regarded as the greatest of the early French pilots, and one of whose mechanics was Georges Carpentier, the open light-heavyweight boxing champion. Garos was the first man to fit a machine-gun into a tractor aeroplane. He used a French *mitrailleuse* and simply fired through the airscrew disc without any synchronizing device. Though a percentage of the bullets went through the airscrew, which he generally had to change after firing, no propeller was shattered.

Later in November I was sent back to England to bring over a new Avro machine. After reporting at the Air Division I went into the Aero Club, still in its original home in Piccadilly. There I found A. V. Roe who was particularly interested to hear about Garos and his machine-gun, at once producing a pencil and on the back of an envelope trying to work out a crank system of mounting for a machine-gun which would enable it to shoot over the top of the airscrew.

I had a few days at home before going to Eastchurch for the new Avro. It was an improvement on the original 50-h.p. Gnome Avro having an 80-h.p. Le Rhône engine, but it was not ready to fly until 1 December. Even then there were various teething troubles and it was 8 December before I got back to Dunkirk.

Activity with the armed cars had come to an end by this time, except for a lorry armed with a 3-pdr. Samson took this to Nieuport from time to time and consulted Colonel Bridges who was British Liaison Officer at Belgian H.Q. Prince Alexander of Teck (later Earl of Athlone) who was serving as a major on Bridges's staff, usually found suitable targets for the 3-pdr. which the Belgians called *l'autocannon du Prince de Teck*.

Samson sent me to Nieuport with this one day. Prince Alexander told me that a French colonel had taken over artillery command there and that I should ask him for orders. I found him at the top of the Crusaders' Tower, an ancient brick tower on the outskirts, where he was using a telephone to spot for some French *soixante-quinze* guns which seemed to be making good practice at a German battery. I was watching through my glasses when I saw another German battery start to fire and five little black dots appear which seemed to be coming straight into my binoculars. Down the winding stairs of the tower I fled. After rounding the first spiral, thinking I was being a bit undignified in front of the French colonel I slowed down, only to be bumped into from behind. It was wise to leave the top hastily when the Germans fired at it, explained the colonel, '*Parce qu'y on a des pierres.*'

There certainly were, for it sounded as if a cartload of brick-bats was rattling down the stairs above us. Continuing down, I was about to go out through the archway at the bottom when the colonel stopped me and made me sit down with him on the last step. He produced a packet of cigarettes and while we smoked, started to tell me what the 3-pdr. was to do. Almost at once there were several explosions just outside and shrapnel bullets rattled against the brickwork. The colonel explained that the Germans always did that when they thought that the tower was being used as an observation post. First they shelled the top with high explosive; then, waiting long enough for the observer to reach the bottom, they put down a shrapnel barrage outside the door. It was a good thing that they were so systematic, he said. If they only did it occasionally they would kill a lot of people; but as they always did it nobody went out until the barrage was over.

The 3-pdr.'s job was to drive along a street running parallel to the canal, stopping where a side street ran down to the canal to fire six rounds rapid at the German machine-gun pits on the other side of the canal, then full speed up the street to the next opening and repeat the process. It was fun seeing the barrage of shells which came down on each street crossing immediately after we had left it.

Admiralty Intelligence reported that the Germans were using Zeebrugge as a submarine base. Throughout December we kept up a constant watch on it and on Ostend, as well as bombing the basin at Bruges where considerable German activity had been observed. Intelligence reports of the airship shed at Brussels being used by the Germans were also received. This shed was too small to house a Zeppelin but it could hold one of the smaller Schutte-Lanz airships the Germans had.

Amongst other new aircraft the squadron had received, was a large Farman pusher, No. 1241, with a Canton-Unné engine. It was a type with which Maurice Farman for some reason did not persist, although as a weight-lifter it was a long way ahead of its contemporaries. The only bombs we had were 20-lb instantaneous-fuzed; but 1241 could carry twelve of them.

On 20 December, Samson sent me off to try to bomb the Brussels shed. My stick of 20-lb bombs certainly crossed the shed diagonally and much smoke appeared but no flames. I hope that it was due to there being nothing inflammable in the shed for I should hate to think that I had missed it. During January we continued with the same work but the weather was bad and for many days we were grounded. German air activity on the coast was increasing and Dunkirk was occasionally bombed, mostly by single aircraft.

It was not until 22 January 1915 that we saw any signs of the submarines reported to be using Zeebrugge. On that morning when I took the Avro over Ostend and Zeebrugge, I passed over a new German landing ground near Ostend on which was a number of German aircraft. In Zeebrugge harbour there were two U-boats. On my way back again I passed over the landing ground and saw all the German aircraft taking off. Thus I was able to report both the presence of submarines and that an air raid was imminent.

The big Farman 1241 being already armed with bombs, Samson sent Peirse off in her to attack the submarines. All other aeroplanes were at once sent up with passengers armed with rifles to intercept the Germans. The Avro was re-fuelled and I took off with Butler as my passenger. While we were on the ground the sky had been full of Germans, but once we were up it seemed that they had all disappeared. Butler and I flew in circles round Dunkirk hunting

113

them, but did not see one. Most of the pilots had the same experience.

Peirse had meanwhile attacked the submarines with his load of 20-lb bombs, coming in at them from seaward. He had straddled the one he had attacked but could not be sure he had hit it. When he got back, there was still time to make another attack before dark. The 1241 was reloaded and I took her off with Butler as passenger. As Peirse had attacked from seaward and had met with heavy fire, I thought I would approach from the landward side hoping to meet with less. To avoid accidents when flying with a load of bombs, we always turned out to sea while gaining height so as not to pass over the town of Dunkirk. Abreast of Nieuport I had gained sufficient height so turned inland. It was a bad mistake as it was an area in which AA guns were thickest. On passing the coast-line we entered the heaviest barrage I had met up till then. I had previously held the view that since German control of AA fire was crude there was no sense in trying to dodge it. You were just as likely to turn towards the next burst as away from it. I abandoned that theory in about five seconds and turned the Farman round heading out to sea again. We soon left the hulla-baloo behind us.

We then took stock of the damage. There was a big hole in the starboard extension of the upper plane but it did not affect the Farman's performance. Something feeling exactly like a well hit hockey ball, which I assumed was the spent nose-fuze of a shrapnel shell, had hit me a crack on the right knee. Butler had a good look round and reported that although there were several small holes visible, no serious harm had been done. He kept re-peating that there was a hole in the back of my coat, which seemed silly. Eventually, feeling annoyed, I shouted back at him, 'Damn the coat, there's a hole in my bloody leg,' after which he said no more about the coat. It was only after we got back that I realized what his worry had been. There was indeed a hole in the back of the coat but only one hole; it looked as if a bullet had come out there and Butler had assumed it must have penetrated from the front.

Crossing the coast-line again farther east without meeting serious AA fire we made the attack from the landward side. Though Butler let go our stick of 20-lb bombs with accuracy and they certainly straddled the submarine, it was not possible to say if there was a hit, or if the little instantaneous-fuzed bombs could do much damage even if they did hit.[1]

When we landed at twilight I found that my leg had stiffened. Hardy-Wells examined it and, finding that it had been hit by a shrapnel bullet, sent me off to the hospital ship *Magic* lying in Dunkirk docks. There I spent a comfortable few days. The shrapnel bullet having been duly extracted, I was sent home on sick leave.

[1] EDITOR'S NOTE

From: Supplement to the *London Gazette*, Friday 9 April, 1915:

Admiralty, 10th April, 1915

The King has been graciously pleased to give orders for the following appointments to the Distinguished Service Order and for the award of the Distinguished Service Cross to the undermentioned officers in recognition of their services as mentioned.

To be Companions of the Distinguished Service Order

For services rendered in the aerial attack on Dunkirk, 23rd January 1915

Squadron-Commander Richard Bell Davies
Flight Lieutenant Richard Edmund Charles Peirse

These Officers have repeatedly attacked the German submarine stations at Ostend and Zeebrugge, being subjected on each occasion to heavy and accurate fire, their machines being frequently hit. In particular, on 23rd January, they each discharged eight bombs in an attack upon submarines alongside the Mole at Zeebrugge, flying down to close range. At the outset of this flight Lieutenant Davies was severely wounded by a bullet in the thigh, but nevertheless he accomplished his task, handling his machine for an hour with great skill in spite of pain and loss of blood.

9

The Dardanelles

By the time that orders came to report to the Admiralty for medical survey, my leg had completely healed. There were rumours of an expedition against the Turks when, shortly before the survey, I had a letter from Samson. He told me that No. 33 Squadron had been recalled to England and was at Dover, the officers living in the Burlington Hotel. No. 1 Squadron under Longmore had relieved us at Dunkirk. Samson was expecting orders for further service and hoped I would soon be fit to rejoin.

When my date for survey arrived, I packed my kit and took it with me to London. After being examined by a surgeon commander at the Medical Department, I asked him if I might rejoin the squadron. Rather pompously he replied that I must go back on sick leave and would receive instructions in due course: I must leave my address while on leave with his writer in the next office. I thanked him, gave my address as the Burlington Hotel and caught the first train to Dover. To the best of my knowledge that sick leave was also never officially terminated.

I reached Dover in the evening to find that Collett had been doing the first lieutenant's job which he said he was only too glad to hand back to me. The administrative machinery of the Sheerness Sub-Depot which was supposed to look after our pay, victualling and stores had completely broken down under the stress of overloading. The men were in lodgings in the town, for which compensation was payable, but neither pay nor allowances had arrived for a long time. Telephone calls to the depot were unavailing. The officers had lent money to the men until their own pockets were empty, now landladies were growing understandably restive. None of the men had a decent suit of uniform and they were going about in ragged overalls. Luckily there was a man from Harrods hanging about, who declared he could supply the whole of the squadron with ready-made suits if we could give him the contract.

I had just about absorbed all this sad story, when Samson arrived from London with the news that we were bound for the Dardanelles. He was to cross the Channel with an advance party next day and drive to Marseilles. He would take old No. 50 B.E. with him and a party including Collet, Marix and Osmond. New French aircraft would be sent direct to the island of Tenedos. I was to take charge of the rest of the squadron and aircraft and move them to Plymouth where we should be embarked.

Loading started at daylight and by noon, we got the advance party away. I spent the afternoon investigating the gloomy situation as regards money and clothing. Collet had not drawn on the original contingency fund and there was enough left to give each man a small advance. I also interviewed the enterprising young man from Harrods and found that he really was able to produce large stocks of ready-made clothing.

Next morning I rang up the Admiralty and asked for the Air Department. Knowing nothing about Admiralty working hours I did this before 8 a.m. A voice answered 'Air Department here.' When I told my sad story the voice asked, 'Well, what are you going to do about it?' I explained that I proposed to divide the remainder of the fund amongst the men and to kit them up by contract with Harrods. 'Go ahead,' came the cheerful reply, 'and if anyone asks questions, say that you have got Admiralty authority.'

'Thanks very much,' I replied, 'but who am I speaking to?'

'Duty commander, name of Groves.'

It was indeed lucky for us that Groves happened to be duty commander that morning.

As there was no landing ground near Plymouth I decided to strip down the aircraft and send everything to Plymouth by train. The station master at Dover was very helpful but there was one major problem: while I had been away the squadron had acquired a Breguet pusher bi-plane, a huge and horrible affair constructed of steel and powered by a 200-h.p. Canton-Unné engine. As most of the framework was riveted very little stripping down could be done. We took the wings off, but the centre section of the top plane turned out to be a permanent fixture. The only way to get the plane to the station was to tow it, so the undercarriage had to remain. By measuring we found the plane's height too great either for passage under the bridges on the road to the station or for travel on any ordinary rail truck. The stationmaster said that his company, the London, Chatham and Dover Railway, had no suitable truck but that the Midland Railway possessed some very low bogey trucks. He set about acquiring one. Meanwhile on exploring the downland near the landing ground, I found a track which led to the town without passing under any bridge. It consisted of slimy chalk mud and was very hilly, no car or heavy lorry that we possessed could possibly tow the blundering Breguet along it. While we were discussing the problem there came a puffing sound, and an ancient steam traction-engine came slowly into sight, its great iron wheels squelching into the chalky mire. We promptly hired it for the day. With the Breguet in tow it made an impressive sight in the streets of Dover.

The other problem was the horse, Nigger. Nigger had been captured from the Uhlans in one of Samson's adventures with the armed cars, and one of his last instructions to me was that Nigger must accompany us at all costs. One of the transport drivers who had become very attached to him had been nominated Yeoman of the Horse. The stationmaster produced a horse-box in which Nigger and his yeoman went off together.

At Plymouth the men went to the naval barracks and the officers to the Royal Hotel. Our stores, aircraft and transport were to go out in a cargo ship, the *Moorgate*; officers and ratings in a Harrison Line ship called *Imkosi*, her cargo holds having been converted into troop decks. Samson's exploits with the armed cars had led to the formation of an armoured-car section for the Naval Division, a company of which was to be embarked in the *Imkosi* with us. It was commanded by Josiah Wedgwood, M.P., holding the rank of lieutenant commander R.N.V.R. As he was much older than I and my orders were to act as O.C. Troops I was afraid that he might feel hurt. I need not have worried as he happily accepted the position and was the greatest help.

The aircraft, cars and lorries were loaded into the *Moorgate*

1. The Author

2. The author's first ship, H.M.S. *Diana*

3. (*a*) Sopwith Biplane No. 33 (80 h.p.)
First aircraft allocated to author after he became
a Flying Officer

(*b*) Henri Farman aircraft with bomb in position:
Sampson at the controls

(*c*) A Maurice Farman with Maxim gun and
wireless reel

France
3. 1. 16

My dear Davies,

Hurrah! I am delighted to read
that your skill & courage have won you
the great prize. Accept my most cordial
congratulations on a feat of arms wh adds
to the splendid reputation of the Naval wing.
May you live long to enjoy the reward.

Yours v sincerely,

Winston S. Churchill

4. Letter from Winston Churchill

5. The author's favourite aeroplane:
Sopwith 1½-Strutter (*Imperial War Museum*)

6. H.M.S. *Campania*:
(*a*) Hauling seaplane out of the hangar

(*b*) Seaplane ready for flight off deck

(*c*) Take off. Note detachable wheels under seaplane's floats.

7.   H.M.S. *Argus*, Aircraft Carrier, October 1918
(*a*) First take off

(*b*) Landing on the flight deck

(*c*) After landing, arrival at the fore and aft
arrester wires

8. The author, Commanding Officer of H.M.S. *Dasher*,
    at the commissioning party at Hoboken 1942

together with large supplies of petrol in two-gallon cans. The Breguet caused more trouble as the bogey truck was too long to take the curve of the railway lines in the dockyard. We had to find a crane to lift her off outside and we then pushed her to the ship. Nigger, being part of the personnel, was to travel in the *Imkosi*. A horse-box was borrowed from the military barracks. Eventually, with all hands on board we were able to sail early one morning.

The normal trials and tribulations of an O.C. Troops which were my lot, were complicated by Nigger collapsing in his box helplessly seasick. Fortunately a petty officer of the Armoured Car Company turned out to be in private life a master of fox-hounds. Under his expert advice applied to various items of nautical equipment such as a sailor's hammock, a 'handy-billy' tackle, etc., and finally after a belabouring with a rope's end accompanied by the strong language customary amongst M.F.H.'s, Nigger was eventually comfortably slung with the hammock passing under his chest to take his weight if he should collapse again. He recovered from his seasickness and became very fond of his hammock.

Getting Nigger ashore when we reached Tenedos was another piece of combined equestrian and nautical expertise. By a combination of towing by the ship's cutter and swimming by Nigger, he reached the beach safely, where he galloped furiously inland dragging the tow rope after him. One of our old Eastchurch hands, Able Seaman Elsden, gallantly clung to it through a maze of thorn bushes until he was able to catch a turn with the rope round the branch of a stunted oak tree, bringing the runaway up 'all standing'.

It was the beginning of April when we arrived. The *Moorgate* came in soon after and with the help of the battleship *Prince George*, which was detailed to help with her ship's company and boats, we soon put everything ashore. The aircraft which had been shipped direct from France were 80-h.p. Gnome Henri Farmans (see illustration). They were badly underpowered and very lightly constructed. Under strong sun they warped; the fabric slackened and soon rotted. Proving incapable of carrying a passenger to a safe height, they were used for photography which could be done by the pilot alone. With us in the ship had come two B.E. 2c's with 70-h.p. Wolseley engines. There were a few

German aircraft and, soon after we arrived, Reggie Marix flying in one of the Sopwith Tabloids succeeded in forcing a seaplane down into the Straits.

Sir Ian Hamilton visited our camp later in the month. As I walked with him down to the beach when he re-embarked, he asked me what I thought of Cape Helles as seen from the air. I said that the Turks had a lot of earthworks there and that the cliffs looked pretty steep. This was not entirely to the disadvantage of the attacker, he said. As we had learnt at Spion Kop in the South African war, the man at the top of the cliff had to raise his head above the sky-line in order to fire down, while the man below was not plainly visible. This point of view was soon to prove tragically oversanguine.

The landing at Cape Helles was about to take place. On the evening of 24 April, the *River Clyde* and a large number of smaller ships anchored off the north shore of Tenedos. It was the same anchorage which had been used by the fleet of Agamemnon over 2,000 years before. Sitting on a cliff looking down on them we felt a deep sense of foreboding about the next day.

After the landing on 25 April 1915, a midshipman named Weblin told me of his personal experiences which must have been typical of many. He was in charge of a cutter, landing men of the Naval Division at Helles, which formed part of a long line of boats in tow of a naval picket boat. On nearing the beach, the tow was cast off and the cutters started to row in. Almost at once they were swept by machine-gun fire. Many men were killed at once: the survivors plunged into the water, holding on to their boat on the side away from the shore, but the fire continued and many more were hit. Eventually Weblin's boat filled with water and the Turks shifted fire to some other target.

Next to Weblin was a sub-lieutenant, R.N.V.R., of the Naval Division who, after they had been drifting about for some time, let go of the boat and started to swim for the shore, but Weblin did not think he reached it. When the boat finally drifted near the stern of the *River Clyde* Weblin let go and swam to a jumping-ladder hanging from the stern by means of which he climbed on board.

The lighters intended to form the landing pier from ship to shore were still secured to her and full of dead men. It was quite impossible for the survivors in the *River Clyde* to do anything owing to machine-gun fire, but below decks they were in no danger from it, and fortunately they were not being shelled. Weblin stayed on board until the landing was made good the next day and it became possible to leave. Amongst the names in the shocking casualty lists that followed was that of Colonel Doughty-Wylie, the gallant consul I had met at the time of the Armenian massacre. Owing to his great knowledge of things Turkish he had been appointed to Sir Ian Hamilton's staff. He died trying to lead a storming party up the cliff at W beach.

My own activities on that day were in a B.E. 2c, with St Aubyn as observer, spotting for the guns of the battleship *Prince George*, which was supporting French troops making a subsidiary landing at Kum Kale on the Asiatic side. The landing was not intended to be permanent but aimed at preventing direct fire on to the Gallipoli beaches from across the Straits. It was quite successful and the *Prince George*'s fire was most effective. We saw the *Queen Elizabeth* close the shore to within a few hundred yards and plaster the cliffs and ruins of Sedd-el-Bahr with 15-inch and 6-inch shells in an endeavour to put an end to the machine-gun fire.

For the rest of the month we were constantly spotting for ships' gun-fire. Accuracy increased with practice, but ships varied very much in their readiness to accept the air reports of fall of shot. The old battleships of the *Magnificent* class were particularly good. Their guns had a lower muzzle velocity and consequently higher trajectory than the more modern guns. The procedure for directing a ship's guns on to a target was complicated by the fact that the maps originally provided were inaccurate. The aircraft passed the map square number of the target to the ship. The ship laid off the compass bearing by the map and then selected a point of aim on that bearing on the shore by eye. The rough range was taken from the map and set on the sights.

The first shot might be anything up to half a mile off the target. The aircraft first corrected for line and, when that was right, for range. If the line was very badly out it usually meant that the ship had to select a new point of aim, which delayed matters. New maps were eventually made from our photographs but that took some time.

We were joined at Tenedos by a French squadron commanded

by Captain Cesari, one of the early French military pilots. They were a very good lot and we soon made friends. We arranged to make a joint raid with them on a German airfield which we had discovered near Chanak. Flying one of the Maurice Farmans, by a terrific fluke I landed a 100-lb bomb right on a hangar. The French squadron was just behind me and saw the bomb burst, so my reputation as a bomb aimer soared with them.

After the Turkish batteries had all been pin-pointed on the artillery map, the gunners asked for an early morning reconnaissance each day to see if any changes had been made during the night. One morning, having started on one of these trips before daylight, I arrived over Gallipoli while it was still twilight. Everywhere in rear of the Turkish trenches there were little points of light. It was evident that morning coffee was being brewed. After that we started the dawn flight earlier each day, carrying as many 20-lb bombs as possible. Wherever we saw cooking fires we dropped a bomb and the fires were at once put out.

In May a supply of Voisin pusher biplanes reached us. They were powered by Canton-Unné engines and were very solidly built, mainly of steel. Though they were rather slow and the engines had to be run full out to make them climb, they were a great improvement on the little Henri Farmans and proved most useful. Butler who had been doing the photographic work in the Henri Farmans was hit in the foot by a rifle bullet. He had to go to hospital and Thompson took over his work.

After the landing we were joined by more military observers for pin-pointing batteries and for spotting. There were Captain Jopp, an Australian, Walser, Edwards, and Knatchbull-Hugessen, all gunners. The latter was very young. He afterwards became Lord Brabourne and died as Governor of Bengal.

By the end of April the front at Helles had been pushed far enough forward for us to be able to land on what had been a field of oats. It was an uncomfortable landing ground as it was in plain view of the Turkish positions from which field guns usually opened up whenever an aeroplane landed. There was a little mound at one side, to which after landing we taxied at full speed to stow the aircraft out of sight. There was generally just time to get behind the mound before the shells arrived.

On 15 May I had an interesting time spotting for the battleship *Agamemnon*. The target she had been given was a gun mounted in the mouth of a valley running down to the shore of the Dardanelles. The ship was off the west coast of the peninsula whence she had to fire across the intervening hills. It was a very difficult shoot; but by placing her early shots well over, so that they splashed into the Straits, we were able to get the line accurate. Then I hoped to be able to spot her down on to the target. Unfortunately when I felt sure that the next round would be a hit, it landed on top of a hill about half a mile short of the target. It soon became clear that the trajectory of her 12-inch guns was too flat and that it was not possible to get the target from her position.

I signalled 'cease fire' and was wondering what to suggest to the ship, when I noticed a string of little black dots moving along one of the valleys. My observer was our Warrant Electrician, Mr McLeod, who though a good telegraphist had no experience of spotting. I was doing the spotting myself therefore; when I pointed out the dots to McLeod he focused his glasses on them and said he thought they were cavalry. I told him to search the valley with his glasses and try to see what they were making for. He found two camouflaged camps, one in that valley and one in the next. There were numerous tents and what appeared to be dumps, all carefully camouflaged and very extensive. We signalled 'change target' to the ship and then passed the map square number of one of the camps.

After a long pause the ship fired a single 12-inch gun. The shell burst a long way from the target but after various corrections one fell squarely on the camp. Two more did the same after which we signalled for all guns and rapid fire. The whole valley and camp disappeared in smoke and dust out of which shot a stream of little black dots going full speed. They did not look like stopping short of Constantinople. We let the ship continue firing for some minutes until everything in the camp seemed to be on fire, when we made 'cease fire' and 'change target', repeating the performance on the second camp. By the time the ship was hitting, we were nearly out of petrol. We had to leave her to it, but the second camp was going up in smoke very satisfactorily.

All through that summer we continued to spot for ships' fire and for the 60-pdr. battery at Cape Helles as well as bombing suitable targets whenever we found them. One evening Samson and Marix started in the blundering Breguet for Constantinople, intending to make a night attack on the arsenal there. The engine of their machine had been giving continuous trouble and I felt anxious about the result. Fortunately the engine gave signs of distress before they reached the Dardanelles and they had to come back. It was about the only flight which that revolting aircraft made.

During the prevailing strong north-easterly winds, landing at Cape Helles was something of an adventure as the wind stirred up a great cloud of dust which trailed away to leeward as a yellow fog. On approaching, it was necessary to plunge into the fog and turbulent air to leeward of the Cape and skim over the cliff edge. At the landing ground, one had to turn without being blown over and taxi hastily down-wind to the spot behind the mound before Turkish shells arrived.

The whole area at Helles including the cliffs at the southern end was honeycombed with dug-outs. The gunner officers had installed themselves on a sort of terrace cut into the cliff where they had made a relatively comfortable mess, half cave and half tent. A road had been made round the base of the cliff connecting the various beaches. Even when the Turks were indulging in a heavy bombardment of the area, it was perfectly peaceful on the road and men would be bathing from the rocks and sitting in the sunshine smoking. As a result of these bombardments we lost some aircraft at Helles, including, to our great relief, No. 1241 Farman.

Plenty has been written about the flies and resulting dysentery at Gallipoli. Although we were much better off at Tenedos, we suffered too, and by the end of July our alert surgeon, Patterson, reported that we ought to be sent away in turns for a rest. In late July therefore, Samson and Collet were sent off to Egypt for fourteen days' leave which left me in charge of the squadron.

10
Serving Two Masters

On 31 July I received a message from the naval C-in-C, Admiral de Robeck, ordering me to fly to the island of Imbros where a piece of ground had been cleared as a base for airships (Blimps). I was to land there and report to him on board the *Triad*, the yacht which he was using as his flagship. When I arrived on board, he told me the outline of the plan for the landing at Suvla Bay. Our squadron was to be turned over to Sir Ian Hamilton during the operation and in order that we should be close to Army H.Q. we were to operate from the airship ground on Imbros if I found it suitable.

We could use the ground, I told him, though it was rather small. He inquired about the state of our aircraft. This, I had to admit, was definitely bad. Many aircraft had had to be grounded for renewal of their fabric. I added that although a number of new aircraft had been sent from England we had no news of when they were likely to arrive. Picking up a signal pad the admiral wrote on it, then handed it to me saying, 'Does that suit you?' He had written a peremptory order to the Vice-Admiral, Malta, to give first priority to all aircraft and stores and to send forward at once any that reached Malta.

Landing at the pier near military H.Q. I reported to General Braithwaite, the chief of staff, and to Colonel Aspinall who would be giving us orders. They undertook to send tents and to arrange rations and water supplies. I expounded our problems and explained that I should have to leave aircraft under repair at Tenedos until completed, but would move operational aircraft to Imbros as soon as possible.

Since German U-boats had appeared off the Peninsula at the end of May 1915, the old battleships *Triumph* and *Majestic* having been torpedoed and sunk, and the naval organization had been altered. Normally only older and smaller ships now took part in bombardment in support of the Army. Called the Inshore Squadron, these were under the command of Rear-Admiral Nicholson, with his flag in the old battleship *Exmouth*, from whom our orders would come.

The shift to Imbros was a real headache. In a motor lighter which was lent to us we put an advance landing party and a supply of oil and petrol across at once. Until that had been done, the programme ordered by Inshore Squadron had to be carried out from Tenedos. Then we had to conduct operations from Imbros while the repair staff was still at Tenedos. With the reduced number of pilots, we were kept hard at it having to carry out the naval programme and at the same time to ferry aircraft from Tenedos as repairs were completed. It was 4 August before we were ready to work entirely from Imbros.

Until that day we had had strict orders from H.Q. that in order to avoid alerting the enemy, we were not to fly over the Suvla area. Now however I was told that we could send one aircraft over the area, provided that the flight was straight across and that we bombed some suitable target near the Dardanelles. I carried out the flight with Walse as observer. We both hung over the side looking for new earthworks but saw none. There were old trenches which had been dug before the April attack, but they were overgrown with scrub and there was no sign of new work anywhere. Beyond the Salt Lake plain lay the ridge called Chocolate Hills on the reverse slope of which existed a line of gun emplacements; but there were no guns and they too were overgrown. On our return Walser reported to military H.Q. that there were no new preparations by the Turks in the Suvla area. We both felt anxious in case we had missed something.

When I landed after that flight I found Commander Nasmith of E 11 waiting at our camp. He had already won a V.C. for his operations in the Sea of Marmora. As he was to go up the mined and obstructed Straits again that night, he wanted to have a look at the narrows at Chanak where the Turks had tried to lay anti-submarine obstructions, so I took him over them in a Maurice Farman (see illustration facing p. 118).

On the 6th a reconnaissance of the Anzac objectives was

ordered. I took Jupp, the Australian gunner, and after reporting at military H.Q. I was given a very full programme for the Army next day: for the Suvla landing was to take place that night. On returning to our camp, I found that a long signal had come from Inshore Squadron giving us an equally full programme in spotting for ships' gun-fire. Admiral de Robeck had told me that he intended the aircraft to be entirely under military control. Evidently Rear-Admiral Nicholson had not been informed of this. I went back to H.Q. where I told General Braithwaite what de Robeck had said and urged that a signal be sent to him pointing out what had happened: Braithwaite was reluctant to comply. Eventually it was decided that I should go on board the *Triad* and try to see de Robeck or his chief of staff, Commodore Roger Keyes.

With last-minute jobs to be done on the aircraft, I wanted to get back to the camp to make sure they were all tackled. I was reluctant to have to spend time in the *Triad* arguing about orders; however it had to be done. I was met by the flag-commander, Alexander Ramsey, who said that I should have to see the chief of staff and took me down to Roger Keyes. It was the first time that I had met him. Roger Keyes possessed a poker face, so that it was impossible to tell whether he agreed or disagreed or even whether or not he had taken in what was being said. I started to explain my problem and to point out the impossibility of serving two masters. Before I had proceeded far, Ramsey came in to say that the captain of one of the ships had come on board to see the chief of staff. Keyes told me to wait on deck where I remained talking to Ramsey.

Keyes and the visiting captain took a long time; I grew more and more impatient. Ramsey did not improve matters by remarking, 'I don't see what you're making such a fuss about, your rotten old aeroplanes will be no bloody good anyway.' There was enough probability of truth in it to make me see red.

At last Keyes and the visiting captain came on deck and the latter departed. Keyes saw me waiting and said, 'Hello, what are you waiting for? You know what you've got to do, don't you?'

I was thoroughly fed up by that time so replied, 'Yes, sir; I understand that I am to go to Sir Ian Hamilton now and say that I cannot carry out any of his orders because I have been given a full programme by Inshore Squadron.'

'You'll do nothing of the kind.'

'Ay, Ay, sir,' I rejoined, 'in that case I presume I am to carry out the general's orders in full and ignore all orders I get from Inshore Squadron.'

'Eh! no, that won't do.'

'Then, sir, am I to understand that I am to give priority to the general's orders carrying them out in full, and if, after doing so, I have any aircraft available, I am to carry out as much of the Inshore Squadron's orders as I can?'

Roger Keyes thought for a moment, then answered, 'Yes, that's what you're to do and I'll give you those orders in writing if you like.'

Still feeling sore I replied, 'I don't need writing, sir, all I need is to know what to do.'

For the first time, the poker face altered. Roger Keyes grinned and said, 'Well, now you know, you'd best get ashore and do it.'

I think that rather stormy interview was a lucky one for me. From then on I met with nothing but the greatest kindness from Roger Keyes.

I landed at the H.Q. pier and reported the result of the interview and that we should hope to meet all Army requirements. I need not have worried about the work on the aircraft as during my absence all the jobs had been completed and our shaky old aeroplanes were as ready as it was possible to make them. Before leaving H.Q. I had been invited to dine with Sir Ian that night.

After cleaning up as well as I could, I went down to the H.Q. mess. There was the same feeling of anxiety everywhere that had been so noticeable on 25 April, but Sir Ian Hamilton was cheerful and appeared full of confidence. Amongst those present were Lord Howard de Walden and Major Jack Churchill (the First Lord's brother), whom I had met on board *Enchantress* during Winston Churchill's week-end parties at Sheerness. Naturally the party broke up early. When I went to say good night to Sir Ian, he said, 'You know, it takes something to throw everything you've got at the enemy just in the hope of doing a bit of good.' It was the only indication he gave of the strain that he was under.

At dawn on 7 August I took Knatchbull-Hugessen on reconnaissance over the Suvla area. The troops appeared to be successfully ashore with no apparent infantry opposition or heavy artillery fire, though we saw a few shrapnel bursts over the beaches. However we could see no forward movement of our troops across the dry Salt Lake. We examined the old gun emplacements in the Chocolate Hills but they were still empty with no sign of activity there. On return, the observer took his report to H.Q. Catching sight of Jack Churchill walking towards the cliff overlooking the harbour, I walked over to join him. He was worried and in a bad temper. He said there was a shortage of water at Suvla. One of the water boats was still in Kephalo Bay, when she ought to have left long ago. We watched the water boat get under way before returning to H.Q.

I told Churchill what we had seen and of the apparent absence of forward movement. The bad organization for water supply has been named as one of the contributory causes of the failure of the Suvla attack, which was a most exasperating business to watch from the air. Over the Suvla position again later in the day I could still see no signs of an advance. Yet the gun emplacements were still empty; the only sign of enemy infantry that we could find was a small party sheltering from ships' gun-fire behind a little mound to the south of the Salt Lake. From my point of view, the only redeeming feature of that day was that all the aircraft remained serviceable so that we were able to complete the full programme for the Army as well as meet most of the demands of the Inshore Squadron.

As a result of Admiral de Robeck's signal new aircraft began to arrive. They consisted of a number of Henri Farmans with 120-h.p. Canton Unné engines and two Nieuports with 80-h.p. Le Rhône engines. During the days following the Suvla landing we were constantly spotting ships' fire and on reconnaissance over Suvla and Anzac. There had been little enemy air activity during the summer but now it increased. On 10 August, when flying the first of the new Henri Farmans with Jupp as observer, we met a German Ettrich Taube over Anzac. The pilot did not see us and I was able to come close behind him. Jupp, who had a rifle, started shooting and must have made good practice for at about the fifth shot I saw the pilot's face as he turned to look behind before going into a vertical dive. We heard afterwards that the Australians had a full view of the encounter from their trenches. Convinced that we had shot down the German, they had all started cheering.

Samson and Collet returned from leave in Egypt on 11 August. I turned the executive job over to Collet and the next day started fourteen days' leave myself.

Returning to Imbros at the end of August, I was saddened to hear that Collet had been killed in a crash. After the crash his machine caught fire. In trying to pull Collet out, Chief Petty Officer Keogh was badly burned and had been awarded the Albert Medal for his gallantry.

The Suvla attack had resolved itself into trench warfare and it seemed there was stalemate everywhere. Samson had employed working parties of Greeks to clear a new stretch of ground for a landing strip. It was much better than the blimp station but was bordered on the harbour side by a steep cliff. We cut a sloping ramp down through the cliff from a hand winch fixed at the top. Stores landed on the beach at the foot of the ramp were hove up to the landing ground on trolleys, while the large aeroplane packing cases were hauled up on rollers. These packing cases made excellent sleeping huts and workshops. We soon had all the officers housed in them, instead of in tents. However the men were still in tents, which were wearing thin. Better housing was essential before the winter set in.

Amongst the Greek working party were a number of competent rough masons. Some Turkish prisoners who had been allotted to us were set to quarrying stones with which the Greeks worked to build barracks and messes. The Turks seemed content with their lot; they came to the camp each morning under a guard of Australians, the guard always giving their rifles to the Turks to carry. I appointed Able Seaman Roper to be foreman of the Turks and he invented a kind of language which they appeared to understand. He reported that one of them, whom he called Abdul, was unfit for heavy work. Abdul appeared to be middle-aged; he was very small, very thin, with a fluffy grey beard round his face and he had a nasty cough. Dr Patterson, after examining him, said there was nothing wrong except overwork and underfeeding. So we detached Abdul from the quarry party, sending him to help the cook in the galley. The cook gave him frequent mugs of cocoa, taught him to peel potatoes and Abdul rapidly improved.

Our building operations proceeded well. We had completed a stone officers mess and nearly half the barracks for the men when the provost marshal decided to investigate the employment of prisoners with a view to ensuring that the Geneva Convention was being complied with. The provost marshal was a colonel obviously brought back from well-earned retirement. I had a long and difficult session with him. He said that quarrying stone conformed to the Geneva Convention provided that the stone was used for road-making. I pointed out that we had no need for roads and that it could not matter to the Turks what use we made of the stone after they had produced it. The argument was growing hot and so was the provost marshal, when he happened to catch sight of Abdul.

Abdul had evidently become conscious of the presence of a brass-hat with red tabs and had determined to make a good impression. He was seated on an upturned bucket outside the galley taking potatoes from one bucket, peeling with speed and dexterity, depositing the naked spud in another bucket and the peel in a third. The next few minutes were critical. It was an outrageous breach of the Geneva Convention; if a newspaper reporter saw that there could be trouble for everybody. I put in a word when I could on the subject of Abdul's weak physical state. He was under medical care, the treatment prescribed was frequent nourishment and a light occupation; it could hardly be called a breach of the Convention if the proper medical treatment was carried out for him.

At that point in our discussion the cook emerged from the galley and gave Abdul a mug of cocoa and a cigarette. Abdul was about to have his elevenses. Fortunately the provost marshal's sense of humour awoke and he began to laugh. He said he wished he could send Abdul home to his wife, as she had to peel her own potatoes. After that the provost marshal accepted a tot of whisky and we had no more trouble over the Geneva Convention.

Evidently the Turks had been reinforced by German aircraft, as they took to bombing Imbros from time to time. Our two Nieuports had proved underpowered as two-seaters but they were fast. We therefore cowled in the passenger seat and made single-seater fighters of them, with a tubular mounting on the top plane in which a Lewis gun could be hinged. It could fire over the airscrew disc and could be swung down on its hinge to change ammunition trays.

As soon as the first was fitted out, Samson took off with two bombs and the gun, intending to attack some suitable target and then hunt German aircraft over the Peninsula. After taking off and when he was at about 200 feet, one of his bombs fell off, bursting directly under him. Though he might have been blown to bits, Samson was unhurt but the Nieuport, including the fuel tanks, was riddled: oil and petrol were cascading out as he landed.

A few mornings after this, while I was turning the hands to before breakfast, a German plane flew over and dropped bombs amongst the ships in the harbour. We tried always to send an aircraft up after raiders, mainly for the sake of earning a good reputation, though there was little chance of reaching the height of the enemy planes until they were back over their own lines. The second Nieuport had not yet been fitted with a gun but I had a pistol. Calling to the handling party, I took off while the German was still in sight. As he seemed to be making towards Cape Helles, I steered more to the north in the hope of intercepting him when he turned for home. Much to my surprise this succeeded. Just as I reached the Peninsula and was at about 8,000 feet, I saw him at the same height and heading towards Maidos.

He did not see me. I managed to approach just behind and below him and started shooting with the pistol. After about four rounds the pistol jammed, but one of the bullets must have gone near enough to attract attention for he turned and let fly with an automatic weapon of sorts from the back seat. Then he was joined by a pal who also started to shoot. I put the Nieuport into a vertical dive and escaped. As a result of this encounter we expedited the second Lewis gun mounting.

Early in October a decree went out that we were all to be inoculated against cholera. The result sent me to bed with a high temperature. Our huts were not yet habitable and I was still sleeping in a tent. Shortly after I had retired to bed a German dropped a stick of bombs across our camp. One fell beside the next tent which was occupied by Samson's steward, Garwood, and Collet's Marine servant, Devlin. Devlin heard it coming and threw himself flat, but Garwood was killed. Since Collet's death, Devlin had attached himself to me and he remained my attendant for the rest of the war. Our old Eastchurch messmate Clarke-Hall, now in command of the seaplane carrier *Ark Royal*, hearing that I had gone sick, invited me to occupy a cabin on board where he made me very comfortable until I recovered.

There was a general reorganization of the R.N.A.S. units during that month. Not only did we receive a number of new pilots in No. 3 Wing, but a second wing under Gerrard was sent out. Colonel Sykes, now holding a commission in the Royal Marines, came out to take command of the R.N.A.S. units. We felt rather unhappy about this in No. 3 Wing. Samson had had the responsibility throughout the most active part of the campaign, and it seemed hard that he should be, in effect, superseded when a stalemate had set in.

The reorganization resulted in a division of duties. Gerrard's No. 2 Wing was to do the spotting and reconnaissance over Gallipoli, while we were to concentrate on long-range bombing. The armoured-car section of the R.N.A.S. had been serving as machine-gunners with the Naval Division. These were Josh Wedgwood's men who had come out with us in the *Imkosi*. After the Suvla landing they were withdrawn and a number were sent to join up with us in charge of a petty officer named Douglas. It was difficult to know how to use them. They were by this time veteran soldiers but knew nothing about aeroplanes: on the other hand it seemed quite wrong to use them as labourers alongside hired Greek and Turkish prisoners. I consulted with Douglas and decided to keep them together as a special party to work under Douglas. I would tell him what jobs required doing and he would undertake to tackle the most suitable.

The first job was to produce weatherproof accommodation for his men. This he did by building a barracks, using the empty wood boxes in which petrol cans had been stowed. When that was done, he proposed that they should dig wells to supply us with fresh water. The only existing supply was an ancient well in the valley which held the military H.Q. camp, whence the water came to us in a cart drawn by mules.

Douglas had been examining the rock formation under our landing ground. He explained that the slope of the surface was at right angles to the lines of strata which came to the surface at intervals forming a rock outcrop. If he sank a shaft between two of these outcrops he would find water. It did not seem possible: the whole place was baked bone-dry in October. However, we provided him with empty oil drums and he set his party to work. Six feet below the surface he found water. Though it tasted of the residue in the oil drums, it was otherwise perfectly good.

The Turkish supplies from Germany passed through Bulgaria by road and rail. Our long-range bombing attacks were therefore mainly against railway lines and bridges on that system. On 19 November, Samson organized all available aircraft for an attack on this railway system at two points, Burgess Bridge and Ferrijik Junction. He passed his order book round at supper the evening before the attack. I was deeply engaged with the operation of building winter quarters and was rather annoyed to find he had put me down to fly one of the Nieuports, carrying 20-lb bombs, to Ferrijik Junction. I did not think those little bombs could do much harm, and I wanted to press on with supervising the building work.

During the attack, the Henri Farman that Smylie was flying was hit in the engine and forced down into the marshes on the far side of the Maritza River in Bulgarian territory. These marshes were very wide, cut up in winter and spring by a large number of water-courses. In November, after a long dry summer, most of the watercourses were dry, the beds being baked mud and gravel. In one of these Smylie had safely landed and I decided to go down to pick him up.

It never occurred to me that we were likely to be interfered with by enemy troops. The marshes were wide and rough with tall banks of reeds and scrub. What did worry me was the possibility of finding two men to rescue, for I knew that some of our military observers had been detailed to take part in the operation as bomb aimers. An experienced gunner officer was much more valuable than a newly trained sub. R.N.A.S. I could only carry one passenger; but I could not imagine Edwards, Jopp, Walser or Knatchbull-Hugessen agreeing to come away and leave the pilot.

As I circled down I could see the Farman burning. I flew low round it looking for Smylie and received an almighty shock when the plane suddenly blew up. I had had no idea there was a bomb still on board and, in case there were any more, I hastily climbed away. Then I saw Smylie emerge from a little hollow in which he had been lying and wave.

I learned later that Smylie had seen a party of Bulgarian troops approaching. He had therefore fired the plane and set off to cross into Turkish territory, preferring to be taken prisoner by Turks rather than Bulgars. On seeing me coming down to rescue him, he had realized the danger if the bomb exploded after I had landed, so he took cover in the hollow, fired at the bomb with his pistol and succeeded in exploding it with his third shot.

To my great relief I found that Smylie was alone. All the same, it was no easy matter to accommodate him in my plane as there was no passenger seat, a cowl now covering the space where one had originally been. He had to climb over me, slide under the cowl and crouch on all fours between the rudder bar and the engine bearers with his head bumping on the oil tank. He managed somehow to stow himself away looking most uncomfortable.

By this time enemy troops were coming close so I lost no time in taking off. There was length in the dry watercourse for a good run and we had no difficulty in getting airborne. The flight back to base took three-quarters of an hour and I felt sorry for poor Smylie, but all went well and we arrived safely.[1]

[1] EDITOR'S NOTE

From the Supplement to the *London Gazette*, 1st January, 1916:
Admiralty, 1st January, 1916
The King has been graciously pleased to approve of the grant of the Victoria Cross to Squadron Commander Richard Bell Davies, D.S.O., R.N., and of the Distinguished Service Cross to Flight Sub-Lieutenant Gilbert Formby Smylie, R.N., in recognition of their behaviour in the following circumstances. On the 19th November these two officers carried out an air attack on Ferrijik Junction. Flight Sub-Lieutenant Smylie's machine was received by very heavy fire and brought down. The pilot planed down over the station, releasing all his bombs except one, which failed to drop, simultaneously at the station from a very low altitude. Thence he continued his descent into the marsh.
On alighting he saw the one unexploded bomb, and set fire to his machine, knowing that the bomb would ensure its destruction. He then proceeded towards Turkish territory.
At this moment he perceived Squadron Commander Davies descending, and fearing that he would come down near the burning machine and thus risk destruction from the bomb, Flight Sub-Lieutenant Smylie ran back and from a short distance exploded the bomb by means of a pistol bullet. Squadron Commander Davies descended at a safe distance from the burning machine, took up Sub-Lieutenant Smylie, in spite of the near approach of a party of the enemy, and returned to the aerodrome, a feat of airmanship that can seldom have been equalled for skill and gallantry.

(See also facsimile of congratulatory letter from Winston Churchill facing page 119.)

By the end of November we achieved good accommodation for all hands. The barrack blocks, fitted with mess tables and hammock rails, in which the men were housed, had stone walls and corrugated-iron roofs. There was a stone-walled galley with an elaborate stone-built mess for meals.

Coal-burning stoves made from empty oil drums had chimneys consisting of steel tubes once the framework for aeroplane tents, the canvas of which had long since rotted away. Amongst the transport vehicles was a lorry, originally intended to carry a searchlight, its engine geared to drive a powerful electric generator. With this we lighted the whole camp. The packing case I shared with Isaac was large enough to divide into three rooms, each 6 feet × 6 feet. The two end rooms we fitted with bunks and used as sleeping cabins, doors connecting with the middle room which we used as a sitting-room. Wash basins were made out of petrol cans fitted on hinged brackets on the side of the case. They were emptied by lifting the brackets which shot the dirty water outside. Windows were made from the glass of old photographic plates.

We improved the oil-drum stove by building a proper fireplace in our sitting-room with fireblocks and fire-clay looted, or rather salved, from the old colliers which had been sunk to form a breakwater for the small-craft anchorage in Kephalo Bay. For fire-bars we used tappet rods from wrecked Gnome engines. In fact we were as well housed as possible to face a Gallipoli winter.

At the end of November the long spell of good weather broke. Starting with a violent south-westerly gale and heavy rain, in the middle of one night the wind suddenly turned north-east and became bitterly cold. The misery it brought to the men in the trenches was awful. Our aircraft were anchored in the open. The main anchorage for each comprised a wooden box full of soil to which a long wire strop was attached, the axle of the undercarriage being lashed to the strop. To the wing tips we secured other boxes full of soil which normally rested on the ground; if a wing lifted it took the whole weight of the box of earth. This arrangement proved excellent in the gale, and until the sudden shift of wind came the planes suffered no harm. When that happened they had all to be turned round head to wind in the stormy night. Before we could complete the operation many elevators and ailerons suffered damage in spite of being well clamped.

The north-easterly gale brought heavy seas into Kephalo Bay. In spite of the breakwater of sunken colliers practically all small craft were driven ashore and damaged. Our own cutter was thrown high on to the beach but without much harm and, having plenty of men, we were able to carry her down and launch her. My old shipmate Spuddy Carver was acting as harbour master and was in his element, bringing his drive and seaman's ingenuity to bear on the problem of salving heavy lighters, barges and other craft which had been driven high and dry.

Early in December came rumours of evacuation. Lord Kitchener had paid a visit to the Peninsula and the rumours were soon confirmed as regards Suvla and Anzac. It seemed a very risky undertaking and we were all most anxious. From 15 to 19 December we flew constantly over the two areas to interfere with enemy reconnaissance. Each night stores and equipment of all kinds were being brought away; but everything appeared normal. In the event we saw no enemy aircraft for the whole period, perhaps owing to the weather conditions. By great luck a low cloud layer formed and made enemy reconnaissance useless. The final evacuation was successfully carried out during the night of the 19th practically without casualties. It appeared to be quite late on the 20th before the Turks realized what had happened.

Towards the end of the month we heard that No. 3 Wing was to be withdrawn. Of the original pilots only Samson, Thomson and I remained and we were ordered to take passage in a transport leaving Mudros in the New Year; the rest were to follow later. Gerrard invited the three of us to a farewell dinner at No. 2 Wing's mess and the next morning we were ceremonially rowed off to the mail trawler for Mudros in our cutter manned by a crew of officers. Before we left Mudros in the transport, we heard of the successful evacuation of Cape Helles.

Samson had not been feeling fit during the last few days at Gallipoli, and during the trip he developed an acute attack of jaundice. At Malta we reported to Vice-Admiral Limpus who invited us to lunch. Before the outbreak of war he had been in charge of the British Naval Mission to Turkey and had been nominated C-in-C of the Turkish Fleet. The whole situation had changed, of course, when the German battle-cruiser *Goeben*, with the cruiser *Breslau*, escaped the British Mediterranean Fleet and entered the Bosphorus, an event which had played a large part in bringing the Turks into the war on the side of Germany. I asked Lady Limpus what she thought would have happened if the British Fleet had followed them up the Dardanelles. She said she thought that the Turks would have flung their fezzes up in the air and cheered. I don't think the Admiral agreed.

While at Malta I heard that I had been promoted to wing commander R.N.A.S., though I was still only a lieutenant R.N. We had a slow trip up the Mediterranean, disembarking at Marseilles for Paris where we spent one night at the Ritz. The head waiter at the restaurant in which we dined had been waiter in one of the Ostend hotels in 1914 and recognized us. The result was a wonderful dinner. Crossing to England the next day I went on leave.

There had been a reorganization at the Admiralty and Admiral Vaughan-Lee had been appointed Fifth Sea Lord, Commodore Murray Sueter remaining at the Air Department as his Chief Assistant. This was a disappointment to all of us as Sueter, our boss for so long, had really built up the R.N.A.S. It was sound, however, that Naval Air should be represented on the Board of Admiralty.

Soon after starting leave, Samson and I were summoned to the Admiralty where the Fifth Sea Lord told us that there were two new types of aircraft on which he wanted us to report. These were the first twin-engined Handley-Page and the Sopwith bomber, afterwards known as the 1½-Strutter (see illus. facing p. 150) because of the arrangement of its interplane and centre-section struts. The aircraft were at Eastchurch where we went by Admiralty car. We lunched in the mess. Although it was pleasant to be back there, we knew nobody in the place except old Horace Short who came over to see us after lunch. Of course we reported enthusiastically on the two aircraft.

Towards the end of January 1916 I was appointed district commander of air stations in the north of England, having being promoted to wing commander at the New Year. The post of district commander had been introduced in 1915 on the ground that, owing to the very rapid expansion of the R.N.A.S., discipline was shaky. I relieved Commander Briggs, a senior commander noted as a strict disciplinarian, a very energetic personality whose nickname was 'The Dasher'. I found him very indignant. He said he had been sent to restore discipline but that there had been nothing wrong with it. He had found a large number of young and newly trained officers and ratings, all keen to do their job, but with no equipment, only rudimentary ration supply, shocking quarters and inadequate transport. Instead of instilling discipline, he had had to spend his time getting his men housed, fed and properly clothed. He had tackled the job with his usual energy and by the time I relieved him the stations were at least habitable.

My first effort was to find out what they were supposed to do. There were four stations in my group, Killingholme on the Humber, Redcar and Scarborough in Yorkshire and Whitley Bay in Northumberland. Redcar was an *ab-initio* flying training school. The other three stations were ordered to carry out a coastal patrol. The object of the patrol was left vague and it did not seem to me to serve much purpose. I thought I had better tackle the stations one at a time starting with Killingholme which was my headquarters.

It had originated in 1914, when the R.N.A.S. had gone there from Eastchurch with the idea of preventing daylight Zeppelin attacks on the Admiralty oil tanks. The landing ground was a small field bounded on one side by the Humber, on another by the oil tanks with their surrounding unclimbable fence, on a third side by a railway line complete with telegraph wires and signals and on the fourth by a disused clay pit. On this unsuitable ground *ab-initio* training with a Bristol box-kite was being carried on. I had that training transferred to Redcar where the aerodrome was adequate. The other activity was seaplane training on the Humber. There was a small single-engine flying-boat of French make called by the mystic letters F.B.A., a Sunbeam-engined Short tractor, quite good but under-powered, and a number of single-seater Sopwith seaplanes called Schneiders, reproductions of the seaplane on which Hawker won the Schneider Cup in 1914. They were powered by 120-h.p. Clerget rotary engines.

The Schneiders appeared to be brand new and never to have been flown. On inquiry I was told that one had been flown but had proved to be uncontrollable and dangerous. This sounded extraordinary so I examined them carefully. They seemed to be perfectly good aircraft, but I saw that the lateral control was by wing warping and I began to suspect the explanation. I had one of them launched and took it up. The moment I was airborne the left wing dropped heavily; most of my strength was needed to hold it up. The trouble was the same from which No. 33 had suffered, but, with a heavier engine and shorter span, the effect of torque was much greater. Similar complaints call for similar remedies. I took the machine back to the slipway and sent for a drill, a length of Sandow elastic and a bottle-screw strainer. Anchoring the elastic to a strength member in the fuselage, I drilled a hole in one of the spokes of the control wheel and attached the bottle-screw. I connected the other end of the elastic to the bottle-screw and then stressed it until it was pulling the left wingtip down to full warp. Leaving a tommy bar in the bottle-screw, I took off again. The machine flew very nearly true and, after a little adjustment of the bottle-screw, completely so. I took her back to the slipway, put a locking wire on the strainer and persuaded one of the young pilots to try her. He came down enthusiastic. Never has my reputation soared to such heights. It seemed to the young pilots to be black magic. I was careful not to let them know that two years before I had had exactly the same trouble and that on that occasion it had taken me six months to find a remedy. With the curse removed from the Schneiders, seaplane training could go ahead at Killingholme.

Whitley Bay station was equipped with Short seaplanes which could carry out anti-submarine patrols over the approaches to the Tyne. The trouble there was that the planes were working from an exposed beach, weather conditions often stopping operations. Scarborough was commanded by Christopher Draper. The landing ground was the racecourse where everybody lived in the grandstand. Beyond the coastal patrols ordered, the only useful purpose for that station was defence against Zeppelin raids. That would have involved night flying, and the racecourse was a most unsuitable night landing ground. Draper was very keen to take it on, but that was a matter of Admiralty policy. Redcar, commanded by Rathbone of the Marines, was for *ab-initio* flying training only and was running smoothly.

My immediate boss was the Admiral East Coast, Rear-Admiral

Ballard, whose headquarters were at Immingham close to Killing-holme. After absorbing the foregoing information, I reported to him. He agreed generally to my proposals, and the question of anti-Zeppelin efforts was referred to the Admiralty. He added that he was constantly receiving reports of daylight sighting of Zeppelins from minesweepers and fishing trawlers off the coast. It seemed that the airships crossed the North Sea in daylight, took a fix by sighting the coast at twilight and then lay off until dark. Raids came nearly always at the time of the new moon. Ballard suggested that if we could get the Schneider seaplanes out to sea we might have a chance at a Zeppelin before darkness fell.

A ferry service crossed the Humber between Hull and New Holland, run by paddle steamers of very shallow draught and designed to carry flocks of sheep. To accommodate the sheep, the upper decks were extended beyond the ships' sides and beyond the paddle-boxes. In plan the upper deck was a circle except for the pointed bow and stern extending beyond it. In fact the bow and stern were interchangeable as the boats went to and fro without turning round. There were two steering wheels and a rudder at each end. This large open deck was capable of accommodating four Schneider seaplanes.

When I reported favourably on these craft, Ballard requisitioned one named *Killingholme* and had her sent to Hull shipyard for a mast and derrick to be fitted to enable Schneiders to be hoisted in. It had to be a rush job in order to send her to sea by next new moon. The Admiral intended to provide a Merchant Navy crew, but it took time to enter them. The mast and derrick were ready in a few days, but not the crew, so I made one up from the air station. The engine mechanics had little experience of oscillating steam cylinders but they managed to make them work and the handling party soon raised a fine head of steam in the boiler. We took our craft down the Humber from Hull to Immingham and secured her in the basin. With her shallow draught and double rudders steering was extremely tricky and she was apt to take wild sheers. There was a compass, but I found that the north point was always directed at the funnel. Then we found that there was no reserve feed water tank, as she always topped up the boiler when alongside the pier. A hasty hunt disclosed a tank which might be suitable, I had a hose put in to fill it up and test for leaks, but the tank did not fill. Presently someone heard the sound of running water in a compartment labelled 'Ladies', so that was no good. Eventually we carried the reserve feed water in two-gallon cans.

The ancient cruiser *Forth* was lying in Immingham Basin acting as a submarine depôt ship. She was commanded by Commander Archdale who said that, as the *Forth*'s seagoing days were over, he would supply me with her binnacle and any other navigational equipment I wanted; so I got a cherub log and a deck watch as well. A few of the original crew joined up, including the chief engineer and an officer who said he had a second mate's coasting ticket. Thus equipped we put to sea. Our destination was the Dogger Bank where a number of Zeppelins had been sighted by trawlers in daylight.

Our course down the Humber was serpentine until the air mechanics got the hang of the tricky steering gear, and by Spurn Head we could keep a fairly steady course. I told the second mate to stream the log, which he did by chucking the log and line overboard. This ripped the innards out of the cherub, leaving only the dial. We then made a hand log which gave us a rough idea of our speed, but the backwash from the paddles tended to give an over estimate.

The *Killingholme*'s performance at sea was unusual to say the least. Each time she rolled, the overhang of the deck hit the surface with a bang which shook the ship and made the funnel wobble. We carried on through the night; got a latitude sight at noon the next day, and in the afternoon picked up soundings with the hand lead on the Dogger Bank. The *Killingholme* was evidently not the sort of ship which could ride out a hard blow at sea. I made up my mind that if it came on to blow, we would make for the Humber if the wind was northerly and for the Tyne if it was southerly; but it was important to know our position. If we could hang on to soundings on the south-west patch of the Dogger, we should be sure of our position; so we went to the patch and picked up soundings there. We ploughed backwards and forwards across the patch, keeping the lead going and watching for Zeps, but none appeared.

Through the following night we continued the sentry go; in the morning watch it started to blow from the north-west. As there was soon too much sea to allow the Schneiders to take off and it looked like blowing harder, I decided to make for the Humber. With the sea on the quarter, *Killingholme* made good progress, though the steering was wild beyond belief. After about an hour, crashes and bangs in the port paddle-box forced us to stop. *Killingholme* promptly fell into the trough of the sea, rolling abominably.

We took off the cover of a manhole in the side of the sponson and peered inside. As crossing the Humber in very shallow water the paddle floats were apt to hit the bottom, to avoid damage to the steel spokes of the wheel the floats were lightly constructed of soft wood so as to break away easily. Several had done so at one end and had been acting as flails against the casing of the sponson. The only thing to be done was to cut away the damaged floats. But each time the ship rolled, the manhole and half the paddle-wheel went under water, while the surge of the sea caused the paddle-wheel to turn. There was a hand-turning arrangement in the engine-room which we connected up. This acted as a brake on the axle and so locked the paddle-wheel. Providentially an armed trawler now came along. We called on her to take *Killingholme* in tow and hold her head to sea. That done, it was possible to put a man into the sponson to cut away the broken floats. He cut away all those above water and came out to allow the wheel to be turned. The gear wheels of the hand-turning gear promptly stripped and round went the wheel. We jammed the handspikes into it and made it stop, then we lashed it with wires and so the cutting was completed.

Casting off the tow we set off again for the Humber, going slowly to avoid breaking any more floats. If the vessel steered badly before with half the floats off one wheel, she steered now like nothing imaginable. We had to man both wheels to keep her headed even approximately in the right direction. Early the next morning we made Spurn Head and anchored under its lee. I demanded a tug to take *Killingholme* up the river as the Humber was not wide enough to allow for her erratic steering.

Personnel became an increasing problem. Conscription was introduced in March of that year, 1916. The result of the delay in its introduction was that the standard of the new intake into R.N.A.S. fell sharply. The volunteers who had come in early in the war had been from the best of the population. Those conscripted in 1916 were most reluctant to join. The Admiralty had taken up land at Cranwell for a large training centre and early in May I flew over and landed there, thus becoming the first person ever to visit Cranwell by air.

On 31 May I received a message from the Admiral East Coast, that he wanted a reconnaissance to seaward at daylight next morning. I did not know what it was for, but as it sounded interesting I took our only Short and flew from Spurn Head for over an hour, but saw nothing.

That flight made me realize some of the problems of over-sea navigation in aircraft. It was a flat calm at dawn and only with difficulty did I get the under-powered Short into the air. I assumed no wind speed and at the end of an hour set course for the Humber. I made landfall near The Wash. A fresh northerly wind must have been blowing a few hundred feet above sea level. The engine now gave out but I managed to beach the plane. The trouble was in the magneto. Until the outbreak of war, all engines, British and French, were fitted with German Bosch magnetos. By 1916 these were wearing out. British substitutes were at first unreliable, but they soon improved.

It was not till the next day that news of the Battle of Jutland began to come in. When the cruiser *Chester* and the seaplane carrier *Engadine* steamed into the Humber, they brought us first-hand news about the battle, but of course they could only relate their own experiences.

The *Killingholme* was sent to Hull to have hard wood floats fitted to her paddles and also some essential alterations made. By the time she was ready for sea a full crew had been entered and a temporary R.N.R. lieutenant had been appointed in command. He proved to be a good one. At the next new moon she was again sent off to the Dogger with her Schneiders, but the Germans evidently knew all about her. A number of Scandinavian ships used the port of Hull and it seems probable that German intelligence managed to make use of them. Two apparently inoffensive fishing trawlers approached her during the night and fired torpedoes at close range. One torpedo was seen to pass right under her, but another hit a paddle wheel blowing it and the overhang deck overboard. The hull remained intact: no one was killed, but several of the crew were hurt.

11
1½-Strutters

Early in June 1916, a letter from the Personnel Captain at the Air Department of the Admiralty advised me that No. 3 Wing was to be re-formed for service in France. Its task was to carry out reprisal bombing raids on German towns in revenge for the Zeppelin raids on English towns. I was to be appointed to the re-formed wing. I thoroughly disliked the idea of reprisal raids. Two wrongs did not make a right. Furthermore, most of us believed that the Zeppelins set out to bomb military targets, only bombing open towns and villages as a result of losing themselves in the dark.

I composed a letter strongly expressing these opinions and had the sense to read it through carefully and then tear it up. Instead I sent one with a paragraph explaining that it was a personal letter written before I had received any official appointment, that if appointed I should of course obey orders and not criticize Admiralty policy. Rewriting that letter was one of the few wise things I have done. It was well received, and in the orders eventually given to No. 3 Wing there was no reference to reprisals.

I was relieved at Killingholme by Arthur Longmore and appointed wing commander of No. 3 Wing about the middle of June. The squadrons were forming at Manston in Kent, where land had been taken over by the Admiralty and a few tents erected. The wing was to operate from Luxeuil, near the French frontier fortress of Belfort, where a large repair base was also to be set up, the whole organization under the command of Captain Elder. At Manston I found Reggie Marix training the first flight which had just been formed. The pilots were nearly all Canadians and were a first-rate lot. The aircraft were to be Sopwith

145

1½-Strutters, which were just coming into production, and it was hoped that they would be followed by some twin-engined Handley Pages.

These were two types of aircraft which Samson and I had been sent to report on when we returned to England early in the year. The 1½-Strutters were a great advance on anything we had had before. The bomber and fighter versions were in essentials identical aircraft. Both had a fixed Vickers front gun firing through the airscrew by means of interrupter gear. In the fighter the rear gunner's seat took the place of the bomb rack. Performance of the two types in the air was so similar that keeping station with one another would be easy. Their operational range was excellent, and to test it Reggie had flown one from Manston to Mevagissey, in Cornwall, and back without landing.

There was nothing much for me to do at Manston as Reggie had the training well in hand. Formation flying was in its infancy in 1916, but we agreed to follow the system that had been tried out before the war, adopting the V formation. I had orders to collect the bulk of the mechanics and to take them out to Luxeuil at the end of June. Lieutenant Peal, who was to be in charge of the repair base, I met in London. We were both staggered by the extent of the equipment which it was proposed to send out, and eventually he persuaded the Admiralty to cancel much of the elaborate repair machinery. It must have been a unique experience to have naval officers asking to have their equipment reduced.

In the last week in June, Peal and I went to the White City which had become an R.N.A.S. Barracks, to collect and muster the men detailed for No. 3 Wing. We divided them into parties under the petty officers. When we reached Luxeuil we found that Elder was already there with a party who were erecting huts on the sides of the very excellent aerodrome. We housed the men temporarily in tents, and found billets for ourselves in a farmhouse near by.

In July the first squadron of 1½-Strutters set out from Manston, led by Reggie. At Paris where they landed he was invited to try a new French machine in which he had a very bad crash and as a result one leg had to be amputated. The surgeons fortunately managed to save the other so that he lived to have a long career in the R.A.F.; his loss was a grave blow to No. 3 Wing.

The first squadron was still not complete, delivery of the new aircraft being very slow. We spent July and August continuing our training in bombing and formation flying. The 1½-Strutters were equipped with the first bomb-sight, a refinement which had been non-existent at Gallipoli. A sighting hole in the floor in front of the pilot was crossed by two transverse wires. The pilot had a reversing stop-watch. The idea was based on the most simple navigational running fix, 'doubling the angle on the bow.' The pilot brought the target into view in the sighting hole and when it came in line with the first wire he started the stop-watch. When the target reached the second wire he reversed the stop-watch; when the hand came back to zero he dropped the bombs. It proved most inefficient. One of the troubles was that the view from the pilot's seat forward and downwards was very poor, being masked by the engine cowling so that the pilot found it difficult to bring the target into view through the sighting hole.

I tried to overcome this with a home-made periscope which, pushed out through a hole in the side of the fuselage, could be revolved in the vertical plane and was long enough to reflect the view ahead, clear of the engine cowling. The effect was as though a slice had been cut away from the engine and cowling making it possible to keep the target in view until it appeared in the sighting hole. Some pilots found it a help, but most found it too complicated to work.

We had another trouble at that time. The original compasses supplied to naval aircraft were ordinary, flat card, liquid compasses, marked in points and degrees. After a steeply banked turn, these compasses usually swung considerably, taking some time to settle down. The reason was that when an aircraft is steeply banked the ordinary compass needle reacts to the 'dip' component of the earth's magnetic field more than to the directional component. Thus during a steep turn the needle ceases to seek north and is held stationary by the 'dip'. On completion of the turn it is released, to swing wildly as it once more seeks north. The scientists had set to work to cure the flaw. They were successful enough, but the compass they produced was an impossible one to use for navigation in a single-seater. There was no visible card and no 'lubber line'. All the pilot saw was a little window showing a number which gave the aircraft's heading. This was basically similar to the arrangement later standardized for aerial gyro-compasses but, as originally displayed, anything better calculated to confuse the pilot could hardly be imagined. I had discovered this before leaving England and had visited the laboratory at Slough, where I engaged in wordy warfare with the scientists. They undertook to produce a more practical compass, but in the meantime we had to make the best of the instruments as fitted. The result of all this was that the newly trained pilots joining No. 3 Wing, convinced that compasses were no good, tried to find their way across country by developing a sort of bird-like instinct. It took a lot of teaching to overcome that idea.

The construction party worked well and we were soon able to house everyone in huts. Delivery of the 1½-Strutters was slow, and to speed up equipment the Admiralty ordered a number of Breguet pusher biplanes to be delivered to Luxeuil. They arrived crated and had to be assembled. When I tested the first I had doubts as to whether we had got the tail incidence correct, the machine seeming rather unstable in fore and aft control. We wrote to the Breguet firm asking them to send a representative to check the assembly. They replied by telegram that their man would arrive by train the next day. I went to meet him and was surprised to see Louis Breguet himself descend from the train carrying a small suitcase and a large yellow crash-helmet. He had booked a room in the local hotel, but I persuaded him to come as our guest to the camp where we gave him a spare cabin. On arrival at the aerodrome he donned the enormous crash-helmet and took up the Breguet with me as his passenger. This was the only time I ever flew with one of the early French pioneers.

After landing he made some slight adjustment to the tail incidence, passing the rest of our assembly as satisfactory. I had an interesting talk with him later in the mess. He was indignant with the authorities in French Military Aviation who, he said, constantly overloaded this aircraft. It had been refused by the French War Office because it would not carry the load on which they insisted. He had had to design a new type for them called Breguet Michelin, but its performance was far inferior to that of our Breguets when properly loaded. He discussed our proposed bomb loads and agreed that they were suitable, but urged that they should not be increased. I thought it tactful not to refer to the 'blundering Breguet' of Gallipoli days, as it was evidently one of his mistakes. He was proud of being the first man to design a streamlined aeroplane and also the first to use metal construction.

We had other interesting visitors at Luxeuil about that time. They were the members of the Lafayette Squadron, the fighter squadron in the French Air Force manned entirely by American volunteers and equipped with Nieuports. The pilots, all graded as sergeants, were fine men and definitely tough. Their mascot was a lion cub which was led around on a string. They had just come from Paris where they had been in lodgings, and were indignant because Paris landladies had refused to accommodate the lion cub.

Elder disliked the reprisals idea just as much as I did and he decided, presumably with Admiralty approval, to act in co-operation with the French 4th Bombardment Group also based on Luxeuil. They were operating under the general commanding the Southern French Army, General Franchez d'Esperet. The C.O. of the group was Commandant Happé, a regular officer in the artillery, seconded to the Flying Corps. He had made a great reputation as a pilot in the early part of the war and was extremely popular with all his pilots. Over six feet tall, with black eyes and eyebrows and a bushy black beard parted down the middle, he always wore the black uniform of the artillery. In spite of this formidable and ferocious appearance, he was light-hearted, with a great sense of humour. His English was as bad as my French and his accent no better. We could understand each other well enough, but things were not made easier by the fact that Happé, who could also speak German of a sort, was liable to confuse the two languages. Soon after we arrived at Luxeuil, the French received a new type of bomb which Happé decided to test for himself on the near-by bombing range. I was at the aerodrome when he came back. As he climbed out of his Farman, he called out, *'C'est formidable. Eas good. Erschrecklich.'* I gathered that he was satisfied with the bomb.

Happé had spent some time in Alsace before the war; he said that the station masters at all the little stations there were pensioned N.C.O.s of the German Army, and that one and all were petty tyrants of the worst description. His great ambition was to take his Farman over one night, land near a station, enter the station master's house, bind him hand and foot and bring him back as a spoil of war.

He was still training his group as we were during August and September, so operations were on a small scale, only one or two raids being made on military targets near the front. By the end of September, when the French had three squadrons of Farmans and one of Breguet Michelins fit for work, Happé planned a long-range attack on a German munitions factory at Obendorf. We could by then contribute two fully trained flights of 1½-Strutters (ten bombers and two fighters). These constituted the Red Squadron. One flight, very newly trained, of 1½ Strutters (five bombers and one fighter) comprised the first flight of the Blue Squadron, the other flight being of Breguets also very newly trained. We had adopted this Red and Blue organization for identification in the air, each aircraft having a different design in the squadron colour painted on the fuselage.

The raid involved crossing the Black Forest where weather conditions were apt to be bad. Happé arranged to send a reconnaissance plane over early each morning to report on conditions, and for several days the cloud was too bad to allow our going. At last the early morning plane reported signs of the break-up of the heavy cloud. Happé sent out another reconnaissance plane, and late in the forenoon he reported that the air was clearing over the Black Forest. We had agreed that the French squadrons should take off first, followed by the 1½-Strutters and finally our Breguets. As the Breguets were likely to be the shakiest of our party, I had decided to go with them, and while the French squadrons were flying off, our party had time for lunch.

At about 1.40 p.m. it was time for the Breguets to take off, and I began to worry about daylight. I took my 1½-Strutter fighter up through the cloud layer which had formed over the aerodrome. In the sunshine above the cloud, there was nothing in sight. Presently I saw a disturbance in the white layer below and the top plane of a Breguet appeared. The machines came out one by one looking like a string of hippos emerging from a pool. As soon as they had picked up formation and the leader was headed for the Rhine Valley I brought the fighter into position just behind the 'V'. By the time they were nearing the front they had still not reached operational height. The leader turned back, quite correctly and according to orders, but the delay meant we would be later returning. While circling and climbing we were joined by the fighter of the Blue flight from which I deduced that the flight had failed to pick up formation owing to the bad cloud layer and that the bombers had returned to base in accordance with their orders. There were now two other fighters with the Breguets besides mine and I felt happier about them.

We eventually crossed the Rhine south of Breisach meeting heavy AA fire, but without harm. Nearing Freiburg a German single-seater appeared and dived at the port-wing Breguet; I was able to fire a burst at him with the front gun and he promptly dived away. Several other Germans appeared but evidently did not like the look of the close-locked formation; after flying with us for a time they cleared off. The Germans had left me too busy to pay much attention to navigation. By the time the last one had disappeared we were well over the Black Forest. There were no good landmarks, but I thought we were drifting too far south. Clearing the forest, we presently sighted a small town ahead. It did not look to me like Obendorf, but the bombers seemed sure it was. They formed into single line, went down and released their bombs. We eventually found that the town attacked was Donau-Eschingen.

The Breguets made a good job of regaining formation and turned on to a westerly course. By this time I was certain we were far south and we were drifting farther in that direction. I could see the line of the Alps and presently made out the deep gorge of the Rhine where it forms the Swiss frontier. I had visions of the whole party being interned in Switzerland. Still in rear of the flight and debating what to do, I saw the other fighter, piloted by Redpath, one of the original Canadians, move in front of the leader and then make a sharp turn to starboard. The leader followed him round, so we kept clear of Switzerland.

About sunset, as we cleared the Black Forest and came to the Rhine Valley, I saw one of the Breguets start to glide down. With no Germans near and no AA fire, it evidently had engine failure. The pilot was Butterworth, an American who had crossed into Canada and joined the R.N.A.S. He landed safely but was taken prisoner. Crossing the lines near Mulheim we again flew into heavy AA fire. I was glad to see it as I thought it meant that there were no German aircraft about. But just then I saw Wigglesworth, flying the starboard-wing Breguet, go into a steeply banked turn and open fire. He seemed to be giving as good as he got from his attacker but, having about 200 feet of height in hand, I was able to put my plane's nose down and go for two Germans both of whom had been attacking him. Wigglesworth continued to circle and engage them and between us we put in several bursts from both front and rear guns before the Germans departed. That was the only determined attack by the Germans, encouraged perhaps by the fact that, being nearly home, our station keeping was a bit slack.

By now it was dark on the ground and the light was dimming even at 10,000 feet. The rest of the Breguets had disappeared in the gloom. More trouble with German aircraft was unlikely, but I wondered what was going to happen when the Breguets landed. There was no proper flare path at Luxeuil, but the handling party had orders that if all aircraft were not back in daylight they were to be ready to start petrol flares directly they heard engines. Since few of the Breguet pilots had had night-flying experience I feared there would be several accidents on the aerodrome. It would be wise to keep away until the handling party had time to clear any debris or illuminate it, so I turned north up the line of the Vosges Mountains.

These are thickly covered with pine woods which show up at night as a blacker blackness. After flying north over them for a quarter of an hour, I turned south, certain of finding the aerodrome because I had noticed that just where the Vosges woods ended, a chain of three little lakes in a line pointed to the aerodrome which was only about a mile beyond the third lake. I sighted them – since lakes are visible at night – and turned towards Luxeuil while still at over 10,000 feet. Then I throttled back to lose height.

The Clerget engine installation in the 1½-Strutter entailed pressure feed, which was done by keeping air pressure in the petrol tank. An air pump worked by a little windmill maintained pressure in normal flight. But at 10,000 feet the atmosphere's pressure is very low, and as after more than five hours' flying the tank was nearly empty, it was necessary to put more air into the tank to ensure correct pressure. To do this when gliding, an auxiliary hand pump was provided. When I throttled back I started to pump but found that the leather washer of the plunger was not biting. Probably it was saturated with petrol and had shrunk. So I could not increase pressure in the tank. Reckoning that I must be close to the aerodrome, though neither flare path nor light was to be seen, I flew a couple of circuits over what I thought must be the landing ground and then throttled back.

When I opened up again after losing about 1,000 feet, the engine failed to respond and presently stopped revolving. I was in for a 'dead stick' landing, and there was still no light on the ground. Then I saw the first petrol fire light up and a flare path gradually grew. I was a little short of the first flare and had begun to flatten out for landing when a queer rumbling noise started. For a moment I could not think what it was. Then I realized that it was the wheels going round. The machine had landed herself.

Some of the handling party ran up: I asked how many Breguets had arrived and was horrified when they replied 'None'. Telling them to keep the flares going and to get the 1½-Strutter out of the way I hurried to the office to find the captain. Elder was there looking anxious. I told him that I had last seen them, all present except for Butterworth, crossing the front and headed for Luxeuil. There was nothing we could do but wait. Then the telephone rang and it was the first Breguet pilot reporting. For the next hour the telephone was constantly ringing with reports from them all. The flight had got completely lost and they had come down all over the district. Some pilots believing themselves to be still in Germany had tried to set fire to their aircraft. Another had landed on a railway line.

It was a tribute to the solidity of Breguet construction that none of the pilots or gunners was hurt, though a good many aircraft were badly bent. The two 1½-Strutter flights of the Red Squadron had bombed Obendorf, arriving back before dark without loss. Their experience with German aircraft had been the same as ours; a few had come near and looked at the formation but had made no serious attack.

The French though had serious losses, the Breguet Michelin squadron and one Farman squadron suffering heavy casualties. It convinced Happé that daylight bombing in slow, heavily-loaded aircraft without fighter cover would not pay. He decided to bomb only at night. Our experience on the other hand showed that a well-locked formation with fighter support was difficult for the Germans to attack. As it also showed that newly trained pilots were apt to lose their way in the dark, we decided to stick to day-light raids.

Towards the end of October, Elder had to go to England for a short time. While he was away I had a note from Happé saying that he was moving his group to Nancy, where he expected to be able to find some worthwhile targets. He suggested that we should come too. He did not say what the targets were, but as I felt sure that he was on to something good we loaded cars with essential spares and tools and the squadron handling parties and set off with the 1½-Strutters for Nancy. There Happé told me he had orders to raid the smelting works and blast furnaces in the Saar iron fields. He was sending his squadrons that night to attack the smelting furnaces at Hagenlingen within easy reach of Nancy. I agreed that we would follow up with a daylight attack next day.

The Hagenlingen raid was most successful. During our share of it there was heavy but inaccurate AA fire near the front, but we saw no German aircraft. The French attacks during the night had obviously done serious damage to the furnaces which appeared to be cold when we arrived. Our aircraft kept excellent formation, moved into single line and went down to bomb in succession, and I could see the bombs bursting amongst the furnace buildings. The return journey was uneventful, with little AA fire.

The Nancy aerodrome was crowded, as besides Happé's group there were French Army co-operation flights there. Hearing from Happé that there was an unused aerodrome at Oche near Toul. which had plenty of accommodation, we shifted there. We found the aerodrome in charge of a Brigadier, a most confusing title. An English brigadier commands a brigade. A French brigadier is a caretaker. Ours was a young lieutenant obviously in poor health and unfit for front-line service. He proved to be most helpful, opened up huts, arranged ration supplies and fuel and we installed ourselves comfortably. Happé brought his group there a few days later.

Billeted in and around the village was a brigade of chasseurs, commanded by Colonel de Sousbiel; chef de brigade – not *brigadier*. The Alpine battalion was commanded by Commandant Joli. We soon came to know them well, particularly Joli, who was a fine officer, and, I believe, rose to high rank in the French Army. The Chasseurs Alpins, who had suffered heavy casualties in the fighting near Verdun were re-forming and training. Joli often took them on long route marches at the remarkable quick step used by the chasseurs. He sometimes invited me and one or two others of our party to ride with him, lending us horses. We generally rode ahead of the battalion until we came to a village where we halted and Joli took the salute as the battalion marched through. He always brought them back past our camp and we would turn out all hands to give them a cheer. It was impressive to watch them go past almost at a run at the end of a 20-mile march.

There were several blast furnaces and smelting works within reach of Oche, the principal being at Volklingen-Dillingen and St Ingbert. When we went to attack we usually met with the same half-hearted interference from German aircraft and the self-confidence of our young pilots rose rapidly. My idea was to keep the flights in close-locked formation, with fighters supporting the bombers both on the outward and return journeys. However the bomber pilots had discovered that once their bomb loads were gone they had the legs of the fighters. So as soon as their bombs had been released, they took to opening throttle and going off on their own in search of Germans. I gave up trying to stop this as it was resulting in quite a number of Germans shot down. Our air gunners, one of whom was Bert Hinkler,[1] were all volunteers from the General Air Mechanic branch, with rating equivalent of able seamen. The gunner I had was a small man named Pinchin, very keen and alert.

Only once did we meet with a really determined German. I had started out with the leading flight, but the engine for some reason not developing full power, I dropped behind and the second flight overtook me near the target. I followed and watched them go down to bomb. As the last machine started down I saw its bomb doors open and all four bombs leave together. I was just thinking that as soon as we returned I must have a word with the pilot, a Canadian named McClellan, when I realized the reason for his

[1] He was to gain fame as an aviator in 1928 when he flew an Avro Avian light aeroplane solo to Australia.

action: there was a German on his tail. Having the advantage of height, I was quickly on to the German, getting in a good burst from the front gun before he dodged and I lost him momentarily.

The Germans at that time were not using tracers but a kind of explosive bullet. Because the sky all round was full of little puffs of smoke as my enemy made good practice with me, I found him again. I took drastic action. Pinchin began firing his gun, and I saw McClellan diving with his gun firing too. Eventually the German went down. I watched him until he was very low, yet he seemed to remain in control. Between us we may have hit his engine or wounded him.

After landing we found many holes in the fuselage of our machine, most of the bullets having apparently gone between Pinchin's legs. The engine had to go to the stripping shop, and the fighter needed patching up.

On the next raid I had a different machine. The Clerget was a French-designed engine which was also being made in England under licence. It was one of these that my new fighter had, the only difference being that the pistons were of aluminium alloy instead of cast iron. I was following a flight in my usual position behind the V when, about fifty miles beyond the front, there was a sudden bang from the engine and an intense vibration started. Throttling back I turned instinctively for home. There was no hope of gliding for fifty miles so I opened the throttle again. There was another loud bang and the vibration resumed but not quite as violently as before. At about a quarter power there seemed hope that the aircraft would not shake herself to pieces, so we headed back with the wing tips flapping like the wings of a bird.

Gradually we lost height but I had enough in hand to get back and after landing, as the engine slowed and stopped, it sounded as if it were full of broken crockery. Two of the pistons had seized up and the wrist pins had torn out of the piston skirting, breaking it all up. While the engine revolved, the bits and pieces remained in the cylinder heads; but when it slowed they fell into the crankcase. All the British-made engines had to be sent home for new pistons to be designed.

In December the weather became bad and opportunities for raids were few. We took the chance of a bad spell to invite the officers of the Chasseurs Alpins together with Happé and his pilots to dinner at a big café in Nancy. As a result of trouble in some French regiments in 1916 army discipline was being tightened up. The chief disciplinarian in Nancy was the commandant de ville, a senior colonel with a formidable reputation. Our dinner party was a great success, becoming definitely noisy as the evening wore on. I was sitting beside Happé when the proprietor of the café, known as Tirpitz on account of his whiskers, came in to say that the commandant de ville with his posse was outside.

Before we could do anything about it the commandant came in. The situation was saved by the Canadians who, not realizing the awful majesty of a commandant de ville, at once gave him three cheers, carried him round the room on their shoulders and, setting him on a table, demanded that he should make a speech. The commandant rose splendidly to the occasion. He saluted the company, said '*Vive la France et l'Angleterre*', accepted a drink and departed taking his posse with him. Tirpitz was much relieved.

Heavy snow after Christmas again held up operations. Happé told me one day that he was taking his squadron commander to a meeting at military headquarters in Nancy. He thought the meeting would be interesting and at his suggestion I went with him. The meeting concerned the results of the French bombing policy and was presided over by a staff colonel. He had evidently taken a lot of trouble in preparing for it, producing a number of graphs and tables concerning the output of iron and steel from the Saar. French intelligence in that area must have been excellent. Starting by showing us the pre-war output and how it had fallen on mobilization, he went on to show the gradual recovery which had resulted in a steady increase in output until the raids had started. Since then, after a marked drop, a decrease had continued to date. The colonel was taking his job seriously, speaking slowly and with great solemnity. When he reached this point he explained that while the results were satisfactory we must not assume that they were solely due to the damage done by our bombs. In order to release men for the Army, he said, the Germans had been employing Swiss workmen in the furnaces, many of whom had recently gone back to Switzerland. The fall was thus partly due to a shortage of employees.

Happé evidently thought it was time he contributed to the

discussion. Wrinkling his brows into a frown of intense thought and speaking in a voice as deeply serious as the colonel's, he leant across the table to me and said, '*Dah-Veeze, peutêtre ce ne sont pas être bombardés.*' His remark produced a shout of laughter from all the French officers, and even the staff colonel relaxed.

As a result of the meeting it was agreed that all pilots, British and French, should be shown round a blast furnace and a smelting works so that they could see what the target was like. It proved very interesting. We learned that with the Bessemer converter, the process once started has to be carried through or the brew is spoilt. A smelting furnace, on the other hand, can be left unattended for about twenty minutes, but if left longer things may happen to its innards: we decided to send the flights off at twenty-minute intervals in future.

Early in 1917 the Air Department circulated a directive which stated, amongst other things, that it was undesirable that officers of wing commander rank and above should take part in routine operations. Ever since coming to Luxeuil I had had a feeling of frustration. I had volunteered for aviation because I thought it would be useful in naval war; but with the war in its third year I had never even seen the Grand Fleet. We had worked with ships in Gallipoli, indeed, but they had really been acting only as floating batteries in support of the Army. My appointment to Eastchurch had been dated 1912, so that the four years for which I had nominally volunteered were more than over. As long as I could accompany the flights there could be no question of asking to change my job, but in accordance with this new order I should have to stay on the ground.

I told Elder how I felt and that I should like to apply to revert to General Service. I found him sympathetic. He said that he felt much the same himself and that if I would write a Service letter he would forward it with his blessing. The answer from the Admiralty was that while I could not be released from aviation during the war, it was intended to give me an appointment more closely connected with the fleet.

The cold weather continued; snow covered the aerodrome, but as it became frozen hard we were able to operate. Having been grounded by the Admiralty order, I was on one occasion watching the flights land on return from a raid. About fifty men of the handling party were standing near the hangers receiving and re-fuelling the aircraft as they landed. The last bomber, flown by a pilot named Stevens, landed safely but its engine stopped out in the field. Two men ran out, restarted it and then came in with the bomber, holding the wing tips as it was taxied. They had almost reached the party of men in front of the hangers when there was a violent explosion. I found myself lying on the snow as was everyone else. For a circle of about 100 yards the snow was apparently blazing: the bomber had disappeared except for a bundle of wreckage in the middle of the fire. I remember yelling as I scrambled to my feet, 'Get the men out.' Then most of the apparent corpses came alive and rushed to the fire.

We dragged out a number of injured and unconscious men who were taken into the officers mess hut. While that was being done there was a sudden disturbance in the pile of burning wreckage out of which dropped Stevens, who rolled across the burning snow with his clothing on fire. We beat out the fire and carried him to the mess hut, but he was in a shocking state. What had happened was that one of his bombs had been caught by its tail and failed to drop. The nose had cleared the bomb rack sufficiently to allow the safety fan of the fuse to unwind. The vibration while taxiing had shaken the tail clear and the bomb had burst under the machine in which Stevens was sitting. The two men on the wing tips were killed and another died of injuries: Stevens recovered, though he lost a leg. He joined the Fleet Air Arm in the Second World War.

It was a sad end to my time in No. 3 Wing. We had not lost a single man or aircraft through enemy action, and all the pilots were quite convinced that they had the better of the German air-craft. I was relieved by Rathbone, then lieutenant-colonel in the Marines and a wing commander R.N.A.S.

12

H.M.S. *Campania*

In the early spring of 1917 I was appointed wing commander in H.M.S. *Campania* (ex-Cunard liner), seaplane carrier attached to the Grand Fleet, joining her at Liverpool where she was completing a refit. One of the Liverpool papers at that time was in the habit of including a small paragraph head '25 Years Ago'. Soon after I joined, an extract from their issue of 1892 stated that R.M.S. *Campania* had arrived from New York having broken the record for the Atlantic crossing by averaging 20 knots. She and her sister *Lucania* could boast of possessing the longest piston stroke and widest crank throw of any marine engines in the world.

The captain was Oliver Swann, who had been the first man to take a seaplane into the air in England, the machine being a privately-owned Avro triplane to which he had fitted floats. The conversion of the ship to seaplane carrier, which had taken place in stages, had reached the final stage by the time I joined her. For the handling of seaplanes the arrangements were remarkably efficient, the chief credit being due to Swann, though many people had helped, notably the senior flying officer, Lancelot Tomkinson, then a squadron commander, whom I relieved. He was given another appointment, but very soon applied to come back to the ship, serving as No. 2 where he had once been No. 1. It cannot have been easy for him, but we got on well together.

The *Campania* had been originally a two-funnelled passenger liner with the first-class saloons, etc., situated between the funnels. The foremost funnel had now been replaced by two funnels abreast, placed right out at the sides of the ship. A launching deck had been built over the fo'c'sle sloping down towards the bows, its after end being about fifteen feet above boat-deck level. At boat-deck level and just abaft the end of the launching deck was the seaplane hatch. Below that, replacing the first-class saloons, was the seaplane hangar at upper-deck level. Below that again, at main-deck level, was the workshop which was large and well equipped. On either side of the boat deck abreast the seaplane hatch were a mast and a steam derrick.

A seaplane could be lifted out of the hangar by either derrick (see illus. facing p. 151) and put on the launching deck or swung over the side. Spreading the wings could be done on the launching deck or, if going into the sea, the seaplane could be lowered temporarily on the boat deck and the wings spread there. For recovery of seaplanes at sea, there was a swinging boom about 50-feet long hinged at upper-deck level some distance forward of the derrick on either side. A long wire with a hemp tail on its out-board end and known as the seaplane wire was rove through a block at the boom-head. The inboard end of the wire was controlled by a steam winch on the upper deck.

At sea the *Campania* always had two destroyers in company. When a seaplane returned from reconnaissance the three ships turned into wind; the destroyers then steamed ahead at high speed to break up the seas and make a slick. When the slick was long enough the seaplane was signalled to land. The pilot tried to touch down about a quarter of a mile ahead of the ship. When the seaplane was down, the ship was manœuvred so as to bring one of the seaplane booms over the aircraft, the pilot meanwhile hold-ing the seaplane head to sea with the engine. Two men went out along the boom, one holding the hemp tail of the seaplane wire, the other a steadying line attached to the hook of the derrick purchase wire. As the boom passed over the seaplane, the pilot stopped the engine. The observer climbed on to the nose of the inboard float where the first boom-head man threw him the hemp tail of the seaplane wire. When he had hauled in the end of the wire and attached it by means of a snap hook to a becket on the nose of the inboard float, the slack of the wire was hove in and the seaplane was in tow from the boom head. Meanwhile the pilot had climbed on to the top plane. The second boom-head man swung the derrick hook to him and he hooked it on to the slings. The sea-plane could then be hoisted in, the seaplane wire acting as a guy to hold her clear of the ship's side. Two men holding long bamboos with padded heads also stood by on the upper deck to bear her off if she swung.

There were many refinements. Derrick topping lifts and purchases had long spiral springs introduced to absorb shock. Special hooks had been designed both for hoisting in and out. The efficient working of these arrangements depended almost entirely on the team spirit of the handling party, and there can seldom have been better team work than that in *Campania*.

I timed the operation of recovery several times during exercises at sea in moderately fresh winds. The average, from the signal to land till telegraphs were put to ahead, was about $4\frac{1}{2}$ minutes.

The ship had old-fashioned through-tube boilers and to keep up with the fleet there had to be a full head of steam in them all. Directly the telegraphs were put to 'slow' or 'stop', every safety valve of every boiler lifted simultaneously. The roar of steam from the escape pipes which came up close to the seaplane hatch was deafening. No verbal order could possibly be heard and everything had to be done by visual signal or left to the initiative of the men concerned.

At sea, aircraft took off from the launching deck, being lowered on to a wheeled axle, held in place by guides on the floats and by a wire span attached to a quick-release gear in the pilot's cockpit. The tail float had a fitting which slid into a split-tube guide set at a height which kept the machine in her flying attitude. After take-off, the pilot released the wheels and axle, which fell into the sea and could be recovered by the attendant destroyers.

At the after end of the ship where the second-class saloons had been, was the kite balloon well. The boat deck had been removed except for a narrow gangway on either side, leaving a clear deck space which was well sheltered, in which the balloon could be housed. There was a hydrogen plant and compressor at the fore end. When not in use the balloon was normally kept flying at short stay and the balloon well was available as a deck hockey pitch. The kite balloon section of the R.N.A.S. attracted members of the stage and the police. The senior kite balloon officer in *Campania* was Stanley Bell who had been stage manager to Beerbohm Tree at His Majesty's Theatre for many years. The handling party were nearly all London 'bobbies'.

162

While the arrangements for working seaplanes in *Campania* were about as good as it was possible to make them, there were still many unsolved problems, the most important of which was communications. During the spring of 1917 the Grand Fleet carried out three large-scale tactical exercises. In each, the first enemy sighting was made by a seaplane, a report being passed by wireless. In none of the exercises did the seaplane's report reach the C-in-C until after surface contact had been made. The trouble was that we were still using spark wireless sets. For some technical reason the fleet flagship could not keep watch on the seaplane wavelength. A battleship in the flagship's division was therefore detailed as aircraft guardship to relay the aircraft's signals to the flagship. There was always a time lag. Linnel was *Campania*'s signal officer. At that time he was a temporary lieutenant, R.N.V.R., but he was also a professional electrical engineer who had specialized in wireless. He was developing a continuous-wave set for aircraft; at the same time the Admiralty had also started development. The first continuous-wave sets became available in the winter of 1917.

Another source of difficulty was the observer. There was no proper observer branch in the R.N.A.S.; *Campania* observers were midshipmen, R.N.R., selected from boys who had trained in *Worcester* or *Conway*. They were excellent material, but the trouble was that they had, one and all, volunteered for the job in the hope of becoming pilots, and Swann felt that it would be most unjust to refuse to recommend a boy for pilot because he was doing well as observer. The result was that just as they were becoming useful observers they went off to train as pilots.

Linnel who did most of the training of the observers had realized that it was essential to enter men who would be content to remain observers when trained. The midshipmen's weakest point had been in signal procedure. Linnel therefore suggested that we should draw on the visual signalling branch of the Navy. As a result a number of signal yeomen were entered and trained. They were all volunteers who were entered on the understanding that, if they made good, they would be advanced to warrant officer, R.N.A.S. They were trained on board *Campania* during the summer of 1917 and as a result mistakes in signal procedure disappeared.

A third difficulty was that of obtaining accurate upper wind speeds. Ashore at Scapa there was a met. station which could obtain upper wind speed and direction by using hydrogen balloons. But the balloons were small and when I tried to use them from the ship at sea the turbulence of the air astern of the ship drove them down on to the water, and we could never achieve a satisfactory result.

Campania's refit ended soon after I joined, when she returned to Scapa. Besides the work with the fleet, there were frequent calls for seaplanes to assist in anti-submarine work round the Orkneys. A small seaplane station had been built in Scapa Bay on the north shore of the Flow where reserve aircraft were kept and repair work could be done. In order to be in close touch with the station, *Campania*'s normal anchorage was near the north shore, whereas the Battle Fleet anchorage was near the south shore. It was mainly due to this fact that the *Campania* had missed Jutland, the visual signals for raising steam and leaving harbour having failed to reach her.

Campania's outfit consisted of five Short two-seater seaplanes with Sunbeam engines, and about four or five Sopwith Baby single-seaters with Bentley rotary engines. The Sopwith Baby was developed from the Schneiders which we had at Killingholme, but had ailerons instead of wing-warp control. Intended for use as fighters, mainly against Zeppelins, they carried one Vickers gun and were excellent aircraft. Their ceiling however was only about 10,000 feet; their rate of climb was slow after about 4,000 feet and the Zeppelins could do much better than that if they shed ballast.

During one of the first big tactical exercises, I took one of the Shorts on reconnaissance. Near the end of the exercise, as the Grand Fleet started deployment, my engine gave out and I had to make a forced landing. Not having had much experience with seaplanes in a heavy sea I tried to put her down too slowly, with the result that I hit the top of a big wave, bounced off it and dropped heavily into the succeeding hollow. Some of the landing struts buckled. The observer put out the sea anchor to which the plane rode, head to wind; but it was a most ignominious situation. Columns of battleships were surging towards us, then wheeling majestically into line and passing a few hundred yards away. I had the most unpleasant conviction that every pair of binoculars in the Grand Fleet was trained on us, broken down and wallowing, helpless and lopsided, in their wash. When the procession had passed, *Campania* came and picked us up.

Later in the summer, information was received that a large number of submarines was expected to pass through the Fair Island Channel between certain dates. To keep a constant watch, working from Scapa, would involve a lot of wasted time in flights to and fro, so Swann decided to make a temporary base at North Ronaldsay. Tomkinson and I took one of the Shorts up there to have a look at the place and see what arrangements could be made. There was a well-sheltered harbour in which moorings could be laid out, with room for a drifter to swing and act as accommodation ship and provide communication with *Campania*. Having reconnoitred the harbour we walked inland to see something of the island. We found that the whole place was a chicken farm. Fresh eggs had for long been a memory in *Campania's* wardroom, so we called at the farmhouse and opened negotiations with the farmer's wife. She at once agreed to sell us a large basket of eggs, showing intense sympathy for us. While packing the eggs she kept murmuring 'Poor things. Oh! poor things.' It took us some time to realize that she thought we lived permanently in the sky, only coming down occasionally for a supply of food.

The patrol of the Fair Island Channel worked out very well, but in spite of constant air and sea patrols no submarines were sighted. One day Swann sent for me to show me an order he had just received for an operation against Zeppelins. Surface attacks had been made on Norwegian convoys and it was thought that their positions and movements as well as those of covering forces were being reported by Zeps. The operation was to take the form of a sweep by *Campania* with a supporting force down the North Sea, the object being to catch airships by surprise and attack them with the Baby seaplanes.

When Swann asked me what I thought, I said that I thought unfavourably of the idea. The *Campania* and her escort would be just as visible, if not more so, to the Zeppelin as the Zeppelin would be to her. Furthermore the Zeppelin could out-climb the seaplanes. The best and easiest place to attack a Zep was at her home base, Tondern or Ahlhorn, both of which we ought to be able to reach with the Shorts. Swann had evidently come to that conclusion himself. He said that he intended to consult the C-in-C.

He came back very disappointed. He had not seen Beatty, but had had an interview with the chief of staff, Brock, and various other staff officers. His urging that we should be allowed to attack the airship bases had got him nowhere. He said that this was due to the memory of the raid on Christmas Day 1914 when seaplanes had attacked ships at Cuxhaven. From the results of that raid, senior officers had drawn the conclusion that attacks by ship-borne aircraft on shore or harbour targets were no good. We should have to do the best we could with the sweep as ordered. We set off accordingly and plunged down the North Sea with Baby seaplanes ranged at the ready. We saw no Zeppelins. After dark I lay down in my bunk and slept, to be awakened by the fire alarm and general fire stations. The executive officer was of course in charge. This was the first lieutenant, a very experienced R.N.R. lieutenant-commander named Wild. I went to find him to see if I could help.

Fire had broken out in one of the unchanged compartments of the ship, the main purser's storeroom, a large space reaching right across the ship. The only access to it was by two trunks on either side of the ship opening on to the boat deck. Just abaft it was the balloon well, and before it was the 4.7-inch magazine. Flames and sparks were pouring up from the two trunks, illuminating the balloon which was riding at short stay.

Wild took the situation in hand very coolly. He informed me that he had thought of closing the two trunks and smothering the fire, but that would take time and might result in heating the magazine bulkhead red hot. He was keeping them open therefore and spraying as much water down as he could to try and keep the bulkheads cool. I agreed, but for a ship which was supposed to be making herself as inconspicuous as possible to Zeppelins and sub-marines we were not doing too well. I suggested to Wild that I should sit in the magazine and watch over the temperature of the bulkhead. I went down, thinking to myself that we were going one better than the Children of Israel. They had only one column of fire: we had two. Fortunately the bulkhead did not become really hot and by daylight the fire was out; though, following in the footsteps of the Children of Israel, we still produced two columns of smoke by day. We completed the sweep as ordered but the result was nil.

The talks that I had had with Swann about the possibilities of bombing the airship bases had made us realize that the Short seaplanes were not the right aircraft for that sort of operation. They had a good range, but were very slow compared to the 1½-Strutter bombers that we had used in France. If we were ever allowed to do it, the 1½-Strutters would be much more suitable than the Shorts, but they had fixed planes and could not be stowed in *Campania*'s hangar. Knowing that type of aircraft very well, I thought that it would be possible to make the wings easily detachable. Arthur Longmore, who was serving in the Air Department at that time, happened to visit Scapa soon after our Zep hunt. I told him my idea, and he agreed to have a 1½-Strutter sent to *Campania* so that we could experiment.

He sent one very promptly, a two-seater fighter, but that made no difference to the experiment as the construction was identical. The conversion worked out well and when it was finished, we devised a drill and then trained a rigging crew. After a little practice they could rig in 45 seconds. Unrigging took a few seconds more. We had made a small landing ground at Smoogroo on the north shore; when ready we landed the machine there and I took her up for a trial. As far as I could see, the conversion had not affected her performance. The Fleet Air Arm's change from seaplanes to aeroplanes was the result of several factors, but the conversion of the 1½-Strutter played its part.

The Zeppelin problem and the unsuitability of the Baby seaplane for solving it, led to the introduction of the Sopwith Pup, a very light plane with a rapid rate of climb. Some light cruisers were fitted with launching platforms, and in 1917 Smart, flying a Pup from the *Yarmouth*, succeeded in shooting down a Zeppelin.

The *Furious* visited Scapa Flow in the late summer of 1917 when I had my first view of her. Her conversion to an aircraft carrier had taken place by stages. Originally she had had two turrets, each mounting a single 18-inch gun. The first conversion had involved the removal of the fore turret and its replacement by a hanger and launching deck for the seaplanes with which she was originally equipped. It was in fact a copy, though a poor copy, of *Campania*'s arrangement for handling seaplanes. The booms and derricks were too short and the booms were placed too low down. Instead of the reliable steam winches for working derricks, she had electric bollards which were violent in action and liable to trip the overload switch at the slightest provocation. Dunning, her first senior flying officer, was thoroughly dissatisfied with the arrangements.

The second conversion had involved the removal of the after turret and the building of an after hangar with a landing-on deck above it. The bridge, funnel, mast and control top remained. A wide gangway either side connected the two decks.

With the introduction of the Pup with its wheeled under-carriage, the question of recovery came to the fore. A dummy landing deck had been built at the Isle of Grain air station where Harry Busteed had been experimenting with Pups. The problem as it appeared at Grain was quite different to that at sea. At Grain, where there was only the natural wind, the problem was to arrest the aeroplane. At sea where a relative wind of 30 knots was available, there was no difficulty in stopping a light aeroplane like the Pup. The real problem was to hold her down after stopping.

I imagine that the second conversion of the *Furious* was based on the results obtained at Grain. During her stay in the Flow, I was able to have a talk to Dunning. His experience at that time had convinced him that deck-landing necessitated clean air, that is to say a smooth flow of air over the deck. The after deck of the *Furious* was a failure because the bridge and other structures before it caused excessive turbulence of the air over it.

I did not see any of the early experimental landings on the after deck of *Furious*. Rutland had had a narrow escape in a Pup which had cartwheeled over the side, falling on to the above-water torpedo tubes on the deck below. Harry Busteed had fetched up in the safety net, giving himself a bloody nose. This safety net which was intended to stop aircraft flying into the funnel, was made of 5-inch grass rope and was hung from a gantry at the fore end of the deck. There had been other gallant efforts, but the result was to prove the deck a failure.

Dunning told me he was sure that deck landing was possible, provided the air over the deck was undisturbed. It was soon after our talk that he was killed experimenting, in accordance with his theory, with landing a Pup on the small fore deck of the *Furious*.

Approaching from the port side with the ship steaming fast into the wind, he was able to hover over the deck with practically no forward speed relative to the ship, and to touch down on the deck. Toggles were attached to the struts and tail, which a handling party caught hold of and held the machine down on deck. The first landing was successful; but on the second attempt, just after touching down, the left wing lifted, the Pup slid across the deck to starboard, and before the handling party could reach her cartwheeled over the starboard side into the sea and Dunning was drowned. I did not see this, but a film was made at the time which showed clearly what had happened.

An American battle squadron had joined the Grand Fleet and during the summer of 1917 the *Campania* was visited by a number of American officers, amongst them Admiral Sims. One party was accompanied by a middle-aged man in plain clothes with whom I talked but whose name I did not catch. After showing them round, I took them to the wardroom for a drink, when I found an opportunity to ask one of the officers who the civilian was. His name was Manly, and he had been the pilot of the 'Langley Aerodrome'.[1] He was, in fact, the first man to take off from the water in a power-driven, heavier-than-air machine.

Submarine sightings were common throughout the summer and seaplanes were frequently called on for emergency sorties. I had taken one of the Shorts out on report of a submarine about fifty miles east of the Orkneys and when about twenty miles out the engine developed a most unpleasant sound. Throttling back, I experimented with various throttle settings until presently the grinding stopped and the engine ran perfectly, but when I opened the throttle, although the revolutions increased the engine did not seem to produce any thrust. It took me a little time to realize that the reduction gear had stripped and that the engine was no longer connected to the propeller. There was a strong wind and considerable sea running. Profiting from past experience I put her down with plenty of speed. We bounced off the first wave, jumped the next trough and settled on the following crest without harm.

The trouble with a broken-down Short in a strong wind was that she drove fast astern, submerging the tail float. Once that was under water she was bound to capsize backwards. To prevent this

[1] An early rival of the Wright Brothers' aeroplane.

it was necessary to get out the sea anchor quickly. This consisted of a canvas drogue with a short length of wire which could be attached to a becket on the nose of the float. Directly we were down, my observer climbed on a float with the drogue, but with the airscrew free-wheeling round like a windmill, he could not reach the nose of the float. Luckily I was wearing a long knitted scarf which I wound round one hand to make a sort of boxing glove. Getting on to the top plane I shoved against the airscrew and persuaded it to slow down and stop, when I lashed it with the scarf. Meanwhile the observer dealt with the sea anchor.

A few miles back we had passed over a destroyer which was still in sight. It was a considerable relief when we saw her turn towards us in answer to signals from our Aldis lamp. Until that time I had believed myself to be immune from seasickness. Anyone who believes that should try a broken-down seaplane riding to a sea anchor in a rough sea. She rolled, she pitched, she yawed and she jerked at her drogue, and by the time the destroyer reached us I was just about as seasick as it is possible to be. We went on board and the Short was taken in tow, but she capsized almost at once and had to be abandoned. As the destroyer was covering the passage of a Scandinavian convoy, we had a trip to Norway and back before rejoining *Campania*.

Towards the end of the year Oliver Swann was relieved by Captain Humphrey Hugh Smith. I was very sorry to part from Swann, but H.H., as he was generally called, was a delightful person to serve with. He seemed to know everyone in the Navy and to have a good story about nearly all of them. At the same time Wild, the first lieutenant, left. The second-in-command of the *Campania* was the navigator, Mackenzie-Grieve, an acting commander. He did not want to take the job of executive officer, so I was given it and was glad to acquire the experience. Mackenzie-Grieve was afterwards Hawker's navigator during the first attempt to fly the Atlantic.

The King paid a visit to the fleet in 1917 and lunched on board his name ship *King George V*, flagship of Admiral Sir John de Robeck, who kindly invited me to the lunch. I think that the King always enjoyed visiting the fleet, and he certainly seemed to be in great form that day. At lunch I sat next to Prince Albert, then a midshipman. He was determined to have correct the names of all captains present, also the names of the ships they commanded, so we spent most of the lunch reciting the names of the guests at the table and their ships. By the end of the lunch he was word perfect.

In his reminiscences, H. H. Smith attributed to me a mysterious instinct for knowing where broken-down seaplanes were. In fact there was no mystery about it. When a seaplane was away on submarine search, the observer reported all courses by W/T; a second observer, in the plotting-room on board, kept a track chart going. As we could obtain pretty accurate wind speeds from the met. station ashore, the seaplane's position was always known.

There was one tragedy that winter due to faulty navigation. To assist in submarine hunting, a small airship station had been set up at Scapa. The airship, a blimp, was commanded by my old *Diana* shipmate, Hayes. Rather late on a winter afternoon, Hayes had taken the blimp out to the east of the islands on report of a submarine sighting. When the wind rose suddenly from the west, he started back but could make very little headway against it. He had not sighted land when it grew dark, and presently reported that he was losing gas. Messages that he was heading west but losing height were received, but finally ceased and nothing more was heard. Destroyers sent to search to the east of the islands found nothing; a day or two later, wreckage was washed up on the west coast of the islands. He must have passed over the Orkneys in the dark without realizing it.

13
Deck Landings

Campania's refit at Liverpool ended in the first week in April. On the 1st of that month we all ceased to belong to the R.N.A.S. and became members of the newly constituted Royal Air Force. The original titles of the R.A.F. were military so that I became a lieutenant-colonel. I was acting as executive officer of the ship at that time and my new title gave H. H. Smith great amusement. He said that when turning the hands to in the morning he would expect to see me in field boots and spurs, not sea boots and a scarf.

Very soon after reaching Scapa I was appointed to the *Furious* as senior flying officer. I turned the R.A.F. contingent of *Campania* over to Tomkinson, and the executive job to the senior lieutenant and joined the *Furious* at Rosyth. By that time the unsatisfactory seaplane arrangements had resulted in seaplanes being given up in favour of the detachable-wing 1½-Strutters and single-seater Sopwith Camels as fighters. The conversion of the 1½-Strutters had originally occurred to me as a means of using the long-range single-seater bomber for attacking Zeppelin bases. The first conversion, though made to a two-seater, had proved so suitable that the type had been adopted by *Furious* as a two-seater reconnaissance plane. The conversion of the standard 1½-Strutter to the detachable-wing type was carried out at Turnhouse by R.A.F. mechanics on the lines produced in *Campania*. The Sopwith Camel was a standard R.A.F. fighter converted to ship use by having the after part of the fuselage made detachable in the same way as was done in the Sopwith Baby seaplane.

Furious was wearing the flag of Rear-Admiral Sir Richard

Phillimore as Rear-Admiral, Aircraft Carriers, and his R.A.F. staff officer was R. H. Clarke-Hall with the rank of lieutenant-colonel. He had been our gunnery officer at Eastchurch, and had commanded the old *Ark Royal* off Gallipoli, so was an old friend of mine. The captain was Wilmot Nicholson. Most of the observers were the ex-yeomen of signals trained in the *Campania* and now holding temporary commissions in the R.A.F. Other old *Campania*'s who had been transferred to *Furious* were Linnel and L. H. Wilkins.

Linnel's efforts in combination with the Admiralty Technical Branch under Professor Airey had produced a continuous-wave wireless set for aircraft which could now communicate directly with the fleet flagship. The time lag which had interfered so badly with the effectiveness of the Fleet Air Arm had at last disappeared. The observer's art was also making progress. Position reporting had been a weak point, but with the larger number of aircraft available it became possible to organize the search ahead of the fleet on a system which afterwards became known as constant bearing patrol. This simplified the navigation problem for the observer, giving him only an opening course and speed and a closing course and speed to worry about.

The problem of getting accurate wind speeds when at sea was still defeating us. Soon after I joined the *Furious* we were ordered out on an operation. A large mine field had been laid just north of the Heligoland Bight and information was needed about German activities in and about it. *Furious* and her escort crossed the North Sea to reach a point at dawn off the coast of Denmark, where reconnaissance planes were flown off to cross the mine field and report any minesweeping or laying which was going on. Aircraft had orders to make the Danish coast and fix themselves geographically after completing their reconnaissance. It was thus possible to check positions signalled by plotting the track backwards from the shore fix. The result of doing this on the first of these operations gave me a shock.

It appeared that after ninety minutes' flying, there was an error of nearly forty miles in positions signalled. This was mainly due to the fact that near the Danish coast there is often a considerable difference between the surface wind and the upper wind. I had gone on trying to obtain results from using met. balloons, but had found much the same trouble as in *Campania*. Bott, the navigator of the *Furious*, was much more skilful with a sextant than I was, so I had sought his help. There were two troubles: one was that once you took your eye off the balloon in order to read the sextant, you lost the balloon. The other was that the turbulent air stirred up by the ship prevented the balloon from rising until it was a long way astern. Bott and I were discussing the problem in the wardroom one day when Hooper, the gunnery officer, came in. He sat listening for a while and then suggested we use the burst of an AA shell which he could arrange at any height we liked. We tried it out the next time we went to sea, with satisfactory results. So that problem was solved.

Reconnaissance over the mine field was repeated several times during the early summer. It involved the aircraft landing in the sea at the end of each operation. Additional flotation gear had been added to the 1½-Strutters in the form of fabric bags under the lower plane, which could be inflated from a compressed air flask. This enabled it to be hoisted in with very little damage to the airframe, though the skin fabric had to be largely renewed after each sortie. On the east side of the North Sea, it was considered to be too dangerous for *Furious* to stop and hoist in, owing to the submarine menace, so the aircraft had to be recovered by destroyers. As they had no long derrick, a good deal of damage was done and the aircraft was under repair for a long time.

As the war in France began to go in favour of the Allies, it seemed to everyone that the High Seas Fleet would be certain to come out for a last desperate effort. It was essential therefore that whatever special operation *Furious* was taking part in, she should always have her full number of action reconnaissance and fighter aircraft on board and ready for fleet action. At the same time it was necessary to keep pilots and observers constantly practised. To achieve this, on approaching the Forth after an operation or exercise, all fleet action aircraft were flown off and carried out an exercise, landing at Turnhouse on completion. A second outfit of aircraft was kept at Donibristle, where there was an organization for swinging compasses, testing guns and checking state of engines. On *Furious*'s arrival in harbour, this outfit was at once embarked, each aircraft having a certificate showing by whom and when compasses, guns and engines had been checked. While in harbour pilots and observers exercised at Turnhouse, but were at two hours' notice to re-embark.

This system called for a large number of aircraft, and I was always in a state of anxiety about the number of 1½-Strutters available. The two-seater fighter of this type was no longer in production, having been out-dated as a fighter by the single-seater Camel. The Air Ministry had made no difficulty about re-leasing all in existence for use in the fleet, but there were no new ones coming along, and there was always a large number under repair.

During one of our expeditions to the Danish coast and the mine field, *Furious* was bombed by a German seaplane, the only occasion during the war that her 4-inch HA guns came into action. Anti-aircraft control in 1918 was extremely crude and there were no sleeve targets available for practice. The guns put up an impressive barrage but the only casualty was the ship's galley funnel (always known in the Navy as the Charley Noble).[1] We always had a Camel ranged on the fore deck and it was flown off, catching up with the German while still in sight of the ship. Hit in the engine, the German came down on the sea a few miles ahead to the great delight of everyone.

The crew were unhurt and were standing on the floats when we reached them. I tried to persuade Captain Nicholson to stop and hoist the seaplane in, so that we could have a trophy; but, no doubt rightly, he refused to stop because of the possibility of submarines being about. The Camel was signalled to come down near a destroyer. The landing resulted in the usual violent pitch forward when the undercarriage entered the water and the pilot came on board the destroyer with blood streaming from his nose. The two Germans were collected, without bloody noses, by a destroyer and the seaplane was sunk. What was left of the Camel was also collected by a destroyer.

Hooper and the Gunnery Department of *Furious* were rather touchy on the subject of the galley funnel. It was dismounted and a temporary erection put in its place, so that it could be sent to the dockyard for repairs. But they were not allowed to forget about it, for the next morning the temporary funnel was found to bear an

[1] After a captain, Charley Noble, whose copper galley funnel was kept brightly burnished.

inscription in chalk: 'Sacred to the memory of Charley Noble. R.I.P.'

The violent pitch forward of the Camels when touching down in the sea had resulted in a lot of damaged noses. The breech of the Vickers gun was in front of the pilot's face, and although we had padded it thoroughly, the pilot nearly always suffered a heavy blow on the nose. There was considerable danger that he might be knocked out. I came to the conclusion that the violence of the pitch was due to the high water-resistance of the wheels. The landing struts and axle were streamlined and were not likely to offer much resistance. The wheels could not be streamlined, but if they could be shed before touching down, I thought the violence of the forward pitch could be much reduced.

The spokes of the wheels were covered by fabric discs and the set of the spokes was such that the outer surface of the wheels was convex while the inner was flush. In flight, the air pressure on the convex surfaces would tend to thrust the wheels inwards along the axle. The wheels were held on the axle by collars outside, each secured by a bolt and nut. I took these off and reversed the wheels on the axle. As the convex surfaces were now on the inner side, the air stream would tend to thrust the wheels outwards. I replaced the collars and substituted for the nut and bolt a long split-pin with a wire attached to its eye, the wire passing through a fairlead in the side of the pilot's cockpit and terminating in a toggle. When he wanted to shed the wheels, all the pilot had to do was to pull on the toggles and so draw out the split-pins.

I had one of the Camels fitted up like this, intending to try it out. The ship was in harbour and there was no wind. Impatient of waiting for a suitable breeze from ahead, I decided I could fly the Camel off the fore deck without it. I think a little wind from astern must have risen just as I was released. At any rate the Camel took charge, slewed round at right angles to starboard and dived straight into the water. I emerged with exactly the same bloody nose that I had been trying to prevent. However the scheme of shedding the wheels proved efficient so mine was the last bloody nose.

Shortly after that incident Clarke-Hall told me that another operation was proposed. It was an almost exact repetition of the previous year's Zeppelin hunt which *Campania* had carried out, and seemed to me to have all the same objections. *Furious* and her escort would be even more conspicuous than the *Campania* had been, and though the Camels had a better air performance than the Baby seaplanes, the Zep had only to drop ballast to out-climb them. I again urged that the place to attack Zeps was at their bases. Clarke-Hall was in complete agreement, as was Swann the year before. If the proposal was to be put to the C-in-C we must be ready to implement it quickly. As we should have to carry a full outfit of aircraft for fleet action, the raiding aircraft would have to be additional. To ask for any special machines for the job would mean delay, so we would have to use those we had. The 1½-Strutters had originally been brought to carriers for this very purpose, but the numbers available were small and as reconnaissance aircraft they were precious. It seemed to Clarke-Hall and me that we should have to use Camels. Their range was not large, making Ahlhorn impossible, but Tondern would be just within range from a point near the Danish coast.

When we had got that far, Clark-Hall said he would put the proposal up to Admiral Phillimore. Knowing Phillimore's penchant for offensive action I had no doubt of the result. Clarke-Hall went straight off to the *Queen Elizabeth* and this time there was no question of not seeing Beatty. He came back with authority to make the attack and the earlier proposal was cancelled.

We fitted seven Camels with bomb racks to take 20-lb bombs, and I selected pilots to train. The attack was to be at low level. The training at Turnhouse had to be a rush job. The six more-experienced pilots soon became proficient, but the latest to join, Youlet, needed longer. Since we could not delay, I had to tell Youlet that he was out of the team; a bitter disappointment to him.

On the day set for the attack *Furious* and her escort of destroyers set out to reach a point off the Danish coast just before dawn. Soon after midnight the weather deteriorated, coming on to rain and blow. The operation had to be abandoned and it was about a week before we were able to try again. In the meantime practice continued, Youlet improved rapidly and I agreed to put him back in the team.

On the second attempt the weather again deteriorated during the middle watch. I again went on to the bridge feeling anxious.

It was a curious position to be in, because this was primarily an R.A.F. operation, and I was in command of the R.A.F. contingent, Clarke-Hall being a staff officer. The admiral said, 'It's for you to decide and I shan't influence you. But I expect you know what I hope.' I replied that it would be decided at 4 o'clock and went down to the intelligence office.

With the wind as it was, it seemed doubtful if the Camels could get back to the ship after the attack. However as the latest met. report did not suggest any worsening, they would certainly have enough petrol to cross the Danish frontier. At 4 o'clock, therefore, I reported that the operation could be carried out. The Camels took off at early twilight: we had then to wait for two interminable hours. At last three of them hove in sight and landed in fairly rapid succession near the destroyers, the pilots, Dickson, Smart and Jackson, reporting complete success.

After hanging about off the coast until quite sure that the rest must have come down somewhere (we hoped in Denmark), we shaped course for the Forth. The result of the attack was that two Zeppelins, L-54 and L-60, were burnt out, both sheds destroyed and the gas plant severely damaged. In fact Tondern remained out of action as an airship base for the rest of the war. We soon had news of three other pilots who had come down in Denmark, but to my great sorrow there was no news of Youlet. The Germans made no claim of shooting down any of the raiders and he must have had engine failure over the sea.

Williams was one of those who landed in Denmark. Realizing that he was nearly out of petrol, he landed near a Danish village on the coast. The villagers gathered round and he asked them where he could find petrol. They were willing to help, but unfortunately the village policeman joined the party. He explained that it was against his orders to allow a British plane to be refuelled in Denmark and requested Williams to come to the police station. There they were joined by an official in plain clothes who said that he would have to take Williams to Copenhagen. They arrived at an hotel in the city, where on entering the official hung up his raincoat and bowler hat on a peg in the hall. He then conducted Williams to a room in which the other two pilots who had landed in Denmark had already been installed.

Soon afterwards when the man left the room, the three pilots began to discuss the chances of escape. Believing he had a good chance there and then, Williams walked out of the room and back to the hall. Donning the official's bowler hat and raincoat he went out into the street. From the first well-dressed passer-by whom he met he asked the way to the British Embassy, and was answered in fluent English. At the embassy they put him into a car and drove him to the docks where a Norwegian ship was on the point of sailing for Aberdeen. Williams's passage was booked, he went on board and the ship sailed. On arrival at Aberdeen he found he could just catch the Edinburgh Express. Expresses don't stop at Turnhouse, but when this one slowed to walking pace while passing through the station, Williams jumped out, went to the air station and got a car to Hawes Pier. There he found one of *Furious*'s boats and came off to the ship, arriving on board less than forty-eight hours after the ship herself had returned.

The Tondern raid did a great deal more than eliminate one airship base. It finally removed the belief held by many senior officers that attacks by shipborne aircraft on shore or harbour targets were no good. The immediate result was that everybody wanted Ahlhorn to be attacked; but it was too distant for any fleet aircraft. There was no longer an Air Department at the Admiralty but Groves (now a brigadier R.A.F.) had an office there, and acted as liaison officer. He came up to the *Furious* and we discussed the possibility of attacking Ahlhorn. The de Havilland biplanes were by then in production. He proposed that some should be given extra tanks and sent to Turnhouse to have the wings made readily detachable. The general idea was that the aircraft should be launched off the Danish coast, carrying on after the raid to cross the western front and land in France. Groves succeeded in getting de Havillands despatched to Turnhouse where we tackled the conversion. However the war was over before they were ready.

The last few months of the war were hectic. As everyone expected the German Fleet to come out, fleet action aircraft had to be always on the top line; in addition there was the Ahlhorn attack to be prepared. The Italian liner *Conte Rosso*, requisitioned while on the stocks, was being completed as the first flush-deck carrier *Argus* at the yard of John Brown on the Clyde. H. H.

Smith, lately of the *Campania*, had been appointed in command. The programme of deck-landing trials had to be worked out; the Sopwith Cuckoo torpedo planes were in production and Pulford had been posted to train and take command of a squadron of them. We had a number of meetings on board *Furious* to discuss the *Argus* trials.

An extraordinary number of ideas had been put forward by people in the fleet as well as by the Admiralty. I remember one officer who said that he had noticed that aeroplanes stopped quickly in ploughed fields. He suggested that the flight deck should be covered with a good sticky loam. Nicholson had watched Dunning's landings and all the early attempts on the *Furious*'s after deck. Convinced that the essential thing was to hold the aircraft after landing and prevent her blowing overboard, he proposed a line of hooks like broad arrow-heads overlapping along the wooden fairing on the axle, which were to engage in fore and aft wires supported above the deck. I agreed in general with that idea.

Eventually we decided to build two wooden ramps about thirty feet apart, the after one to be about half-way up the deck. They were to slope upwards from aft forward, the top being about two feet above the deck. Between them, fore and aft wires were to be stretched. The idea was that the aeroplanes would land on the clear deck aft. The pilots should then keep full controllable speed, taxiing forward and up the after ramp, when the aircraft would drop off the ramp into the trap and the hooks would engage in the wires. As the aircraft ran up the forward ramp the hooks would pull on the taut wires, the resultant friction arresting the aircraft.

Admiral Phillimore, who as Rear-Admiral Carriers was responsible for conducting the trials, told me to take charge, and Rosyth Dockyard was instructed to do whatever I asked. The *Argus* actually arrived in the Forth just as the Grand Fleet was about to go out on a sweep and tactical exercises, so I had to leave the *Furious* R.A.F. unit in the hands of Wilfred Acland during the trials. It was not possible to take any of the regular *Furious* pilots to help as they were needed in the ship; but there was a thoroughly experienced 1½-Strutter pilot at Turnhouse, named Cocky, so I roped him in.

On board *Argus* at a conference with H. H. Smith and his navigator, Clark, we agreed that *Argus*, her deck not yet filled with the ramps and wires, should go down the Forth next day to a point near the mouth and then turn into the westerly wind. She would then be manœuvred to give a relative wind of about 20 knots along the deck. A 'negative' flag being displayed would be replaced by an 'affirmative' as soon as H. H. was satisfied. Cocky and I, each in a 1½-Strutter, would meet the ship, and take it in turns to make six landings. We would not attempt to stop but would touch down, taxi forward, and fly off again. Two sailors equipped with a paint pot and brush were to be stationed in the nettings aft. After each landing they were to emerge and put a blob of paint on the deck where the machine touched down. We executed the operation as planned.

The *Argus*, as originally converted, had no round down and the square transom at the after end of the deck was rather alarming. I took first turn, my first white blob of paint appearing about half-way up the deck. I succeeded in getting the later ones reasonably far aft. But when Cocky's turn came, to my intense annoyance he put all his red blobs alongside the best of my white ones. We went on all that morning, by the end of which we were confident that we could touch down well aft.

The *Argus* was then taken to the dockyard and an army of ship-wrights started work on the ramps. By the time the fleet came back I reported that we were ready for the trials. Unfortunately Cocky now went down with flu. Groves and a number of naval constructors came up from the Admiralty, Brigadier Drew from the Air Ministry, and Harry Busteed from Isle of Grain. The admiral and his staff came on board from the *Furious* and a 1½-Strutter fitted with hooks was embarked.

I did the first landing with a 20-knot wind (see facing p. 182). The machine dropped into the trap and pulled up easily. The natural wind was then about 10 knots, so for the second landing *Argus* worked up to full speed providing a relative wind of about 30 knots. At the higher wind speed I found matters easier. Then Groves said he would like to see a landing at a low wind speed. The natural wind was dropping, and by the time the machine was ready to fly off again we reckoned that it was about 4 knots which, with the *Argus* at slow speed, would give us a relative wind of about 8 knots. In fact the wind continued to drop and the third landing was made with the wind well under 8 knots. Gymnastic mats laid on the fore ramp increased the friction. The machine ran the full length of the trap and up the fore ramp; but the braking effect of the ramp was enough to pull her up on top. That concluded the trials for the day, but as the constructors were working on plans for the *Eagle* and *Hermes* they wanted some further trials carried out later.

In *Argus* the funnel gases were led into horizontal ducts and driven out at the stern by fans. With the higher boiler power in *Eagle* and *Hermes* it was not thought practical to make similar arrangements. Instead the constructors proposed to put the funnel right at the side of the ship, building an island round it to contain bridge, chartroom, etc.

Argus went back to the dockyard where a dummy island was built with wood and canvas on the starboard side of the ship. This narrowed the deck very much: considering that the span of the $1\frac{1}{2}$-Strutter was too great and that I might easily foul the island with a wing tip, I fitted a Sopwith Pup with hooks for the second lot of trials. As these went off satisfactorily it was decided to complete *Eagle* and *Hermes* with islands.

The wooden ramps which we had built on the deck of the *Argus* were of course purely temporary for experiment. It was necessary to give her something permanent. I wanted some arrangement of hinged steel plates, which could be pushed up electrically or by hydraulic ram to form ramps and which, when not in use, could lie flush on the deck. An arrangement of this sort was eventually provided; but as aircraft became heavier, with faster landing speeds, the fore and after wire system of arrester gear proved unsatisfactory. It was abandoned in 1925 and, until the system with athwartship wires was adopted in 1931, deck-landings were made without arrester gear, relying upon a high wind speed down the deck to stop the aircraft.

During all these trials I had been working with H. H. Smith and could not have had a better person with whom to collaborate. He was enthusiastic but always ready to see both sides of a question and never lost his temper. After the first lot of trials, the first lieutenant of the *Argus*, who was very keen to be the first to land on a deck as passenger, asked me to take him. I sought permission from H. H. who said, 'What do you ask me for? It's your aeroplane, isn't it?'

'Yes. My aeroplane, but your first lieutenant.'

'Pooh! Plenty more first lieutenants.'

Furious took part in the final operation – the surrender of the German Fleet. The Grand Fleet and Battle Cruiser Force formed into two columns and between these the German Fleet was to follow the light cruiser *Cardiff*, which had been sent ahead to meet them. With all ships at action stations, the Grand Fleet steered eastward into the North Sea. In the *Furious*, aircraft were ranged on the fore deck, the wind-break palisades raised to shelter them. It was a calm hazy day with pale winter sunshine. I was on the fore deck looking ahead through the palisades. Presently a little pencil of light appeared in the haze. It was the winter sunlight reflected on the *Cardiff*'s side. More and larger gleams were sighted and then at last those silhouettes that we had studied so often for so long: it seemed unbelievable.

Turning sixteen points together the Grand Fleet ranged itself on either side of the line of German ships and escorted them into the Forth, where they anchored in Leith Roads. The fleet went to Divisions and Prayers and when I went into the wardroom I found a copy of Beatty's signal posted on the notice board: 'At sunset German Ensigns will be hauled down and will not be rehoisted.'

It is interesting to speculate on what might have happened if the war had lasted into 1919. With the new enthusiasm for air attacks on shore and harbour targets, the Cuckoos and de Havillands would certainly have been used and there might have been a Taranto twenty-one years sooner.

The old *Campania* had come to an end shortly before. The first fleet carrier, she set an example which has been faithfully followed by all carriers; she learned how to drag her anchor. Beatty had based the Battle Fleet at the Forth and *Campania* was berthed at Burnt Island Roads. When it came on to blow hard one night, she dragged on to the bows of the *Royal Oak* and sank, fortunately without loss of life.

The rest of my time in the *Furious* seemed like an anti-climax. The Spanish flu epidemic which broke out was defeated in *Furious* by sending the men out on constant route marches.

Demobilization started and produced outbreaks of unrest in some ships and stations, but in the *Furious* we had none.

As regards the R.A.F., it was decreed that all regular officers of the Navy and Army would receive permanent commissions in the new Service unless they opted to return to their old one. Being quite sure that I did not want to leave the Navy, I put in an application to revert to General Service. Nothing happened for some months, but one morning early in 1919 I found two letters on my desk in the Air Office. One was in an Admiralty envelope and the other in an Air Ministry envelope. Opening that from the Admiralty I found an appointment to the battle-cruiser *Lion*. I shifted into naval uniform and put the Air Ministry letter in my pocket. After turning over the R.A.F. unit to Wilfred Acland, I said goodbye and went over to the *Lion*. There I opened the second letter to find that I was posted to the Air Ministry. I acknowledged it, but regretted that I was unable to comply as I had already taken up a naval appointment. A few days later poor Acland received a rude letter from some official at the Air Ministry, protesting that the whole procedure was irregular. He sent it over to me, so I put a minute on it: 'This must not occur again.' Then I sent it back to him.

The *Lion* was wearing the flag of Rear-Admiral Sir Roger Keyes, who, years later, told me that it was his application which got me appointed to the ship. The captain was Wilfred Tomkinson, and J. D. Cunningham[1] was the navigator. The *Lion* had only one commission in the entire eight years of her career and when she paid off in 1920 there were several petty officers who had joined the ship as boys. Before the Grand Fleet was reduced and became the Home Fleet, it assembled off Southend and a section from all ships' companies took part in a march through London. All captains and commanders took part; I as first lieutenant remained in command.

Later in the year we met the *Argus*. Mackenzie-Grieve, her navigator, asked me to dinner and in the course of it told me about the first attempt to fly the Atlantic when he had been Hawker's navigator. He had no bubble sextant but had used the cloud horizon and had been quite confident of his position all the time. They followed a Great Circle track all the way which took them

[1] Admiral of the Fleet Lord Cunningham, First Sea Lord 1943–6.

into much higher latitudes than the normal shipping route. They were near the apex of the Great Circle when the engine lost power, which Hawker attributed to a partial choke in the petrol pipe. They turned south until they reached the shipping track and then followed it; but it was about half an hour before they sighted a ship. They landed near her and were picked up, but as she was a small Norwegian ship with no wireless, it was about ten days before she reached port, by which time they had been given up for lost.

The battle-cruiser *Hood*, now completing, was to commission early in 1920. Roger Keyes's flag was to be shifted to her and Tomkinson was to go in command. From something he said, I gathered that he intended to take me with him, but I was promoted to commander at the New Year.

One of the first things that Beatty did on becoming First Sea Lord was to form a committee to examine current questions. It was called the Post War Questions Committee and Admiral Phillimore was its chairman. Having been made Rear-Admiral Carriers, the first question he took up was that of the Navy's air component. I was called to give evidence and spent one forenoon at the Admiralty. But when the committee reassembled after lunch, a Government directive was received, decreeing that no major change in the air organization was to be proposed for a period of four years from the end of the war. Phillimore had to comply, but I knew that it had been his intention to urge vigorously that the Fleet Air Arm should revert to the Navy.

The only argument which had carried weight with the Government up to that time had been that unless naval officers acquired air experience, the flag officers of the future would be badly handicapped in meeting the air menace and in making the best use of the air. To avoid this, a certain number of naval officers were to be seconded to the R.A.F. where they would be given temporary commissions and serve in the general list of the R.A.F. The scheme did not prove attractive and very few naval officers volunteered.

Early in 1920 I was appointed commander of the *Eagle*, Wilmot Nicholson having already been appointed captain. The *Eagle* was built by Armstrong-Whitworth on the Tyne. Designed as a battleship for Chile, she had been taken over during the war.

When half complete as a battleship, the Admiralty decided to turn her into an aircraft carrier. At the end of the war, she was still incomplete and, as arrester gear and aircraft-handling arrangements generally were still in an experimental stage, it was decided to take her to sea before completion, carry out experiments and decide on the final lay-out after trials. Final completion was to be done by the Royal Dockyard.

In March 1920 I went up to Newcastle. Nicholson was already there. We had a small office in Armstrongs' yard. The ship was to be taken to sea with only half boiler power, one funnel in place (the other one was eventually dumped on the flight deck), no lifts, temporary boat-hoisting arrangements and very little accommodation. The island structure followed the shape of the temporary wood and canvas erection that had been tried out in *Argus*.

Standing by a ship under construction is apt to be a dull business, but Northumberland in spring is very pleasant country. However the chief significance of Newcastle for me was that I met my wife-to-be there. L. A. Montgomery, my great friend of pre-war years since we had met when serving together in the *Dominion*, had been killed at the Battle of Coronel in November 1914. His father, Major General Sir R. A. K. Montgomery, was commanding the North East District of England; so of course I called on the family. Before the time came to leave Newcastle, I was engaged to the only daughter, Mary.

By the time the *Eagle* reached Portsmouth, Wilmot Nicholson had been promoted to rear-admiral and had turned over the command of the ship to Captain Dugmore, but he remained in general charge of the trials as Admiralty representative. The ship was based on Portsmouth, and Nicholson was frequently visiting the Admiralty to discuss programmes and results. After one of these visits in July he told me that it was proposed to add a Naval Air Section to the Naval Staff at the Admiralty. He had mentioned my name to the Assistant Chief of Naval Staff, Rear-Admiral Sir Ernle Chatfield, and asked me if I would like to go. We discussed the proposal for some time, and eventually I agreed.

14
Nineteen Years of Friction

Turning over to my successor on board the *Eagle* in July 1920, I went directly to London. On the following morning I reported at the Admiralty to the Assistant Chief of the Naval Staff. Lord Beatty was First Sea Lord, Vice-Admiral Sir Osmond Brock, Deputy Chief, and Rear-Admiral Sir Ernle Chatfield, Assistant Chief of the Naval Staff. I was given a desk in the office of the A.C.N.S.'s Naval Assistant, Commander Hugh Binney, and told to spend the first few days in gathering a general idea of Admiralty procedure and the relations to Naval Air policy. This would have been somewhat overwhelming without the help I was given by Binney and Paymaster-Commander Jerram, the A.C.N.'s secretary.

During the next four years and at intervals during the following nineteen years, I was to be involved in arguments and disputes between the Air Council and the Board of Admiralty. It is to be hoped that this friction is a thing of the past and most of the details are best left to oblivion; but for two reasons, I think it is advisable to record what I remember. The first is that if similar conditions are allowed to arise in the future, similar friction is likely to occur, which would be deplorable. The second is that I have heard it stated that Boards of Admiralty during the inter-war years were uninterested in the development and use of aircraft for naval purposes and in the Fleet Air Arm. The record of their part in these disputes shows this to be untrue.

In the course of studying the situation as it stood in 1920, I came on the report of Admiral Phillimore's Post War Questions Committee, before which I had given evidence the year before. He had intended to report on the Naval Air situation as thoroughly as possible, but it had been struck off his terms of reference because of a Cabinet decision. This decision governed the Naval Air policy until 1922 and consequently dictated my course of action in the Naval Air Section for the first two years. It was to the general effect that from 1919 for the first four years after the end of the war the Admiralty were not to propose any drastic change in the organization but were to do their best to make the existing state of affairs work.

The procedure agreed upon was for the Admiralty to set out their requirements for the year and for the Air Ministry to meet these by selecting and embarking the necessary squadrons. The aircraft and personnel of these squadrons were, of course, entirely R.A.F. This seemed straightforward enough, but at the time it was generating a great deal of correspondence between the two departments.

Disarmament and economy were the order of the day and the Air Estimates had been stringently cut. The only carrier available for the fleet was *Argus*, as *Eagle* was employed on experimental work and was incomplete; *Hermes* was still being built and *Furious* had been taken in hand for reconstruction. *Argus* could carry about eighteen aircraft of the 1920 types which consisted of Camel, a single-seater fighter; Panther, a two-seater spotter-reconnaissance; Cuckoo, a torpedo plane. The R.A.F. organization however was in homogeneous squadrons of twelve aircraft each.

The Admiralty wanted to employ all three types in fleet exercises in order to study the effect of air power on naval tactics. But to lock up three whole squadrons for the use of a carrier, which at best could stow one and a half, appeared to the Air Ministry a shocking waste of a big portion of their total strength. Eventually it was decided that units of the R.A.F. selected for service in carriers should be organized in flights of six aircraft each. This minor dispute was nearing its end by the time I had succeeded in acquiring a general grasp of what was going on. I was duly installed in an office in the attic of Admiralty House. I had the title of Head of Naval Air Section; but for six months N.A.S. resembled a tadpole; it was all head, there was not even a tail.

I found that the branch of the Air Ministry with which I had mainly to deal was that presided over by the Deputy Chief of the

Air Staff, at that time Air Vice-Marshal Sir John Steele. He had been first lieutenant of the *Minotaur* in 1911 and I had met him often since, both during his service in the R.N.A.S. and at the two clubs of which we were both members. This was fortunate for me and it was thanks to him that things worked as smoothly as they did for the next two years. His personal assistant was Squadron Leader Lancelot Tomkinson, my old *Campania* shipmate. As a result I found that much of the work could be done on the telephone and the number of inter-departmental letters was reduced.

September 1920 had been fixed for my wedding and I was given ten days' leave subject to the Naval Air Requirements for 1921 being ready for sending to the Air Ministry. Needless to say I took care that they were. Mary Montgomery and I were married at Alnmouth in Northumberland where my parents-in-law were then living, spending our honeymoon in Merioneth. The ancient Sunbeam car which I had bought in 1913 carried us most of the way round England and brought us back to London the day before my leave expired. We took rooms in the Vernon Court Hotel in Buckingham Palace Road while my wife set about furnishing the flat we had taken in Ashley Place.

Soon after I got back to the Admiralty another possible source of trouble between the two departments made its appearance. The Grand Fleet had become the Home Fleet and, under the command of Admiral Sir Charles Madden, had resumed its peace-time routine of three exercise periods during the year, separated by three periods at home ports for leave and refit. The *Argus* was attached to the Home Fleet and conformed to this routine. In a report to the Admiralty, the C-in-C stated that during the last exercise period, he had not been able to carry out as many exercises with aircraft as he had hoped, because of the amount of time *Argus* had had to spend in training the pilots in deck-landing. So many pilots were changed at each leave period that this was likely to be the usual state of affairs and he requested that it be remedied. I discussed this on the telephone with Steele who asked me to try and stop any official letters passing until he had had time to find out what was possible as the question was one for the Air Member for Personnel. I told the A.C.N.S. about it and a day or two later Steele explained what the situation was and what could be done.

Owing to drastic reduction of the R.A.F., the Air Council had decided they could not afford to have specialist categories of pilots: if they did their posting problems would become impossible. This policy however necessitated frequent changes of posting, including to carriers, for each individual. The D.C.A.S. said that he had explained the difficulty this produced in the fleet and that the Personnel Department of the Air Ministry would try to reduce the frequency of changes for the immediate future. But they could not change their policy which, the Air Ministry believed, would in the long run benefit the Admiralty by producing a greater number of pilots with deck-landing training. I put this down in the form of a minute which the A.C.N.S. passed on to the C-in-C Home Fleet, and the incident closed without friction; but it undoubtedly left an uneasy feeling at the Admiralty.

The fact was that the reduction of the country's Armed Forces at the end of the war affected each service quite differently. A vast Army had been swept out of existence. A strong Air Force had been reduced to a skeleton. A powerful fleet had been reduced to a moderate one. But the air component of the new moderate fleet was dependent on what could be spared by a skeleton Air Force.

Soon after this I was the unintentional cause of friction. Among my other duties I was to watch the development of new types of aircraft and keep the Board informed of any that might be of value in naval operations. To this end I had asked for and been supplied with an Air Ministry periodical which set out the state of development of all new types of aircraft under production. Amongst these new types at that time were two large flying-boats which had been projected at the end of the war as experimental types and which appeared in the periodical at each issue, but with no indication that any advance had been made in the interval. Although aircraft engines were much more reliable than they had been during the early part of the war, they were still regarded as very temperamental machines and it was generally accepted that land aeroplanes would not be expected to make long flights over sea. Flying-boats therefore were the only shore-based long-range aircraft which the Navy expected to have available in naval operations.

I made inquiries of the D.C.A.S.'s office as to what was happening to these new flying-boats; it happened that one of his assistants was an enthusiastic flying-boat pilot. He knew all about them and told me that in spite of protests by flying-boat enthusiasts at the Air Ministry, the Air Council had reluctantly come to the conclusion that there was insufficient money available to continue with their construction, and that the contracts were suspended. He added that if only the Admiralty would raise the question it might result in this decision being reconsidered. I wrote a minute to the A.C.N.S. enclosing a memorandum on the value which flying-boats would have in naval war and proposing that the Admiralty should write to the Air Ministry urging their development. Admiral Chatfield sent for me and said that as he did not propose to open the question on my unsupported opinion, he was sending my minute over to Coastal Area, proposing that the Air Officer Commanding or his representative should come to the Admiralty and give his views at an informal discussion.

The Headquarters of Coastal Area were at that time in Tavistock Place and the A.O.C. was Air Marshal Sir Vial Vivian. His chief of staff was my old chief, Air Commodore C. R. Samson. I felt pretty sure what their opinion would be. At the meeting both Vivian and Samson strongly urged the development of flying-boats; as a result a letter was sent to the Air Ministry in the general sense that the Admiralty believed in their future and would be glad to know what developments were in view. The answer was a strong protest from the Air Ministry against the Admiralty's action in consulting Coastal Area. They pointed out that the proper advisors of the Admiralty were the Air Council and not Coastal Area. The Admiralty had to accept the rebuke as they were technically in the wrong, though their action was taken in all good faith. The practice of sending Admiralty minutes or dockets over to Coastal Area for their remarks had to be stopped and later Coastal Area was shifted from London to Lee-on-Solent. Thus direct touch between the Admiralty and the Air Command who would co-operate with them in war came to an end.

At about the same time as the flying-boat incident, I had raised another question which indirectly led to the establishment of the Naval Observer Branch. On demobilization at the end of the war, the comparatively small number of young, direct-entry observers serving in the fleet had gone back to civil life. The only trained observers remaining were the ex-naval yeomen of signals trained in *Campania* in 1917. They had all become warrant officers, R.N.A.S., had transferred to the R.A.F. as second lieutenants and by 1921 were mostly flying officers. They were essentially experts in signals whose handling of their wireless sets was of a high standard. They were also experts in ship recognition. However, they were not trained from early age in navigation problems. Since they were much older than the majority of R.A.F. officers of their rank it was more than could be expected of them that they should suddenly become enthusiastic pioneers in the problem of air navigation from a moving fleet.

Reports from *Argus* seemed to suggest that the system which we had evolved in *Furious* during the war was being forgotten. Intercourse with Coastal Area had not then been stopped so I made out a summary of the methods we had developed in *Furious* (smoke-burst wind-finding, compass adjustment procedure, plotting organization, etc.) and sent it to Coastal Area with a minute asking whether the same system was in force and what developments had taken place. The minute in reply was signed by the air marshal himself and was quite frank. Progress had not been made and he was not satisfied. He hoped to improve matters and would keep the Admiralty posted.

On the skill of the observers depended the accuracy of reconnaissance reports and as longer-range aeroplanes became available, accurate navigation would become increasingly important. The A.C.N.S. therefore was deeply interested in this subject. He considered raising it with the Air Ministry, but as Coastal Area had taken the matter in hand decided to await developments.

Some months later the question of observers was raised, this time in connection with fleet gunnery. The C-in-C Home Fleet, Sir Charles Madden, was not satisfied with the progress being made in air spotting. He proposed to come to the Admiralty and discuss it. The Air Ministry was informed and a meeting arranged. Lord Beatty was away but the Chief of the Air Staff, Lord Trenchard, decided to attend. The meeting was held in the D.C.N.S.'s room; Lord Trenchard, Sir Charles Madden, Sir Osmond Brock and Sir Ernle Chatfield were present; as there was no secretary I was told to make notes and draft the report.

The Chief of the Air Staff explained the reluctance of the Air Council to create specialist branches. He pointed out that spotting for batteries ashore had been successfully performed by pilots throughout the war and suggested that the same arrangement could be made to work in the fleet. Madden, who gave a summary of his experience up to that date, was strongly of the opinion that observer specialists were needed. Eventually on Lord Trenchard's proposal it was decided to put the matter to a practical test. An Air Force officer with long experience of spotting for Royal Artillery heavy batteries during the war was to be selected and sent up to the fleet. The C-in-C was to arrange for a series of test shoots for which this officer was to spot while acting as pilot. The decision on whether or not a specialist Naval Observer Branch was necessary was to depend on the result.

Both before that meeting and since, I have noticed that in the Navy and in the Air Force (possibly in the Army too) the more exalted the rank of an officer, the less marked is the tendency to stick strictly to the point at issue. This meeting was no exception to that rule and my duty as amateur secretary was no sinecure. It was further complicated by my being sent from time to time to fetch copies of reports and letters required for reference. I had to guess what had been discussed during my absence. But though the point at issue, the control of the fleet's gun-fire, was not always in the forefront of the discussion, the talk never wandered very far from the general question of the observers, about which the Air Council's policy was made clear. It was based on their reluctance to create specialist categories within the R.A.F. and therefore was along the lines of using General Service pilots both for observation and for navigation. The test firing duly took place and when the report submitted by the selected officer insisted that specialist observers were a necessity, the Naval Observer Branch came into existence.

When I first joined the Admiralty, Admiral Chatfield had told me that on all matters of any importance I was always to consult him verbally before adopting any policy or initiating any proposal, and this I had always done. During the period in which the observer question was being thrashed out I was constantly consulting him or being sent for by him. I had soon realized his method of dealing with complicated questions. He always sought the essential point or points and, having firmly grasped them, never allowed any subsequent red herring to confuse the issue.

Consequently his policy was always clear cut and easy to understand. No matter how many other subjects he was dealing with at the same time, he seemed always to be able to come back to the matter with which I was dealing, with the essentials of the question clear in his head. The method sounds easy and I have always tried to imitate it, but have found that the difficulty has been to recognize the red herring when I see it.

This insistence on a clear-cut policy on all matters made working under him very pleasant and I also greatly appreciated his accessibility. However busy he was he would always find time to discuss any point I wanted to raise and invariably had the essentials in his head. The observer discussions also brought me in touch with the Gunnery Division of the Naval Staff whose director was Captain F. C. Dreyer.[1] He had been one of the officers mainly responsible for the development of naval fire control. As Director of Naval Ordnance, he had been successful in remedying the dangerous naval shell situation disclosed by Jutland and he had been Lord Jellicoe's flag captain throughout his period as C-in-C Grand Fleet. Naturally, his opinion carried a lot of weight with the Board and to gain his support in air matters was an immense help. Under his leadership the Gunnery Division was even more of a hive of industry than it usually was and for a while I was alarmed lest it should swallow the Naval Air Section. Captain Dreyer put this right very early in the discussions on the observers. Calling me into his room one morning he remarked, 'Look here, Bell Davies, don't imagine I intend to put any spokes into the Naval Air wheel. It seems to me much more likely Naval Air will be able to put spokes into the Gunnery wheel before long. Let us work together in this.'

I have said before that Admiral Chatfield had considered the reconnaissance side of the naval observers' work before the question of gunnery observation was raised. The agreement reached with the Air Council had not of course included reconnaissance, but the Board of Admiralty felt that once an observer branch had come into existence it was inevitable that they would eventually take over reconnaissance duty as well as gunnery observation.

About nine months after I joined the Admiralty, the head of

[1] Later Admiral Sir Frederick Dreyer.

N.A.S. was allowed an assistant. There was at the time hardly another naval officer who had had any flying experience and none with carrier experience, so I suggested to the A.C.N.S. that my assistant should be a paymaster with experience as secretary. Paymaster-Commander J. L. Syson was appointed and from then on N.A.S. activities became much more methodical and orderly. We moved house from the attic, first into an annexe overlooking Whitehall and then into another annexe built into the central courtyard and opening into South Block, both of which have since been pulled down.

In carrier construction much was going on. The drawings for *Eagle* and *Hermes* were complete but there were constant questions of detail. Drawings for the reconstruction of *Furious* were still in production. During the war I had from time to time come in contact with members of the Royal Corps of Naval Constructors who attended trials on board carriers and appeared to have something to do with their construction. I had vaguely heard that they were from the Admiralty and were members of a body known as the Aeronautical Sub-Committee. Soon after joining the Admiralty I was invited to become a member of this. I suppose it had been started in the early airship days and so earned its title; but by 1920 it was concerning itself entirely with carrier construction and deck-landing equipment. The chairman was Mr J. Narbeth, Chief Constructor, who was a member of the Director of Naval Construction's Department, Admiralty. The director himself was Sir Eustace Tennyson-D'Eyncourt.

Mr Narbeth was an ideal chairman, an enthusiast in his job and particularly in the development of carriers. He was always ready to listen to the opinion of younger men and to give everybody except himself full credit for any development that succeeded. The sub-committee was at that time dealing with such matters as experimental arrester gear, palisades, dimensions of aircraft lifts, petrol supply systems, aircraft salvage equipment, stowage of equipment of all sorts, and a mass of similar detail. To deal with all this, it co-opted members from Coastal Area, from Farnborough, and from various Admiralty and Air Ministry departments. The recommendations of the sub-committee were then passed to the main Aeronautical Committee for approval. I am not sure what the composition of the main committee was, but it contained several heads of Admiralty departments and I think the chairman was the D.N.C.

One day a paper came to me shortly before lunch-time on the subject of the Aeronautical Committee. It contained a minute over the signature of Sir Eustace Tennyson-D'Eyncourt pointing out that the recommendations of the sub-committee were not being acted on sufficiently promptly and that unnecessary waste of time was occurring. To remedy this it was proposed to strengthen the main committee and it was suggested that the chairman in future should be the Controller of the Navy. A meeting to discuss this was to be held that same afternoon in the controller's room. Admiral Chatfield was away so that I could not consult him, but I felt pretty sure that the remedy proposed was not the right one. The more exalted the members of a committee are, the less frequently they are likely to meet. Controllers and heads of departments are very busy men and have a lot more than the details of carrier equipment to worry about. I thought that the right solution was to do away with the main committee altogether and to allow the old sub-committee, reconstituted, to report in an advisory capacity direct to the Admiralty department concerned. The head of department could always refuse advice if he thought it unwise and was just as capable of vetting a recommendation as a main committee would be.

It was an imposing meeting, including Sir Eustace, Director of Naval Construction, Admiral Sir Frederick Field, Controller, the engineer-in-chief and the Director of Naval Equipment. I put forward my view rather anxiously; it seemed to me there was a rather uncomfortable pause. Then the D.N.C. with a laugh, called to me across the table, 'You want to get rid of the controller, the D.N.E. and me and run the show yourself, isn't that what you mean?' I hastily tried to deny it but he cut me short and turning to the controller said that though the proposals had come from his department and he supported the need for speeding things up, he was not wedded to the proposed remedy. If the controller agreed, he would like to withdraw the original proposal and adopt that of N.A.S. I came to know Sir Eustace much better afterwards and have always thought his action on that occasion typical of his broad-minded attitude.

The sub-committee was duly reconstituted with new terms of reference as an Admiralty committee with the imposing title of Joint Technical Committee for Aviation Arrangements in H.M. Ships. The title took a bit of living down but we got over it by shortening it to J.T.C.

The J.T.C. accomplished an immense amount of work and, to my knowledge none of its recommendations was ever questioned. The worldly wisdom of its genial chairman, Mr Narbeth, probably prevented any foolish recommendations going forward. Besides the chairman, there were other constructors on it at that time, Forbes the secretary and Hopkins who was working on the *Furious* design. There were a succession of representatives from Farnborough including Major Penney (an old *Campania* pilot) and Dr Coles, while from Coastal Area and Air Ministry most of the early deck-landing pilots attended, including Harry Busteed, Wilfred Acland, Dickson, Evill and Kirke.

It had been decided to have an island lay-out in *Eagle* and *Hermes* as a result of the experiments made with the dummy island in the *Argus*, but there was still a body of opinion among the pilots which would have preferred flush-decked ships. When the *Furious* design was first considered, it was believed to be impractical to carry exhaust gases from so many furnaces along horizontal ducts and to pump them out at the stern. She was therefore to have an island too. My own view was that as it was impossible to foresee how the requirements of aircraft would develop, anything which limited them in span or otherwise was undesirable, so I was reluctant to see islands in the early carriers. Further examination of possibilities showed that *Furious* could be completed without an island and the J.T.C. recommended that this should be done.

At the time, we knew that the Japanese were becoming greatly interested in aircraft carriers. They had already started on the *Hosho* and were in a position to convert ships under construction to carriers. It was important for us to keep ahead. It seemed that flush-deck carriers the size of *Furious* might enable us to use much bigger aircraft than the Japanese were likely to be thinking of. Mr Narbeth, the chairman of the J.T.C., suggested that if we could attract Japanese attention to the smaller *Eagle* and *Hermes*, which were new ships, it might be possible to distract them from *Furious* which was an old ship being altered. He thought that by keeping some timber framework and unfinished plating over the starboard side until the *Furious* was nearly complete, the impression could be given that she was going to have an island, to attract attention to *Eagle* and *Hermes*, these two ships should be classed top secret.

The proposal, put to the Board, was approved and presently a string of Admiralty Fleet Orders appeared; *Eagle* and *Hermes* with special police guards were barricaded off while in dockyard; special identification methods for men working on board were instituted; no cameras were to be allowed on board when the ships were in commission; special permission for visitors had to be obtained. The scheme apparently worked well, for it had the desired result of attracting hordes of queer-looking tourists many of whom no doubt were Japanese agents. They fairly buzzed round those two ships while no particular notice seemed to be taken of *Furious*. When I returned from sea to the Admiralty in 1926, *Furious* was in commission and all the world could see that she had no island and got rid of her smoke at the stern. But the secrecy regulations were still in full force and everyone had forgotten why they had been introduced. It took a long time and hard work before those A.F.O.s were cancelled and cameras and visitors allowed on board aircraft carriers.

As it happened, our efforts at cunning were to no avail, perhaps fortunately. The early Japanese carriers followed the *Furious* arrangement. On the other hand, the island arrangement proved to be a better one and all our carriers after the *Furious* incorporated it.

The interest in air matters taken by the Gunnery Division of the staff in 1921 and 1922 resulted in my being pressed hard by them to obtain some form of towed target for anti-aircraft practices. Letters and personal inquiries to the Air Ministry produced no result. I don't suggest that the Air Ministry intended to be obstructive about AA gunnery but they were certainly not enthusiastic. Their reply was that towing a target by an aeroplane was not a practical proposition. However I came across an article in a Norwegian technical magazine, illustrated by a photograph of an aeroplane towing a sleeve target. I had the descriptive article translated, cut out the photo, and sent both over to the Air Ministry 'With reference to previous correspondence'. No doubt we should have had the sleeve target eventually, but we had the Norwegians to thank for speeding up its production.

When the sleeve target proved a practical success, the Admiralty began to press for some streamline form of target capable of being towed at a greater speed, but none was produced owing to the difficulty of stabilization. Some seventeen years later, in 1939, as a result of the early experiences of the war, the First Lord of the Admiralty, Mr Winston Churchill, found it necessary to intervene personally to secure the supply of higher speed AA targets.

The development of AA targets led some years later to the production of the most spectacular trial ever staged by the J.T.C. – that of the pilotless, wireless-controlled target aeroplane known as the Queen Bee. In the early experiments the difficulty was to land the aircraft without wrecking the expensive instruments inside it. It was therefore designed with a buoyant fuselage and no undercarriage, with the idea that it should glide on to the water at the end of its flight. As there were no catapults then available to assist in its launch, it was decided to use *Argus* with a good wind speed down the deck. The aircraft, mounted on a trolley from which it would rise when flying speed was reached, was to take off under its own power. As there was danger of the tail striking the trolley just after the aircraft became airborne, the trolley was constructed to collapse at the correct moment and allow the tail to pass clear. The trolley was thus too complicated and expensive a piece of mechanism to be allowed to fall over the bows and be lost in the sea, so a buffer was devised to catch and retard it when the aircraft was clear, Sandow elastic being used to absorb the shock.

There were many people interested in that trial – gunnery experts who hoped for a target, wireless experts interested in the control, designers of aircraft, Farnborough, naval constructors, and the members of the J.T.C. Committee who had supplied a photographer with a cine-camera on legs to record it. The engine was started and the contraption moved forward along the deck. The aircraft lifted successfully but for some reason the trolley failed to collapse; the tail struck the trolley and the aircraft dived steeply, landing on its nose in the bows of *Argus* where it remained in a state of unstable equilibrium with its valuable cargo of instruments. Naturally all the experts rushed to the rescue. The trolley meanwhile continued on its course until caught by the buffer. The stretched Sandow elastic then reasserted itself, the trolley was shot to the rear scattering the experts in its course and finally knocking away the legs of the tripod of the cine-camera.

There was one other occasion when monotony of office work was relieved by a little comedy. It was due to a Hungarian inventor with a quite unpronounceable name. He was a rather stout, beady-eyed little man capable of producing the most astounding flood of broken English I have ever heard. Raymond Fitzmaurice (our original torpedo lieutenant at Eastchurch) and I were ordered to investigate and report on his invention. Fitzmaurice was attached to the Directorate of Torpedoes and Mining and we sat in his room opening into the main entrance corridor of the Admiralty.

The inventor appeared and the flood submerged us. It appeared that he and the Regent of Hungary, Admiral Horthy, were almost brothers. Masses of papers showing the closeness of his acquaintance with His Excellency the Regent were scattered round the room. It further appeared that he shared with His Excellency such a profound respect of 'der crate Prietish Navy' that they were both accustomed to spring enthusiastically to their feet whenever it was mentioned. As he contrived to mention it in almost every sentence he was bobbing up and down like an exhaust-valve tappet.

Gradually the mysteries of the invention were unfolded. Called 'der see refolfer', it appeared to be the result of a *mésalliance* between a submarine and an aircraft carrier. In the torrent of words the technical details were hard to follow, but apparently the apparatus could poke its nose above water, sneeze and eject an aircraft from its interior. For some reason which I could not follow, in order to repeat the process it had to roll over on its back. The explanations did not come out in sequence but were inclined to get mixed up with Admiral Horthy. It was confusing but I had just managed to establish clearly that it was 'der see refolfer' which rolled on its back and His Excellency who sprang to his feet, when I noticed Fitzmo and was seriously alarmed at the colour of his face. I managed to stop the flood and explained that my colleague and I were so deeply interested in what we had heard that we needed a little time for private discussion. Perhaps our visitor would not mind waiting in the entrance hall for a few minutes. I led him out of the room and was just in time, by slamming the door, to cover the explosion of Fitzmo.

During my first two years at the Admiralty, I had worked constantly under the A.C.N.S. and had only occasionally come into touch with other members of the Board. It was only towards the end of my time there that I had any personal contact with the First Sea Lord, Lord Beatty. It was the period when relations with the Air Ministry were at their worst. I suppose that most men of very strong personality have a certain streak of the actor in them. In Lord Beatty's case it was probably quite unconscious but he seemed to adapt his personality to the occasion and even to the clothes he was wearing. Normally he wore a blue serge suit in the Admiralty and looked and behaved like a brisk and alert senior officer. Meeting him in a corridor you naturally stood to attention and were accorded a glance, a nod and usually a 'Good morning'. On the other hand when he attended a Cabinet meeting or the Committee of Imperial Defence he usually wore a black coat and heavy black satin stock. If you met him then, he appeared to be walking slowly, hands behind his back, chin sunk on his stock, and he did not look up as he passed you.

I only once experienced an exception to this custom. There was a certain very eminent politician whom he delighted to score off. I had to prepare a memorandum one day for Lord Beatty to use at a meeting of the C.I.D. On his return he sent for me. He was still in the 'elder statesman' clothes, but was grinning broadly and rubbing his hands. He said, 'By gad, I had him today. I got him properly. I made him go as red as a turkey cock.'

15
Airships, Personnel and Others

From the middle of 1922 relations between the Admiralty and Air Ministry became, as I have said, very strained. The period of four years during which no major change was to take place had expired, and the Admiralty was thoroughly dissatisfied with the quality and quantity of its air arm. The dispute was one of principle and rendered acute by the totally inadequate size to which the R.A.F. had been reduced after the war. Disagreement existed over quality of personnel and both quality and quantity of material. In the case of the former, the Navy, accustomed to a system of specialization which ensured continuity in progress and eventually provided senior officers with a knowledgeable outlook, wished for aviators with specialist nautical experience and knowledge. The R.A.F. considered specialization a system wasteful of personnel and was loth to allocate pilots or observers to the Fleet Air Arm except on a strictly temporary basis.

This had its effect not only upon the serving personnel but also upon the reserve. The war-trained reserve of the R.A.F. was gradually dwindling, with merely a handful to take its place. It could not afford to lock up a part of its reserve as specialists in naval work. The Admiralty consequently felt that there would be no reserve on which the Navy could rely in war.

With regard to material, not only did the R.A.F. naturally concentrate its very limited funds on development of aircraft suited to its own purposes rather than on maritime types but, responsible for the defence of the country against air attack, it shrank from allocating much of its exiguous strength to support of the Navy. The Admiralty on the other hand, responsible for the defence of sea communications, naturally felt that the air strength allowed it was inadequate. I have often thought since, that if the R.A.F. at that time had been numerically stronger, the Air Staff would have been much more willing to meet the wishes of the Naval Staff. As it was they felt they simply could not afford to. With such opposed views held by the two staffs, no agreement was possible and a Government ruling was eventually inevitable.

The relationship between the two staffs was not improved by a campaign taking place in the Press about this time on the subject of bombs versus battleships. The French had conducted experiments in which an old battleship anchored in shallow water had been attacked with live bombs. At an early stage in the attack the ship had sunk, and the reports tended to show that this had been accomplished not by bombs which hit, but by bombs which missed. In the United States, where General Mitchell was urging the claim of the long-range bomber, trials of a similar sort took place. There the battleship was an ex-German vessel of more modern construction and the trials took place in deep water. The same result was obtained, though not quite so quickly, and again it was definitely shown that it was the near misses which sank the battleship.

These results quite rightly gave great encouragement to the supporters of the long-range bomber in England. But they also unfortunately gave great encouragement to another and much more dangerous group, the economizers. The two groups often appeared indistinguishable and no doubt many people belonged to both: but their two theories were distinct. The bomber enthusiasts wanted to spend money on building bombers – a very laudable wish at the time. The economizers wanted to save money by cutting down the Navy. Their argument was simple: Bombs can sink battleships; why waste money on the Navy? Obviously the next step along that line of thought was: Bombs can sink battleships; therefore they can sink all ships; therefore Great Britain can be starved into surrender. Why waste money on any form of defence? The near-miss discovery was very attractive to both groups and was naturally well aired in the Press. Apparently it was not even necessary to hit the ship; a bomb somewhere near would do the trick.

The bomb-versus-battleship controversy was much too serious

to be disregarded by the Admiralty which decided to do two things. The old battleship *Agamemnon* was then in use as a gunnery-target ship for the fleet. It was proposed to stage a series of attacks on her with practice bombs, giving maximum facilities to representatives of the Press to witness the trials. It was also proposed to carry out a series of trials with underwater charges against a specially constructed float, afterwards called the Chatham Float, with the object of testing as thoroughly as possible what degree of damage was to be expected from the near miss. The Air Ministry was invited to collaborate.

When the *Agamemnon* trials took place, it was agreed that journalists should be accompanied by officers from the Admiralty and the Air Ministry. I was sent by the Admiralty and Lancelot Tomkinson by the Air Ministry. We were old friends and had a most interesting day. Not having met many journalists before, I assumed that the representatives of the various great papers would somehow suggest by their appearance and manners the kind of paper they represented. This proved quite wrong.

At that time the *Daily Mail* was generally regarded as the *enfant terrible* of the London Press. Its representative was a serious, middle-aged man with a wide knowledge of naval affairs. *The Times* was represented by a young, smartly-dressed man with an unending supply of good stories who obviously intended to enjoy himself. But the man in whom Tomkinson and I were most interested represented a small paper of the extreme Left. A convinced economizer and an extremely conscientious man he buttonholed first Tomkinson and then me and pumped us. He wanted to understand about the near miss. How near must it be and how big must the bomb be to do harm?

It was largely a matter of guesswork to answer but apparently the answers we gave corresponded, as he later collected us both together to explain that he had worked out a kind of formula which he intended to apply to the trials. It was a good formula, taking into consideration as far as possible all the doubtful elements which, he had gathered (from his pumping of the two of us), existed. The Admiralty had undertaken to supply the party with the results of the trials, giving the number of hits scored; but he checked up on these personally, comparing his observations with those of the other journalists. At the end of the day he came up to us obviously depressed. He was afraid it was no good. We should have to go on spending money.

He explained that by his calculation, which allowed for the probable increase of range and carrying power of bombers for some years ahead, the percentage of certain sinkings to bombs dropped would not justify him in recommending the cutting down of naval expenditure. Tomkinson asked him if he had really expected that the introduction of a new weapon would result in reducing the country's defence expenditure? He said he had hoped it would. Tomkinson replied that it had never happened yet and that new weapons always meant more expenditure, not less. This coming from an R.A.F. officer depressed him still further. He was obviously an intelligent man, an honest man and I believe a patriotic man. He was anxious to prove that bombers could always sink ships and that ships could not be protected from them. But he would not fake his evidence and was determined to tell the truth.

It had apparently never occurred to him that if his theory were in fact true Great Britain would be at the mercy of Germany, since by the time British bombers had sunk all the German ships, and German bombers had sunk all the British ships, the Germans would still be alive, but the British would have starved to death. After all, the basic reason for sinking enemy warships is to protect your own merchant ships (or to be able to sink the enemy's); but the bomb-versus-battleship controversy never progressed beyond the first step in the process.

The Chatham Float experiments went forward, but were not completed when I left the Admiralty for a seagoing appointment early in 1924. I believe they proved of great value in the design of the watertight sub-division of ships, the development of damage control, the design of bombs, and perhaps not least the correct selection of types of weapon for the attack on ships of different types and in different circumstances. I attended some of the preliminary meetings on the subject and noticed that the state of tension between the Admiralty and Air Ministry had spread to their scientists, who were apt to hurl terrific formulae across the table at each other.

It was a relief during that period to find that there was one subject on which the Naval and Air Staffs were in complete agreement:

the Burney airship scheme. The sponsors of the scheme proposed to spend a considerable sum of public money on the development of airships. The project was primarily commercial but was supported by arguments which, amongst other things, aimed to show that airships would be of great value in war, more particularly as aircraft carriers. Eventually a committee was appointed to investigate the claims as regards the possible war value of airships, the chairman being Mr L. S. Amery, then Civil Lord of the Admiralty. There were some Parliamentary representatives, the remainder of the committee coming from the Admiralty and Air Ministry. Before the committee met, I accompanied Mr Amery and some others to Pulham where the R33 was secured to the mooring mast. Major Scott, the captain of the ship, was much the most experienced captain of a rigid airship that Great Britain produced.

I have never been a great believer in the future of airships, but I think one of the reasons that they failed to do better than they did was due to the difficulty of giving long enough training to their captains. The master of a merchant ship has usually spent ten years or more in a subordinate position before he is given command. He has seen the ship berthed literally hundreds of times and has seen her handled in every sort of weather. I suppose in the whole world there has only been one man who had experience with airships comparable to the ship experience of the average British master mariner. This was Dr Eckener when he commanded the *Graf Zeppelin*. She had no accidents and made, I think, two trips round the world.

R33 lay at the mast with her bows clamped into a fitting which was free to revolve round the masthead. Her stern was moored to a great pair of heavy wheels which had scored a circular track on the ground round the mast as she revolved. Scott said she had made frequent flights during the last six months returning each time to the mast without meeting any difficulty in mooring. The only incident during these flights had occurred when one of the hydrogen ballonets had developed a leak and a rigger had gone up the framework of the hull to put on a patch. He had somehow lost his hold and had fallen through the ballonet bringing up, swathed in fabric but unhurt, on the cross-bracing at the bottom of the hull structure. The ripping of the ballonet released instantaneously about three tons of lift. Scott said he had had no difficulty in keeping control. He had re-trimmed by releasing ballast and the ship had only lost a few hundred feet of height.

We climbed the mast, entered the ship over a gangway leading to a port cut just under the bow and walked down the central gangway. The slack lower parts of the ballonets were overhead. I went aft as far as the crew's mess deck which was about amidships. The floor of the hull had been reinforced at this point and there was quite a good mess deck with stools, lockers and a hammock netting, the hammocks being slung from the full framework. The crew had been living on board all winter.

Joining Scott and the others in the control car I saw the ship cast off. The engines were started and as there was no wind the screws were put slow astern. Scott gave orders to slip aft first and then as the stern began to rise, to slip forward. She cleared the mast with a little sternway on. This was my only trip in a rigid airship: I found it very impressive, giving a feeling of solidity and space.

We went out over the North Sea at about 3,000 feet. I climbed into the hull again, and aft to the rear-gun position in the stern. The central gangway was about two feet wide with a wire life-line rigged above it but no side rails. The fabric floor of the hull stretched away beneath it on either side. I had been walking along quite happily without bothering about the life-line, when through a tear in the fabric floor I could see the North Sea about 3,000 feet below. After that I held on to the life-line.

As we came back to the mooring mast I watched from the control car. The main mooring wire led from the main winding drum of a converted traction engine, up the mast and out through the centre of the revolving nose cap. From there it ran down again to the ground along which it was played out directly to leeward of the mast, the position of the end being marked by a flag, with a man standing by it. Scott explained the procedure as we approached. He first trimmed the ship a little light so that to maintain horizontal flight we were slightly nose down. As we drew nearer he flew her still more nose down so that we were losing height, but always well above the height of the mast. Shortly before we reached the flag, the airship's own mooring wire was released. This was a long wire secured to the nose, with at its free end a special fitting to enable it to be rapidly attached to the main mooring wire on the ground.

The end of the airship's wire now trailed along the ground until near enough for the man at the flag to run to it with the end of the main mooring wire in his hand and snatch the two together, signalling to the ship when they were fast. The engines were reversed bringing the ship to a stop whereupon, being light, she at once began to rise. As soon as the way was off the engines were stopped. meanwhile the traction engine was heaving in at full speed. I estimated that the ship rose to a little under 1,000 feet before the mooring wire came taut, by which time we were almost vertically above the mast.

While the engine continued to heave in at full speed, two more wires were dropped from the bow of the ship, one on either side. When these reached the ground they were led through blocks, one on either side of the original marking flag, and taken to two secondary drums on the engine. As the ship came lower these wires were kept taut, thus hauling the ship astern, away from the mast, and preventing her from impaling herself on the masthead. Hauled in by the engine, the nose of the airship entered the cup-shaped fitting on the mast into which it clamped itself. Finally a stern line was dropped which was secured to the heavy wheels. Scott said that the absence of wind made the operation more difficult. Even so it was remarkably simple, requiring far fewer men than does the berthing of a big ship in dock.

Soon after that trip the committee met. Admiral Chatfield who was representing the Admiralty nominated me to it. Sir Geoffrey Salmond and Sir John Steele were the Air Ministry representatives; Major Locker-Lampson was one of the Parliamentary members; Mr Amery was chairman. We were concerned only with the possible use of rigid airships in war, for which both naval and R.A.F. members were convinced they were too big and too vulnerable to have any real value. Furthermore we were anxious lest the already inadequate Naval and Air Estimates be burdened with a contribution towards the building of airships. We were all rather afraid of the chairman, who had obviously been impressed by what he had seen in R33, and we were doubtful what line he meant to take.

The chief weakness of the German Zeppelins, their inflammability, seemed to offer the best hope of avoiding having them thrust upon us (and the Estimates) for war purposes. In the early stages of the meeting all went well. It was shown that helium, the only non-inflammable substitute for hydrogen, involved a considerable loss of lift or alternatively a big increase in size. Also the possible sources of supply in the British Empire were inadequate. The possibility of an envelope of non-inflammable gas round the hydrogen containers was next examined and again showed a big loss of lift.

I was feeling pretty confident, when one of the witnesses asserted that there was a possibility of a new gas. He was very cautious, but said there was reason to suppose that the atomic weight of the new gas which was non-inflammable lay between helium and hydrogen. Mr Amery at once started to cross-examine, objecting that no element could exist between those two. The witness agreed but nevertheless denied that he had in mind a mixture. This was an entirely new gas. By that time I was quite out of my depth and I suspect that all the other Service members were too. Locker-Lampson who was sitting next to me admitted it.

Fortunately the chairman was not. He went on pressing, suggesting an analogy in the relationship between ozone and oxygen. The witness agreed that the new gas was of a similar nature. Mr Amery suggested that such gases were liable to be unstable and could not be relied upon to keep their characteristics under all conditions of temperature and pressure. He said that the committee felt that if they were to accept the existence of such a gas they must be given some evidence of its stability. (I was very glad to know that we felt like that.) In the end the chairman's victory was complete. The new gas was traced to its lair in a laboratory experiment at a temperature of some thousands of degrees. It was of the stuff that chemists' dreams are made of, but not suitable for inflating airships in 1923. The committee reported that the Burney Airship Scheme must stand or fall by its merits as a commercial proposition and could not be supported by the Defence Services.

The Board of Admiralty's final decision to refer the matters in dispute with the Air Ministry to the Government was taken as the result of a letter from the C-in-C Mediterranean, Admiral Sir John de Robeck.

It was a magnificent letter, clear and incisive, depicting the situation in the Mediterranean as he then saw it. More and more our vital sea communications through the Mediterranean would have to depend on the combination of surface and air strength, and there was no air strength. He finished with an appeal to the Board. He regretted that his own time on the Active List was nearing its end. With even more regret he realized that members of the Board were in a similar position. Were they, the generation of flag officers who had served throughout the war of 1914–18 and who could speak with authority, to pass on to the Retired List leaving to their successors a state of affairs which they knew to be unsatisfactory?

The various directors of staff divisions, including myself as head of the Naval Air Section, having written unanimously supporting these views, the Board decided to put their case to the Government. Before taking action, it was necessary to decide in detail what claim the Admiralty should make. There was general agreement that they should claim full possession of the Fleet Air Arm, that is to say the air component of the seagoing fleet, including full control of its operational training, much of which took place at stations ashore. It appeared also that a strong case could be made either for possession of, or control over, the coastal stations, that is to say that part of the Royal Air Force which is now Coastal Command.

Sir John de Robeck's criticisms of the state of affairs in the Mediterranean had been aimed more at the weakness of the flying-boat unit which, in spite of Samson's vigorous efforts, remained weak in number and old in composition, and at the lack of shore facilities both for training and operations, rather than at the numerical strength of the Fleet Air Arm. I was opposed to the idea that the Admiralty should make any claim for the coastal stations, for two reasons: First, during the first German War, these stations although they had been built purely for naval purposes, had been required for the defence of the country against attack by Zeppelins. I thought that this fact could be used so effectively in a counter-claim, that to claim them for the Admiralty would weaken the case for possession of the Fleet Air Arm. Secondly, while the Navy in 1923 was in a position to find officers and men in sufficient numbers to man the Fleet Air Arm with comparatively small additions, it was not in a position to man the coastal stations as well. Therefore we should have to ask not only for the transfer of stations and aircraft but of the greater part of the personnel as well. They had all been in the R.A.F. for five years and I felt that such a transfer would be unpopular. A discontented auxiliary Service would not produce efficiency.

The Admiralty eventually decided to restrict their claims to the Fleet Air Arm only. The preparation of these claims was carried out by Plans Division with whom I was constantly working. Captain Tom Calvert was appointed as additional to Plans Division and he and I worked under the Director, Captain Dudley Pound,[1] on the preparation of Admiralty memoranda, which were presented to the Committee of Imperial Defence by the First Sea Lord. In the early stages the claim was set out on general principles and we believed that the case was unanswerable.

Had it been possible to confine the presentation of the Admiralty's case solely to general principles, we should have been on firm ground and much of the subsequent friction might have been avoided. Unfortunately it was not. The question of finance came in, inevitably raising a host of economic spectres. It was stated that under the Admiralty's proposals, the Fleet Air Arm would cost more. We had to try and show that it would cost less. Some of the Navy's skilled artificer ratings drew higher rates of pay than some of the R.A.F. technical N.C.O.s. This was a serious stumbling block to us. The fact that the Air Council were trying to secure better rates of pay for their men did not help us. We had to demonstrate that there was overlapping on board carriers by the technicians of the two services. For instance if there were naval coppersmiths and R.A.F. coppersmiths in the same carrier, we had to show that under the Admiralty proposal we should be able to save a whole coppersmith. Or if vice benches were installed for the use of R.A.F. mechanics, and also vice benches for naval artificers, then by the Admiralty's scheme we should save a whole vice bench.

This part of the dispute seemed to me to be farcical. The cost to the country might be a few pounds more or less, but the difference could be only a minute fraction of the whole. Compared to the importance of the safety of our sea communications, it was negligible. None the less we had to go on with it. The climax came when I remembered that the R.A.F. possessed a category of

[1] Later to be First Sea Lord for the greater part of the Second World War.

professional tailors paid by the State. The Navy did not. In the Navy, tailoring is carried out by gifted amateurs who are paid by their customers. Here was a magnificent economy of which we made full use.

The work of preparing all the detailed memoranda whether farcical or not was heavy and, since they had to be presented mostly in printed form by a given time and date, frequently involved long hours. The Director of Plans seemed to enjoy working into the small hours. While I was living in London this was simple enough although dinner became a chancy meal.

By this time Mary and I were starting a family, our daughter Anne being born in November 1921. The next summer, I bought a house called Walhatch at Forest Row, Sussex, which was to be our permanent home in a wandering, sailor's life for the next twenty-three years. So I now became dependent on catching trains.

My wife and I arranged to move house on a Friday and I was to take the Saturday forenoon off to install furniture, lay carpets, etc. Of course on the Friday there came an urgent call for a memorandum for the C.I.D. and no possible chance for me to leave the Admiralty. The decorators were found to have broken their promise to be clear of the premises. My wife arrived to find the furniture piled outside the front door with no chance to make the house habitable and I was not there to help. With a two-months-old baby on her hands it was a sorry situation for Mary, but she overcame it somehow.

As the investigation before the Committee of Imperial Defence dragged on throughout the summer and autumn of 1923, inter-departmental irritation increased and the good relations which had been established between the Deputy Chief of Air Staff's office and the Naval Air Section began to feel the strain. There was no let-up in the normal work of the Naval Air Section; in combination with the work for the committee, this was often gruelling.

That autumn, for instance, trials were taking place on board the *Argus* which, as a member of the J.T.C. Committee, I had to attend. On one occasion, as we had arranged to get away from London and to go on board the ship at Spithead early the following morning, I had booked a room at the Keppel's Head in Portsmouth. During the morning before the trials, a call for another C.I.D. memorandum detained me all day at the Admiralty in the Plans Division with the Director and Calvert. They broke off for supper and I caught the 7.45 train. On arrival at Portsmouth I was met by the flag lieutenant from Admiralty House with a message from the Admiralty that I was to return at once and report to Plans Division. There happened to be a train just leaving. Of course it was a slow one and it was midnight before I reached the office. Pound and Calvert were still at work on some technical point for which they wanted me. It was after 2.30 a.m. by the time we had finished.

The Committee of Imperial Defence eventually decided to appoint a sub-committee to investigate the Admiralty's claim verbally and in detail. It was known as the Balfour Committee, though Lord Balfour who was to have been chairman went sick, and it consisted of Lord Weir and Lord Peel. Admiral Chatfield having been succeeded as A.C.N.S. by Rear-Admiral Fuller, it fell to Fuller to put the case verbally to the committee. I always accompanied him, but was not supposed to do any talking.

Lord Weir had been the first Air Minister. A brilliant engineer and a great industrialist he was, I think, greatly influenced by the material side of the problem. The Admiralty had made no claim to find their own source of supply of aircraft, remaining content to obtain supply through the R.A.F. machinery. Lord Weir did not think that would work.

It was some time after the committee finished hearing the case before they produced their report. The first news I had of it was a telephone call from Tom Calvert to come to Plans Division. Pound was sitting at his desk studying the report with a scowl on his face; Tom Calvert was walking about swearing: evidently it was bad news. I was given the substance of it by Calvert: The air units in the fleet were to remain R.A.F.

While we were discussing the matter I was sent for by the D.C.N.S., Roger Keyes. I found him with a copy of the report in front of him. 'I suppose you think the Board ought to resign over this,' he said. 'So do I.' But he went on to explain that it was not possible at that time. The big axing scheme to reduce the number of officers in the Navy was imminent. Lord Beatty felt that it was impossible for him to resign leaving his successor the unpleasant task of taking responsibility for that measure. I thought it was uncommonly good of Roger Keyes to tell me all this himself.

When I went back to Plans Division I found the atmosphere less gloomy. Pound and Calvert had had time to digest the report more fully. The Navy was to decide the strength and composition of the air units and was to pay for them by a grant in aid. Furthermore the Navy was to provide all the observers and up to 70 per cent of the pilots. This suggested that providing we could produce the full 70 per cent the Fleet Air Arm would eventually become naval in fact, if not in name. Incidentally the name Fleet Air Arm was first proposed during that discussion.

It still remained to implement the report. Shortly before I left the Admiralty, Roger Keyes sent for me again. When I went in to him he asked, 'What sort of a chap is this fellow Trenchard?' I must have looked as astonished as I felt for he went on, 'I know he's my brother-in-law, but what sort of a chap is he?' I could only say that my impression of the 'chap' was that he was very able, very determined and in fact formidable. That cannot have been much help to him, but between them they produced an interpretation of the report which was known as the Trenchard-Keyes Agreement, on which the organization of the Fleet Air Arm depended for the next fourteen years.

16
At Sea Again

Early in 1924 I turned over the Naval Air Section to Tom Calvert, and was appointed executive officer of the *Royal Sovereign*. I joined her at Sheerness in April 1924. About a week after this, Captain St G. Collard,[1] generally known as Sammy, relieved Captain Napier in command. He had the reputation of being a very taut hand; in fact I found in him a good friend. When he was relieved by Barry Domville in the following year I was sorry to see him go. He had an explosive temperament but his bark was always worse than his bite. My own time in the *Royal Sovereign* came to an end early in 1926 and, after some leave which coincided with the General Strike of that year, I was again appointed to the Naval Air Section as assistant to Tom Calvert.

Things had been developing fast in naval aviation. The Japanese were converting the battle-cruisers *Akagi* and *Kaga* into aircraft carriers, and the Americans the *Lexington* and *Saratoga*. We had *Eagle* and *Hermes* in commission besides *Argus*; the *Furious* was completing.

Tom Calvert had always been determined to maintain the 70 per cent of naval pilots in the Fleet Air Arm which the Balfour Committee had allowed, but it was proving difficult to do. Calculations showed that the requirements of the specialist branches, including destroyers and Fleet Air Arm, would eventually absorb the whole of the lieutenants' and lieutenant-commanders' lists without leaving any for 'salthorse'[2] duties. Calvert wanted to ease the situation by making use of petty officer pilots;

[1] Later to be involved in the notorious *Royal Oak* courts martial in 1928.
[2] Non-specialist executive naval officer.

correspondence on the subject was taking place with the Air Ministry.

The Earl of St Vincent once urged the Secretary of the Admiralty of his day not to allow his subordinates to 'mingle gall with their ink'. A great deal of gall was getting into the ink in the course of this correspondence. The Air Ministry claimed that the only reason for the admission of naval pilots into the Fleet Air Arm had been to ensure that some future senior naval officers should have some air experience. The introduction of petty officer pilots would not do this. If non-commissioned pilots were needed the R.A.F. could provide them. The Air Ministry won that battle.

Catapults were now being developed. The first of these were operated by compressed air, but experiments were being made with cordite propulsion. One of the early cordite experiments produced a spectacular result. The catapult concerned was installed at Farnborough and had been designed for operation with compressed air supplied from a high-pressure cylinder and admitted directly into the nest of rams. The rams were lubricated with mineral oil. To convert it to cordite operation, an explosion chamber had been added below the ram cylinder and connected to it by a port through which the explosion gases entered the cylinder. After a series of cordite shots, the volume of the explosion chamber being found to be too big it was reduced by inserting some wood blocks, after which the cordite experiments continued.

The Farnborough catapult being at the time the only one available for training pilots in a catapult take-off, the compressed-air cylinder was reconnected when it became necessary to do some training. An aeroplane was mounted and the first of the pilots for training took his seat. When the valve was opened there was a shattering explosion; the rams extended with such violence that they wrenched off the catapulting points, hurling them and most of the undercarriage across the aerodrome while the rest of the aeroplane complete with pilot sat down on the catapult and stayed put.

The Joint Technical Committee suffered severe headaches before they found the explanation. During the cordite experiments, a quantity of lubricating oil had run down into the explosion chamber. Though the oil had been wiped out from time to time it had thoroughly saturated the wood-blocks. When not in use the cradle of the catapult was secured by a locking pin. On this occasion the crew had forgotten to remove the locking pin before the launch. On the valve being opened, the rams failed to move at first because of the locking pin and pressure rose to the full pressure of the reservoir. The normal air content of the explosion chamber had become impregnated with oil vapour, so that when high pressure air entered through the port compressing the original air content and thereby raising its temperature, the vapour exploded as in a diesel engine. The combination of full air pressure plus the explosion was too much for the locking pin which sheared. The rest of the performance followed as a matter of course.

G. P. Talbot having succeeded Tom Calvert as Head of Naval Air Section, I worked under him for the rest of my time at the Admiralty. Some time before he left Calvert was told that he would be given command of the cruiser *Frobisher*. We were making out the programme for installing catapults in cruisers. Naturally the newest ships had been given first priority putting *Frobisher* low on the list. Tom at once insisted that I should find some excellent reason for revising the list. F. C. Dreyer was then Assistant Chief of Staff and though no doubt he saw through that manœuvre, the amended list received his blessing.

I ended my time in the Naval Air Section in the summer of 1928, having been promoted to captain at the New Year. Throughout that time at the Admiralty the First Sea Lord was Sir Charles Madden, who had been Jellicoe's Chief of Staff throughout the latter's command of the Grand Fleet. He was also Jellicoe's brother-in-law. He had a house at Forest Row quite near ours. Whenever the Jellicoes came to visit the Maddens, the latter always asked us to come to a meal or to tennis and so gave us the opportunity to meet Lord Jellicoe, a kindness which we greatly appreciated. I never served under Jellicoe, but from those short meetings it was easy to realize the reason for his immense popularity.

In September I was appointed flag-captain to Rear-Admiral H. W. Parker and in command of *Frobisher* where I was to relieve Tom Calvert. As we should be in the Mediterranean for the next two years, my wife and I rented a house on Malta at Guarda Mangia and arranged for the children to follow us.

When we reached Malta, the fleet was scattered in the Levant for the latter part of the summer cruise. Sir Frederick Field, the C-in-C, sent his yacht *Chrysanthemum* to collect Admiral Parker and staff including me, and take us to the *Frobisher* which was at Skiathos. Parker relieved Admiral Boyle, while I took over from Tom Calvert. Most of *Frobisher*'s quarter-deck was taken up by the circular catapult pedestal, but there was no catapult on it. My command of *Frobisher* was to be comparatively short as the new cruiser *London*, nearing completion, was soon to relieve her. I enjoyed my time in her however. She was a delightful ship to handle and we had a first-class ship's company.

For the spring cruise of 1929, the First Cruiser Squadron consisted of *Frobisher* and three D-class cruisers until we reached Gibraltar at the end of the cruise, when the *London* arrived from England. As her captain, H. H. Rogers, and I were to exchange ships and the admiral's flag was to be transferred, we arranged to set off simultaneously in our galleys, passing and politely saluting each other in the harbour, being received on board our new ships with traditional ceremony.

London was one of the 10,000-ton cruisers built under the Washington Treaty rules; the first four to be built had been sent out to China. We had very little information in the *London* as to how they had performed, but the first few shoots which the *London* did filled me with horror; in none of them did we get through without several turrets having jams and breakdowns, mostly after the first salvo.

The trouble could be traced to the provisions of the Washington Treaty. Prior to that, British policy had been to develop a reliable hydraulic system of loading for the big guns of battleships and to rely on hand-loading for the lighter guns. The 7.5-inch, hand-loaded guns of the *Frobisher* produced a high rate of fire and were thoroughly reliable. But at Washington the Japanese had said that their sailors were little men and were not strong enough to handle 7.5-inch projectiles. They insisted that the guns in new cruisers must either be small enough for Japanese sailors to load by hand, or else so big that British and American sailors could also not lift the projectiles. Hence the power-worked 8-inch guns of the *London* class.

The well-tried hydraulic system for 15-inch guns in battleships was too slow for the lighter guns of the cruisers. It could not produce a high enough rate of fire. An entirely new system of power loading had to be produced, starting from scratch. The teething troubles which resulted were appalling. Turner, the *London*'s gunnery officer, was able and energetic and the commander was my old *Royal Sovereign* shipmate, Pat Brind,[1] a gunnery specialist of eminence. After discussions with them I proposed that *London* should not take part in any competitive shoots for the first six months, but that we should spend the time and ammunition in doing slow-time, experimental shoots and try to eliminate the troubles. At the end of six months we should be able to do a 20-rounds-per-gun shoot.

The proposal was approved and carried out; but even after six months of careful work we failed to do a clean shoot of 20 rounds per gun. A great deal of detailed redesigning had to be undertaken before these mountings were satisfactory.

When the First Sea Lord, Sir Charles Madden, was nearing the end of his term of office, the C-in-C Mediterranean, Sir Frederick Field, was called home for a conference. *London* was ordered to take him to Marseilles where she was to wait while he travelled to the Admiralty and back. As a result of the meeting, Sir Frederick Field relieved Sir Charles Madden as First Sea Lord and Sir Ernle Chatfield became C-in-C Mediterranean.

One of the events of 1929 was the Barcelona Exhibition. *London* and *Ramillies* were sent there to take part in the ceremonies. On arrival, a young Spanish sub-lieutenant named Prado reported himself to Admiral Parker as liaison officer. The Spanish people have very many admirable qualities, among them, I have always understood, is a cheerful disregard for times and timetables. Prado was obviously the exception to the rule. He at once set about arranging the paying and returning of official calls. These were innumerable as besides Spanish officers and civil officials there were ships of nearly every nationality present. The linguistic strain was considerable. I struggled along in lame French and lamer German, but the limit was reached when I found myself trying to converse with a Portuguese captain in schoolboy Latin.

The first event was the arrival by train of the Spanish King and Queen and Royal Family. Prado had arranged for cars to take us to

[1] Later Admiral Sir Patrick Brind.

the station half an hour before the royal train was due. We got there exactly on time to find the station completely empty and the platform barricaded off with scarlet poles and ropes. During the next half an hour a large crowd gathered outside the barricades. A number of officers from foreign warships then arrived and finally well after the royal train was due, Spanish officers and grandees. The latter could be recognized by the gold key they wore on the hip.

Just before the royal train came in, nearly an hour later, the crowd stepped over the barricade and pushed on to the platform. When the train stopped the King stepped out first and by using his elbows succeeded in clearing enough room for the Queen and his suite whom he formed up into a sort of phalanx, then putting himself at the head he slowly ploughed a passage for them through the crowd. Whenever he sighted a grandee he halted his party, plunged into the throng and shook hands with the grandee.

I had been squeezed up against one of them to whom this happened when the King seeing my uniform remarked, 'Hullo! is a British ship here?'

'Yes, sir. The *London*,' I replied.

'Oh your new 10,000-ton cruiser; I shall want to see her.' He resumed his place at the head of his party and eventually forced a passage to the waiting cars.

Prado escorted us back to the landing place and we sat down to lunch on board at about 3 p.m. Before we finished, Prado appeared again to say that the King and Queen with most of their suite would be coming on board in about half an hour. There was barely time to parade the guard and band, man ship and saluting guns, before they arrived. One of the ladies-in-waiting remarked to me, 'I hope you are satisfied. We have only been allowed just time to swallow some food before being dragged off to your ship.'

The admiral took the Queen round and I followed with the King. He showed great interest and made some very pertinent remarks. We took them into the after-cabin for tea, where the King said to me, 'I'm a very happy man today; my young son John has always said he was going to be an engine-driver. I've kept telling him it's no good and he'd much better be a sailor.

Well, this morning I had a letter from him to say he wouldn't be an engine-driver but would be a sailor.'

The Exhibition was to be opened the next day. Prado arranged for a car to take us to the main hall, again with half an hour to spare. Soon after starting, the car was brought to a standstill by the huge crowds of people in the street. Getting out, Prado plunged into the crowd, returning accompanied by two Guardia Civiles. He stationed one on each running board and climbing in beside the driver gave the order: 'Charge!' We went through the crowd like a tank, reaching the Exhibition Hall dead on time. Of course there was nobody else there.

During the next hour notables of all sorts arrived; I was proud to see that the British Ambassador was the last to arrive before the King. After a number of speeches the King left to perform the opening ceremony, which involved going to a platform in the grounds and pressing a button to release hundreds of pigeons dyed all the colours of the rainbow. The notables in the hall were to watch the display from the portico and steps; but there were a great many notables and very little room. We found ourselves alongside the Spanish C-in-C, Admiral Morales, and his daughter, but there seemed no chance of seeing anything owing to the crowd. However Miss Morales said that if I and Mainguy, the flag-lieutenant, would hoist her up on our shoulders she would be able to see over the heads of the crowds and could describe what was happening. So we did and she broadcast events in English and Spanish.

The final event at Barcelona was a banquet given by the King at the palace. My place was on the opposite side of the table from the King and next to one of the ladies-in-waiting, so I begged her to see that I behaved in accordance with accepted custom. The King kept up the custom of drinking wine with his guests, and she told me that when that happened it was necessary to stand. He had a small, silk royal standard near his place which he raised from time to time. Each time he raised it a very dignified official, gorgeously uniformed, stepped forward and bent over his chair. From his dignity and uniform I thought he must rank with a field-marshal at least.

Half-way through dinner I saw the King look at me and raise his glass. When I stood he asked how many officers' messes there were in the *London*. I told him, and he said that he intended to send them a present of wine but would make one stipulation: When the officers drank his wine they must drink his health. I said that it would be done. We then drank and I sat down. I saw him raise the little standard and the official stepped forward. Presently I was aware of a presence behind my chair and looking round saw that it was the official. He bent over me and said, 'Beg pardon, sir, but would you mind telling me where your boats come in? The King says I've got to send some cases of wine aboard.' He was a gentleman's gentleman from London.

In the autumn the First Cruiser Squadron carried out a series of shoots while based on Skiathos. In the last of these the *Devonshire* was the last ship to fire, the *London* following astern of her during the shoot. Watching through my binoculars I saw the roof of 'X' turret suddenly fly into the air in a great burst of flame. The old sad story: there had been a hang-fire in the right gun of that turret. In the shock of the broadside, the breech workers had evidently not realized that the gun had failed to fire and had thrown open the breach. It was the Marines' turret and they suffered heavy casualties. The squadron sailed to Volo where there was a cemetery in which the dead were buried.

In November 1930 I was relieved by Burrough. My wife and I came home overland, the rest of the family having preceded us by sea. After foreign service leave at Walhatch I was appointed liaison officer at the Air Ministry. As there were many old friends from the R.N.A.S. there I enjoyed the job. Director of the Operations Directorate to which I was attached was Mills, whom I had known in the R.F.C., and Reggie Marix was one of his assistants. Clarke-Hall was Director of Equipment, Wilfred Acland Assistant to the Deputy Chief of the Air Staff, both Mitchell and Brownhill Directors of Personnel. Sir John Salmond was Chief of the Air Staff.

The programme for installing catapults in ships had at last got into full swing and inter-departmental correspondence on the subject was becoming voluminous. One morning soon after I joined, one of the Assistant Secretaries came into my room bearing a great pile of dockets strapped together with a piece of tape. He dropped it on to my desk remarking that he had been wading through it all. Included were twenty-three letters from the Admiralty about catapult installation and all highly technical. He was the individual who was supposed to draft the answers.

Could I not produce some better method of dealing with the problems instead of ponderous official correspondence? he asked. We discussed the situation and he agreed to leave the great bundle of dockets with me. I attached a minute to it explaining what it contained and proposing to set up a committee to deal verbally with all the problems. It was to be called the Catapult Aircraft Committee and was to include Admiralty representatives. The bundle of dockets carried weight in more ways than one and the proposal sailed through the Air Ministry without opposition. When it was sent to the Admiralty I took a bus down the Strand and started lobbying on its behalf.

I found that Turle, the Head of Naval Air Section, was strongly in favour but several staff directors, suspicious of inter-deparmental committees, opposed it. Fortunately F. C. Dreyer was Deputy Chief of Staff and after I had briefed him he squashed the opposition and pushed through my proposal.

As it was to be an R.A.F. committee the chairman would have to come from the Air Ministry. I tackled all the directors in turn starting with the senior one. All said they had far too much to do as it was and anyhow knew nothing about the subject. I finished up with my own boss, Mills, telling him that as all his seniors had refused it looked as if he was for it. Mills's reaction was even more violent than the others', so I suggested that he need not do it personally but could put in a nominee.

'But who on earth can I nominate?'

'Why not nominate me?'

'I say, will you take it on?'

Thus I found myself chairman of an Air Ministry committee.

It proved highly successful and we polished off the twenty-three outstanding problems at the first meeting. In theory an advisory committee has no power to get things done, and action is supposed to await approval by the Air Council, or Ministry concerned. But in practice it is easy to extract a recommendation and pass it to the department concerned with a minute: 'In anticipation of approval, please say what you will do about it.' The task always is accomplished before approval is received.

In another matter I was not so successful. The Short seaplanes which we had used in the *Campania* had been able to put down on to quite heavy seas without difficulty. But they had poor air performance. The aircraft which had been produced for cruiser catapults, the Osprey, had an excellent air performance and carried a reasonable armament but had a high landing speed. In any seaway I felt sure that it would crack up on landing, and would thus prove to be a one-flight aircraft in wartime. But for cruisers operating on trade routes, the air requirement was for constant search for submarines or surface raiders and there was little likelihood of air combat. I urged the Admiralty to request, and the Air Ministry to produce, a seaplane for cruisers whose main attribute should be low landing-speed, even if this meant poor air performance and little or no armament. Until the production of helicopters, it was extremely difficult to persuade anyone that a comparatively slow-flying aircraft would be of any use in war.

Late in 1932 when my time at the Air Ministry was nearly up, I was offered the cruiser *Cornwall* in China. She was due to come home and re-commission late in 1933, but as the Naval Secretary assured me that, by direction of the First Sea Lord, Sir Ernle Chatfield, captains given a command were not to be relieved until they had completed a full term of about two years, I accepted with enthusiasm.

My wife and I travelled to Hong Kong by P. & O. in company with the new C-in-C, Admiral Sir Frederick Dreyer, and his staff. He absorbed me as a temporary addition to the staff, with the result that I had to work. However it had the advantage that we got to know the staff and the flag captain, Algy Willis,[1] well. The children remained behind, living with their Montgomery grandparents.

At Hong Kong I relieved Knowles in command of the *Cornwall*. After a cruise to Amoy and Tsingtao followed by a refit at Hong Kong in the hot, steamy climate of early summer, we went north to Weihaiwei to scramble through a full programme of gunnery and torpedo exercises during July, preparative to going to Hankow, a thousand miles or so up the Yangtse River. Hankow in August is a most depressing place. The river is still running down

[1] Later Admiral of the Fleet Sir Algernon Willis.

in flood from last year's snow in Tibet. It is a thick yellow colour and runs at about 7 knots. Temperature varies between 95° and 110° F. and the air is moist. Mosquitoes resemble dragons and have forgotten to clean their teeth.

The Chinese Festival of Lanterns took place while we were there. After dark, hundreds of little rafts, each with a lighted candle, are set on the water from sampans in midstream. As they float downstream one after the other, they produce a long ribbon of light bent about by the variations of the current. With twenty or more of these ribbons, the effect is striking.

As a rule a stay at Hankow in August produces a heavy sick list; but the fact that the *Cornwall* was about to go home to pay off had a wonderful effect on the health of the ship's company. We came down-river with hardly a man sick. We anchored for one night off Nanking where the consul general, Blount, was an old school-fellow from Bradfield, while the Assistant Minister, who shared a house with him, was also an old friend, so I dined with them. As Blount was going to stay with the C-in-C at Weihaiwei, it was arranged that he should take passage in *Cornwall* and that off the Saddle Islands we should transfer him to a destroyer bound for Weihaiwei.

A Roman Catholic mission at Ziccawei near Shanghai had established a meteorological station, and one of the Fathers had become an expert on the subject of typhoons. During the passage down the river we received reports from Ziccawei of the formation of a typhoon to the south and forecasts of its possible course. It appeared to be travelling westwards towards the coast of China, but there was a probability that it would turn north towards the mouth of the Yangtse. We made for the Saddle Islands at increased speed and Blount was transferred to the destroyer which left for Weihaiwei with utmost despatch. Though she managed to keep ahead of the typhoon, Blount had a pretty uncomfortable trip.

The *Cornwall* now had a problem. Our course to Hong Kong would hit approximately the centre of the typhoon if it held to its westerly path, in which case we could steam eastwards out to sea and then turn south and pass behind it. On the other hand there was a strong chance that the typhoon would curve round to the north and north-east. The Sailing Directions specified a good typhoon shelter with a bottom of stiff mud, called Beale Harbour, formed by a group of islands just south of the Saddle Islands. I decided to go there and anchor until it was clear which way the typhoon intended to go.

It was a lovely afternoon when we anchored, with little wind, but a heavy swell. It seemed that every fishing junk in China was making for the anchorage, all crowding into a little cove on the south side.

In the middle watch, as the glass started to fall rapidly, the wind rose and by morning was blowing a full gale. We had both bower anchors down and steam on the engines, but during the forenoon when the wind increased with violent squalls and rain, we started to drag. Cable was veered on both bowers and the sheet anchor let go. We then had fourteen shackles of cable[1] on one bower, ten on the other and the sheet anchor at short stay. Though we did not drag any more after that, the ship yawed wildly in spite of the sheet anchor under foot. A strong tidal stream ran through the harbour and in spite of the immense wind pressure, when wind and tide were contrary, the ship did not lie head to wind. We tried steaming to the anchors, but found that did little good and was liable to produce jerks on the cables. At the height of the typhoon, the squalls came down with a wild trumpeting sound, the rain reducing visibility practically to zero. In the afternoon the glass, which had been falling rapidly, suddenly started to rise and the squalls shifted direction from north-east to south-west. It was surprising how quickly after that the weather improved. By the evening the rain had stopped, the sky had cleared and the wind had moderated. It took most of the following morning to weigh the anchors.

Soon after this the *Cornwall* returned to England to re-commission. My wife followed me home and, when the time came to set off for China again, she saw the children safely aboard a P. & O. liner in charge of their Swiss governess before she herself left to travel out via Canada. Reunion of the various sections of the family did not take place as planned owing to the unscheduled movements of the *Cornwall*. After a rendezvous between my wife and myself at Shanghai had failed, we finally met at Singapore where the family lived until the end of the commission.

Not long after the *Cornwall* returned to the station the fleet moved to Weihaiwei for the summer exercising period in which

[1] One shackle of cable = 12½ fathoms = 75 feet.

Cornwall acquitted herself well. In the winter we paid a visit to Manila, meeting the *Augusta*, flagship of the American Admiral Upham. His flag captain was Chester Nimitz who was to gain renown as the Commander-in-Chief Pacific, during the Second World War. The Americans were most hospitable and we thoroughly enjoyed our stay. Early in the year we paid a visit to Japan, where we were entertained by the Assistant Chief of Naval Staff, Rear-Admiral Toyoda, who was to command the Imperial Japanese Fleet during the latter part of the war. It was a curious coincidence that we should have been entertained by those two future adversaries.

17
Another World War

A busy and successful commission in a very happy ship reached an end in October 1935 when I went home to become Commodore of Devonport Barracks, relieving Lane-Pool who had been sub of the *Magnificent*'s gun-room when I was a midshipman. I soon realized how shockingly ignorant I was about everything connected with the barracks and my job.

Things were in a mess through no fault of my predecessors. During the period of economy and 'no war for ten years', the numbers in all branches of the Navy had been run down to a bare minimum. When Mussolini had attacked Abyssinia, the Admiralty had decided to bring the complements of ships of the Mediterranean Fleet to war strength without mobilizing. The resultant drain on the barracks and the technical schools had checked the flow of new men into the higher grades, while the wastage of men retiring on pension continued. Steps to increase recruiting had already been taken, but that necessitated larger training staffs. The first step towards an increase, therefore, was to withdraw from the fleet a large number of the best petty officers, leaving ships short of complement. This was most unpopular.

Besides an increase in the boy entry, it had been decided to enter a number of short-service ordinary seamen. The country was only slowly emerging from the bad depression of the early thirties; there was still much unemployment and many of the short-service recruits came from the depressed area. They lived in huts on the parade ground with their instructors and were looked after by the training commander and his officers. Soon after joining, when I was inspecting some of these lads I noticed that their uniforms were much too tight. I told the training commander to have the clothing contractor on the mat and to threaten him with loss of contract if he continued to skimp the cloth. A few days later the strongly protesting contractor brought his measurement book to me and was able to show that measurements had been properly taken, and the clothes made accordingly.

It was clear what was happening. Many of these lads had been unemployed since leaving school and now, for the first time in their lives, were enjoying full meals with plenty of exercise and fresh air. The result was that their chests were expanding and muscles swelling at a surprising rate. The contractor undertook to make allowance for this in future.

The commodore was ex-officio chairman of the mobilization committee of the port, a subject that I knew nothing whatever about. The committee met once a quarter and the principal matter discussed was the condition of ships in reserve, with the object of making out a timetable for completing them with fuel and stores and bringing complements to full strength on mobilization. It was only after several of these meetings that I began to realize how big the problem really was.

One of its main features was the provision of accommodation and kit for the flood of reservists which would swamp us. On the previous occasion, in 1914, many of them had had to sleep in the open on the parade ground—no great hardship in fine summer weather, but next time we might have to mobilize in winter. The organization of the victualling yard for kitting up the men was, on paper, splendid; but no stocks were held, all having been expended during the lotus years when 'no war for ten years' had been the yardstick applied. When at last I got an idea of the extent of the various problems, I went to the Commander-in-Chief, Admiral Sir Reginald Drax, to suggest that a retired officer should be selected to act as a permanent mobilization secretary and expert. Drax had been studying the problem too. He replied that there were already two individuals in the port who ought to be mobilization experts. He was one and I the other.

Similar activity had been going on at Portsmouth and Chatham and the Admiralty was being bombarded with letters on the subject from all three manning ports. In my view Mussolini did us a good service by creating a crisis in 1935.

The relations between the Navy and the city authorities were excellent at Plymouth. We could always rely on the help of the Lord Mayor when Navy Week came round, and I was always invited to civic functions. One of these was the ancient Fishing Feast. It consisted of a luncheon banquet in a large marquee tent which was set up beside the reservoir. After luncheon, two ancient silver cups were produced, one filled with water, the other with wine. The Lord Mayor and Aldermen tasted the water by sipping at the first cup, followed by a good swig at the wine in the second to take away the taste.

In 1937, the Trades Union Congress was held at Plymouth. The C-in-C invited the members of the Council and their wives to a luncheon to which we were also invited. I went to the party determined to avoid talking home politics at all costs. After the ladies had been taken into the drawing-room by Lady Drax, Sir Walter Citrine, then the Secretary of the T.U.C., carrying his glass of port, came and sat down in the vacant chair next to me. 'What do you think of the situation?' he asked.

Suspicious of politics I said, 'What situation do you mean?'

He replied, 'The European situation generally.'

'I believe the only hope for peace lies in a strong England,' I answered.

Clenching his fist, Citrine brought it slowly down on to the table and affirmed with great emphasis, 'That – is – precisely – my opinion.' Then after a pause he added, 'But you've no idea how hard it is to make some of these chaps realize it.'

At the end of the conference a resolution was passed in support of rearmament. It has been my belief that the credit for that was largely Citrine's.

Besides official and civic entertainments, the Commodore and his wife were drawn into a great many social functions and entertainments both in Devon and Cornwall. People were extremely hospitable. In the winter I had some of the best shooting I have ever enjoyed. In the summer we were always invited to attend the Cawsand and Saltash regattas. It was a busy and a pleasant existence.

In 1937 I was promoted to Rear-Admiral and early in 1938 was relieved at Devonport by A. T. Curteis. Being without an appointment, I went on half pay, but was told that I should be given a job later in connection with the Fleet Air Arm which by this time had finally been restored to the Admiralty. It seemed a good opportunity to take a holiday, so chartering an old 15-ton motor cruiser *Marjorie*, my wife and I set off to explore the canals of Holland. After a happy and interesting trip, lasting about a month, we reached home. I then found that half pay had been abolished so that I had been on full pay all the time.

In the autumn I was put on the Selection Board for entry of candidates for the new Air Branch of the Navy, and we toured the country interviewing young men. Later in the year I was appointed Rear-Admiral of Naval Air Stations (R.A.N.A.S.) with Lachlan Mackintosh[1] as chief of staff and Eric George as secretary. As there was no headquarters yet available we worked at the Admiralty. A certain measure of agreement had already been reached with the Air Ministry on how the transfer of the Fleet Air Arm was to be carried out. Lee-on-Solent, which was to be my headquarters, was still the headquarters of Coastal Command, but when the new site was ready in the summer of 1939 for the latter, Lee-on-Solent air station together with Worthy Down and Ford were to be transferred to the Navy. Land at Yeovilton and Arbroath had been secured and work started. At the Southampton aerodrome at Eastleigh which was in use by the Cunliffe-Owen firm, accommodation for a naval air station was in progress.

The biggest problem was the provision of technical ratings. The Air Ministry had agreed to lend a certain number of air mechanics, but until naval ratings could be recruited and trained we should have to rely largely on civilian mechanics for workshop staff. We were working on these details all that winter. Then Bowhill, who was C-in-C Coastal Command, said that he could evacuate the R.A.F. squadrons at Lee-on-Solent in the spring of 1939 which would set free the air station and also the building known as Wickham Hall, which had been used as squadron offices. I installed the family in rooms in the Belle View Hotel on the front and took possession of Wickham Hall as my headquarters. Tom Bulteel assumed command of the air station, the naval observers' school being already situated there. As Lee was also to be the manning depôt for the Fleet Air Arm, the drafting office was also established there.

[1] Later Rear-Admiral The Mackintosh of Mackintosh.

The little aerodrome at Donibristle on the north shore of the Firth of Forth had been established during the First World War to enable aircraft to be embarked in carriers and ships of the fleet. It was now handed over to the Navy and used as a repair base and for storage of reserve aircraft, Captain Robinson assuming command with the rank of commodore. Up to the outbreak of war the only naval air stations which were working were Lee, Ford, Worthy Down, Eastleigh and Donibristle.

As regards aircraft, the Swordfish had replaced the Shark as the Fleet Air Arm's torpedo-reconnaissance plane and was in full supply, though many of the latter remained for training purposes. The fighter position however was very bad. In earlier times, it had been the custom to adapt for fleet work the type of fighter current in the R.A.F., the latest example having been the Gladiator, some of which were still in use. But with the advent of the monoplane fighters – Hurricanes and Spitfires – this arrangement had for some reason been dropped. The only aircraft which by any stretch of the imagination could be called fighters were the Skua and the Roc. The Skua was really a dive-bomber but could be used as a single-seater fighter. The Roc was similar, but with a machine-gun turret in the rear position, and was counted a two-seater fighter. The performance of both was far below that of the Hurricane, not to mention the Spitfire. The Fulmar two-seater fighter which was eventually to replace the Skua, was in the design stage, but again it was below contemporary fighters in performance. By July all branches of training were going well, but it was uphill work and it seemed probable that naval aviation would, for the second time, plunge into war immediately after a major reorganization.

Summer leave started at the end of July but I did not take mine until mid-August. The family had become so attached to the *Marjorie* on our Dutch trip in 1938 that I had bought her and given her a square rig as brig in place of the original fore-and-aft steadying sails. With the coxswain as crew, we loaded her up and took her to Yarmouth, Isle of Wight, for the first night. The next morning we headed for Plymouth.

After a carefree few days we started back via Salcombe and Dartmouth and when half-way across Lyme Bay, sailing with a pleasant westerly breeze, a Walrus amphibian aircraft appeared, circled us and dropped a tin. Picking it up I found a message ordering me to return at once. It was 22 August. The quickest way to get back was to go to Portland and by car from there to Lee. Then the old battleship *Iron Duke* appeared from the west. She was on her way to Scapa to act as depôt ship. By semaphore we asked her to pass a signal to Lee telling them to send cars to Portland, but she answered that wireless silence was in force. She offered to give me a passage to Portsmouth, but I could not leave the family adrift in Lyme Bay. We went on into Portland, therefore, and arranged matters by telephone.

Ross House had been bought by the Admiralty as a residence for the Captain of Lee. Tom Bulteel, a bachelor, had suggested that we should use it until the Bowhills left Manorway Grange. I reached it in the small hours of 23 August.

Ten days later war was declared. My appointment in command of the naval air stations continued for the first twenty-two months of the war, my constantly expanding parish being scattered between Lee-on-Solent in the south and Hatston in the Orkneys in the north. From the start, with new squadrons being formed for whom accommodation had to be found or improvised, training to be organized and kept going through that first bitterly cold winter and a flood of recruits to be housed and trained, I was kept strenuously busy.

Equally busy was my wife who had found herself appointed in charge of the W.R.N.S. of the Lee-on-Solent station. Soon after the outbreak of the war she had received a message from the Admiralty to say that she was to recruit nine naval wives or daughters as cypher officers and take them to a certain office in Portsmouth to be signed up. This she duly did, only to be told that she too must sign up – for reasons which were not made clear to her. A few days later she was surprised to receive an appointment as a first officer, W.R.N.S., in charge of the section at Lee. She remained in this post for the remainder of the war, being promoted in 1942 to the rank of chief officer, having eventually 1,000 women under her at Lee and a further 300 at various out-stations.

In the spring of 1940 I found time to tour the northern stations of my command and was at Edinburgh when the news came in of the German invasion of Norway and Denmark. From Donibristle I flew north to Hatston arriving just as the naval Skua squadrons operating from there received orders to attack German warships located at Bergen. I saw them off in the early dawn at 4.30, led by Captain Partridge, Royal Marines. Bergen was at the extreme limit of their range. The slightest miscalculation and they would run out of petrol over the sea. I awaited their return with deep anxiety.

Only one aircraft was lost. Discovering the cruiser *Königsberg* in Bergen harbour, the Skuas had dive-bombed her and though they were not sure of having sunk her, they had certainly hit her. It was not until, during the course of my tour, I reached the R.A.F. station at Leuchars that I received the splendid news that the cruiser had been sent to the bottom.

There followed the months of German air attacks with our air stations taking much of the assault. Dispersal of aircraft and personnel and organization of defences were our chief preoccupation. Invasion was in everyone's mind. An organization was worked out for our training squadrons to be armed and sent into action if the worst came to the worst. The operation was given the code name 'Elah' which stood for 'England's last hope'.

At the height of the Stuka raids on the Portsmouth area, the King came to visit the naval establishment and stations. Red warnings seemed to worry him not at all. They did me however and I wondered what the right procedure was if a bunch of Stukas dived at us. The King settled that.

'I like Hampshire,' he said. 'They have good deep ditches. If we have to take cover I'll take this ditch and you take that one.'

'Aye, aye, sir,' was all I could reply.

By the spring of 1941 I was near the top of the Rear-Admirals' list; not having flown my own flag at sea I realized that the bowler hat was approaching. It came in the form of a kindly-worded letter from the Admiralty. It was signed by the Secretary but I suspected that the kind words were Dudley Pound's. I was promoted to Vice-Admiral but continued to serve until November 1941. Shortly before being relieved by Clement Moody, I visited the Admiralty. Having finished my business there, I went to see the Naval Secretary and suggested that on retirement I might be given command of one of the new escort carriers being built in the United States under the Lend-Lease agreement. He explained that it was impossible. They were to be commanders' commands, and I should be keeping some young commander from getting a ship. So I asked him to put me down for convoy commodore.

Having some points to raise with the Second Sea Lord, Admiral Whitworth, I went to see him. Amongst other things I suggested that there must be a number of destroyer and submarine C.O.s needing a spell ashore who would be most suitable executive officers at air stations. They would have more influence with young 'A' Branch officers than the retired officers who were the only alternative. Whitworth said that though he quite agreed, he was so short of commanders and senior lieutenant-commanders that he could not find reliefs. When I asked him where he expected to find C.O.s for the new escort carriers, he answered 'God knows.' Using his telephone I made an appointment to see Dudley Pound, the First Sea Lord, to whom I explained that the Second Sea Lord was very short of suitable officers to command escort carriers and that there was nobody more suitable than I was. Pound was much amused and though he would not commit himself, he promised to look into the matter.

Newly recruited convoy commodores served for their first trip as vice-commodores. Soon after being relieved by Clement Moody, I was appointed vice-commodore to Admiral A. J. Davis. We were old friends and I was glad to serve under him. The trip to Halifax, Nova Scotia, with a fast – 10-knot – convoy and my return voyage from Sydney, Cape Breton Island, as commodore of a slow – nominally 7-knot – convoy were devoid of any encounters with the enemy. The only hazards were the usual ones supplied by the savage Atlantic weather, the return trip taking nineteen days from Sydney to Loch Ewe at an average speed of 6½ knots, a good performance by slow-convoy standards.

Soon after I arrived back I heard that I was to command one of the escort carriers being built in America. No senior flying officer having been selected for her, I wanted Lieutenant-Commander Esmonde who was commanding 825 Swordfish Squadron, then at Lee. I asked him if he would like to come. He was eager, but said his squadron had been warned to stand by for an operation. A few days later the *Gneisenau* and *Scharnhorst* made their dash up Channel. Esmonde led his squadron of slow 'stringbags' in a desperate and gallant attempt to torpedo the ships, losing his life and being awarded a posthumous Victoria Cross.

I duly received my appointment in the rank of commander to the *Dasher* completing in a shipyard at Hoboken, New Jersey, so I took passage in S.S. *Orbita* to Halifax. The ship, which was acting as a troop transport, was crowded and I shared a cabin with Commander Dickens. Reaching Halifax on 8 March 1942, I took a train to New York where I put up at the Knickerbocker Club, which gave honorary membership to all senior British officers on duty. There I received orders to proceed to Charleston in order to hold an inquiry into a curious accident which had happened on board the escort carrier *Archer*.

The American system of dealing with fires in carriers was to flood the compartment with carbon dioxide. While the *Archer* was in dry dock, the gas flooding system for her engine-room had been accidentally set off, the engine-room filling with gas. It was found that the only method of clearing away the gas was to make a hole in the ship's bottom and allow the gas to escape into the dry dock. Reporting the facts to a representative of the Bureau of Ships, I pointed out to him that we could not use that method of getting rid of the gas at sea. 'No, captain, I guess you can't,' he replied. As a result, a new system of expelling the gas was evolved.

Until the end of June 1942 *Dasher* was in the small shipyard in Hoboken. I and the other officers standing by her lived in the Barbizon Plaza Hotel in New York. Besides the other captains of escort carriers, there were a good number of British officers and civilian residents in New York. Soon after I arrived there, the convoy system was extended through American coastal waters and British convoys used New York instead of Halifax as their western terminus.

Archie Cochrane, an old friend of mine, was in New York. He was captain of the auxiliary cruiser *Queen of Bermuda* which had damaged herself on a rock near Halifax. He had been a submariner during the First World War and I had flown him over the Dardanelles before he took his submarine into the Marmora where she had been sunk and Cochrane taken prisoner. He had organized a remarkable escape from Turkey, he and his party walking to the Mediterranean coast, only to find that Turkey had already given in. I now had to sit on the court martial which tried him for stranding his ship. We dined together afterwards.

Between the wars Cochrane had been Governor of Burma

where he had entertained Miss Ruth Draper, the actress. She invited us both to lunch. She and her brother, Dr Draper, who was staying with her, were both keen to hear what living conditions were really like in England. Amongst other things I mentioned the reluctance of hens to lay eggs when they were given no corn, and the vast improvement which had resulted from a bag of it I brought back from Nova Scotia when I was convoy commodore. Dr Draper exclaimed, 'That's just what I've been looking for. My personal contribution to the Allied war effort shall be to supply feed corn to your chickens.' He had a farm in Connecticut and a few days later a large sack of corn arrived at the Barbizon Plaza Hotel. American hospitality was unbounded and to make some sort of return, Cochrane and I gave a cocktail party at the hotel.

When *Dasher* left the Hoboken yard she was taken to Brooklyn Navy Yard to have guns and equipment fitted. There the ceremony of handing over the ship to us took place. The Americans always have a commissioning ceremony in their own ships and of course H.M. Ships have a christening ceremony on being launched. We decided to combine all three ceremonies (see facing p. 183). The ship's company had arrived and been accommodated in barracks. Admiral Marquart was in command of the Navy Yard so I asked Mrs Marquart to do the christening part, and invited an American naval chaplain to conduct the short service. Unfortunately it rained, so all the ceremonies had to take place in the hangar, but everything went off quite well.

Having completed, *Dasher* went into Long Island Sound for trials, but as she produced an engine defect had to return to Hoboken for a time to overcome it. While there I had a telegram from Dudley Pound telling me that owing to a reorganization in Fleet Air Arm affairs, I was recalled to serve at the Admiralty. It was a bad blow just as *Dasher* was about to become operational. I handed the ship over to Commander Lentaigne and took a train to Montreal where I reported to R.A.F. Headquarters for air passage to England, setting off from there on 10 August.

A vast expansion of the Fleet Air Arm was being undertaken. Admiral Sir Frederick Dreyer had been put in charge, but as he was on the Retired List he was not made a member of the Board, so the title of Fifth Sea Lord was done away with and he was entitled Chief of Naval Air Service: short title C.N.A.S. I was to be his assistant, with short title A.C.N.A.S. It meant another change of rank, upwards this time as I became commodore, R.N. Soon after starting work at the Admiralty, the Board issued a directive to the effect that the aircraft carrier was in future to be regarded as the principal unit of the fleet. We had come a long way from the days of the *Killingholme* and *Campania*.

The expansion originally envisaged was on such a scale that it proved impracticable. Broadly, what had to be done was to ascertain and tabulate the numbers of aircraft which would become available in 1943 and 1944, to estimate the number of recruits suitable to become pilots and observers during those years, and then to estimate the necessary increase of training establishments. It was largely a question of mathematics.

During my first few months at the Admiralty, Operation Torch, the landings in North Africa, was being prepared. When the operation was finally launched, the flow of signals into our office became immense. The senior messenger attached to the office was a naval pensioner of long standing named York whom I had known for many years. One morning when he dumped in front of me a tray piled high with signals, I exclaimed, 'Good Heavens! Have I got to read all those?'

York replied, 'I got to bring 'em to you. Whether you reads 'em or not is up to you. That reminds me of Mr Churchill early in the war when 'e was First Lord. I was First Lord's messenger and one day I brings 'im a lot of signals, same as I 'ave you. 'E looks up and 'e sez, "Take 'em away, York," 'e sez. "I don't want no more signals today," 'e sez. Well o' course I didn't bring 'im no more signals; and d'ye know, sir, the war went on just the same.'

The last two months of 1942 marked the turning point in the war: Alamein, the successful invasion of North Africa and the Russian victory at Stalingrad. Early in 1943 Dreyer's task was completed. The proposed rate of expansion had been cut to what was practical. The training organization had been expanded to meet it largely by setting up training stations in America. I felt that as I had been deprived of one escort carrier in order to help at the Admiralty, I was entitled to another when the job was done. I put the idea to the Naval Secretary and was given the *Pretoria*

Castle, a Union Castle liner of 23,000 tons in process of conversion to a carrier. This time I had the rank of captain, R.N.

The ship was in Swan, Hunter's yard on the Tyne, and I was standing by her all that summer. In fact it was a repetition of my time in *Dasher*; but I prefer New York to Newcastle. Knowing the family habit of carriers of dragging their anchors, I persuaded the firm to supply her with a seven-ton anchor in exchange for one of the five-ton anchors that she originally had.

Pretoria Castle completed in the summer and we went north-about to the Clyde. The ship was used for experimental work: testing new types of aircraft, working out acceleration with the rocket-assisted take-off, measuring take-off runs at different wind speeds and different loadings, launching glider targets, etc. No doubt we accumulated a vast amount of statistics and I can only hope that the information obtained justified her cost. For the next fourteen months she spent her time going up and down the Clyde with occasional visits to Belfast Lough, anchoring off Gourock for the week-ends and usually off Rothesay during the week. The Tail-of-the-Bank was the most crowded anchorage that I have ever seen and during the frequent gales a particularly anxious one. Our seven-ton anchor was a treasured possession.

We had only two trips to break the monotony. The first was to Scapa, to take up some spare aircraft for the fleet carriers. Moore was then C-in-C Home Fleet and he invited me to dinner in *Nelson* where I was given news of the fleet's doings. The *Royal Sovereign*, my one-time ship, had been handed over to the Russians. They had renamed her *Archangel*, but of course to our people her name was only changed to *Royalski Sovereignovitch*.

Our second diversion was escorting a convoy to Iceland, the only occasion on which *Pretoria Castle* took part in an active operation. The convoy consisted of American transports under an American commodore. There were no detailed orders laid down for the use of the carrier's aircraft so at the convoy conference it was agreed that we should act independently, notifying the commodore of our intentions. On the trip to Iceland the weather was good all the time and we were able to keep a continuous search round and ahead of the convoy throughout daylight hours. No submarines appeared.

The month was November, and Iceland was living up to its

name. We had some spare Swordfish to bring back which were flown-on off Reykjavik, after which we anchored in Hval Fiord to await the return convoy. During those days I held the 'Crown of the Denmark Strait'. This was a trophy made of copper, which some humorist had prepared as compensation to the unfortunate individual who happened to be senior naval officer afloat in Icelandic waters. Our return trip was mostly in fog.

Pretoria Castle continued to amass statistics throughout 1944 and in October I was relieved by Caspar John, who was later to become First Sea Lord, the first naval aviator to do so. That concluded my service, but I believe that I hold the record for the number of different ranks I patronized in the course of two wars.

In the first I had been:

> Lieutenant, R.N.
> Squadron Commander, R.N.A.S.
> Wing Commander, R.N.A.S.
> Lieutenant-Commander, R.N.
> Lieutenant-Colonel, R.A.F.

In the second I had been:

> Rear-Admiral
> Vice-Admiral
> Commodore, R.N.R.
> Commander, R.N.
> Commodore, R.N.
> Captain, R.N.

Index

241